"The Inside Light"

"The Inside Light"

New Critical Essays on Zora Neale Hurston

DEBORAH G. PLANT, EDITOR

 PRAEGER

AN IMPRINT OF ABC-CLIO, LLC
Santa Barbara, California • Denver, Colorado • Oxford, England

Library of Congress Cataloging-in-Publication Data

The inside light : new critical essays on Zora Neale Hurston / Deborah G. Plant, ed.
    p. cm.
  Includes bibliographical references and index.
  ISBN 978-0-313-36517-1 (alk. paper) — ISBN 978-0-313-36518-8 (ebook)
1. Hurston, Zora Neale—Criticism and interpretation. 2. Women and literature—United States—History—20th century. 3. African Americans in literature.
4. Folklore in literature. I. Plant, Deborah G., 1956–
  PS3515.U789Z745   2010
  813'.52—dc22   2009048611

ISBN: 978-0-313-36517-1
EISBN: 978-0-313-36518-8

14 13 12 11 10   1 2 3 4 5

This book is also available on the World Wide Web as an eBook.
Visit www.abc-clio.com for details.

Praeger
An Imprint of ABC-CLIO, LLC

ABC-CLIO, LLC
130 Cremona Drive, P.O. Box 1911
Santa Barbara, California 93116-1911

This book is printed on acid-free paper (∞)

Manufactured in the United States of America

This work is dedicated to the new generations of readers of the works of Zora Neale Hurston and to the Spirit of the Aquarian Age, whose other name is Forgiveness.

Contents

Acknowledgments

First, I would like to thank Editor Suzanne Staszak-Silva for asking me to consider editing a volume of essays on Zora Neale Hurston—it was a very good idea. I thank Anthony Chiffolo, Director of Praeger Publishers, Editor Elizabeth Potenza, Project Manager Denise Stanley, and all the staff of Praeger, ABC-CLIO, and Cadmus Communications who facilitated the completion of this project. I am especially appreciative of Senior Production Coordinator Mark H. Kane. You have my deep and abiding thankfulness.

I offer heartfelt thanks to each and every contributor to this volume. I appreciate your enthusiasm for the project—your industry in writing and revising your essays in the midst of a thousand other work demands and family responsibilities. Please know that I am filled with gratitude for all you have done in creating this singular work.

For their constant support and good cheer, I thank my colleagues at the University of South Florida, especially Dean Eric Eisenberg, Associate Dean John Cochran; Drs. Cheryl Rodriguez, Edward Kissi, Eric Duke, Roy Kaplan, Kersuze Simeon-Jones, Dawood Sultan, Christine Probes, Shirley Toland-Dix, Gurleen Grewal and Ms. Daphine Washington; Office Manager Ms. Irina Ramirez-Fuentes; Event Coordinator and Community Liaison Ms. Clara Cobb; Ms. Marianne Bell; Ms. Susan Hall; Ms. Sharon Johnson-Hamilton; Ms. Cynthia Smith; and Ms. Kendra Nicole Bryant. I thank my colleagues and friends outside the University, with whom I have ongoing Hurston talks and with whom I discussed various aspects of the book—Ms. Phyllis McEwen, Ms. Valerie Boyd, Dr. John Lowe, Ms. Lynn Moylan, and Ms. Lucy Ann Hurston. I thank my neighborhood community of friends who always express interest in my work and well-being—Ken,

Jean, Lynn, Julie, Hunter, Vickie, Gary, MeCeal, Charlie, Gg, Mike, Cindy, Jason, Cynthia, Scott, Mr. John, Ms. Nina, and the Lake. And an extra special expression of gratitude to my dear friends Catherine Tardif and Peter León.

Genius has nothing to do with time. So we still find food for thought, inspiration for the soul, and light for our paths in the words of Zora Neale Hurston. For that, I am eternally grateful.

Introduction

Deborah G. Plant

This volume of critical essays brings Zora Neale Hurston fully into the 21st century. As it expands on the body of existing knowledge and critical analyses of the work of this author, it highlights posthumously published works that bring new insights, perspectives, and interpretations of previously published works. Some of the authors herein are distinguished scholars of Hurston's work. Some are new voices. As this volume introduces those whom will be numbered among the new generation of Hurston scholars, its objective is also to introduce Hurston to a new generation of readers.

As indicated by the thousands of Hurston festival attendees, the selection of *Their Eyes Were Watching God* as one of the "Big Read" books of the National Endowment for the Arts, and the television movie production of "Their Eyes Were Watching God," the interest in the life and work of Zora Neale Hurston is not only phenomenal, but promises to be enduring. This volume, therefore, aspires to contribute to the continuation of the Hurston legacy.

In the last ten years, there has been a phenomenal resurgence of scholarly and popular interest in the life and work of anthropologist and writer Zora Neale Hurston. The posthumous publications of Hurston's folklore manuscripts, letters, poetry, plays, and dramatic works offer scholars and lay readers a more in-depth look into the mind and heart of this writer whom Alice Walker described as "a Genius of the South." In 1999, Pamela Bordelon edited *Go Gator and Muddy the Water: Writings by Zora Neale Hurston, From the Federal Writers' Project*; Carla Kaplan edited *Every Tongue Got to Confess: Negro Folk-Tales from the*

Gulf States in 2001 and *Zora Neale Hurston: A Life in Letters* in 2002; and Valerie Boyd published her highly acclaimed biography of Hurston, *Wrapped in Rainbows*, in 2003. Following these book publications was Lucy Anne Hurston's 2004 collection of Hurston memorabilia in *Speak, So You Can Speak Again: The Life of Zora Neale Hurston*; Tiffany Patterson's *Zora Neale Hurston and A History of Southern Life* in 2005; and Deborah G. Plant's *Zora Neale Hurston: A Spiritual Biography* in 2007. In 2005, Oprah Winfrey produced a movie version of Hurston's best-known novel *Their Eyes Were Watching God*, which suggested the widespread celebrity of this important figure.

Newly discovered facts, texts, and film footage have allowed us a fuller appreciation of the life of Zora Neale Hurston. These discoveries give us new materials to examine as they also necessitate new assessments and interpretations of Hurston's previously published works. This collection will do both. In addition, it will give attention to aspects of Hurston's life and work that are still considered problematic or otherwise controversial. For example, Hurston's stance on desegregation and her relationship to her community of origin and the black community at large continue to be points of interest and controversy for readers. Hurston's autobiography, *Dust Tracks on a Road*, continues to be described as apolitical and questionable as to the truth of black life in the early 20th century. And some question whether attention directed to Hurston borders on the excessive and believe that, in an ironic twist, this attention effectively silences negative criticism and, equally problematic, renders other writers invisible.

If voices have been silenced, how can one know? Either the silent voice will eventually become a strident one and/or the privileged voice will be quiet long enough to listen with an empathic ear. If we are truly "crazy for this democracy," we will welcome points that differ from our own. Intellectual growth and expansion demands this. As this volume illustrates, there is so much to celebrate about Zora Neale Hurston. *And* there are aspects of her life and work that invite a less than celebratory interpretation. As Hurston herself would say: That's just being human. Whether the marketplace of ideas will be in the classroom, in libraries, in the media, at conferences, in the Laundromat, or at the water fountain, all voices should know their privilege.

The essays in this collection both celebrate a woman of remarkable achievement and question her motivations, choices, and perspectives. As well, they highlight the added dimensions of Hurston's work and life as suggested by newly discovered materials. Ethelbert Miller's opening poem and Kendra Nicole Bryant's closing poem frame this work. They each speak to the essentiality of creativity in human existence, as our creativity is our direct connection to the divine—within and outside us. In Section I, Piper Huguley-Riggins explores Hurston's life in terms of the labor market and the expectation of black women in early 20th-century America; and Kersuze Simeon-Jones has us look at gender issues as they are treated in Hurston's work. Hurston is best known to the majority of people as a writer. Whereas Hurston stands as a literary giant of the 20th century, she also made major contributions to the social sciences. Lucy Anne Hurston (Hurston's niece, who is also a cultural anthropologist) informs us of Hurston's significance as a social scientist. Hurston's work as a social scientist—an anthropologist and a folklorist—is less known, but is equally important, given Hurston's accomplishments in this area and given that African American folklore is the source of her fiction. Elizabeth Binggeli sheds light on Hurston's experiences in Hollywood and her pecuniary motivations to have her work adapted to film.

In Section II, the reader gets a sense of the breadth of Hurston as a Renaissance woman. Anthea Kraut shares with us Hurston's significance as a choreographer—a descriptive not available to a black woman in her time. Through comparative analysis of other Harlem Renaissance luminaries, Emily Hinnov discusses Hurston as a modernist in terms of her fiction, and John Lowe does so in terms of Hurston's plays. Hurston also wrote poetry, but was she a poet? Phyllis McEwen offers insight into Hurston's poetic sensibility and poetry.

Michelle Jarman discusses one of Hurston's relatively unknown novels, *Seraph on the Suwanee*, in Section III. Whereas most critics focus on the fact that the main characters are white, Jarman focuses attention on Earl, the disabled son. As Jarman questions whether Hurston achieved racial harmony at the expense of the disabled, Shirley Toland-Dix questions whether Hurston sacrificed the possibility of a pan-African identity to national identity. And through her discussion of Hurston's fieldwork in the Caribbean, in context of the Black Atlantic, she extends our appreciation of "the South." Gurleen Grewal brings fresh interpretations to *Their Eyes Were Watching God* through her discussion of Hurston's appreciation for the spiritual inherent in nature, and Scott Hicks re-visions Hurston as a Southern writer whose work should be assessed for its environmentalist dimensions—can a black woman be "green"? As authors in this section trumpet the geographical beauty of the South as Hurston represents it, they are also aware of the vulnerability of the region and the racial politics that exacerbate that vulnerability. Dawood Sultan and Deanna Wathington explain the political economy of security as they compare the hurricane in *Their Eyes Were Watching God* with Hurricane Katrina.

In the last section, authors explore Hurston's relevance in the 21st century and her legacy. Catherine John scrutinizes Hurston's reference to "the man in the gutter [as] god-maker." Her analysis highlights Hurston's focus on the process of creativity, which she identifies as the source of the creativity among inner-city youth who reflect and continue the creative genius of their forebears. Kendra Bryant's letters to Zora Neale Hurston speak of the innate wisdom of the youth in 21st-century America who, often in spite of external, elitist, and academic invalidation, know and embrace their brilliance. They are the New Literati. As the film version of *Their Eyes Were Watching God* speaks to the popularity of Hurston's novel, Hurston biographer Valerie Boyd sees the movie production of *Their Eyes*, which attracted 24.6 million viewers, as instrumental in the continuation of the Hurston legacy. Linda Tavernier-Almada reminds us in her article that the legacy of Zora Neale Hurston must also include voices that have somehow been repressed or outright silenced by the shear magnitude of the Hurston Renaissance. As Hurston's work speaks to the importance of community, Tavernier-Almada's essay suggests that readers and critics might consider anew the reality of Hurston's community of origin in 21st-century America. As scholars assess Hurston's relations with her community of origin, they have reassessed her relations with the larger black community. Lynn Moylan, for example, examines Hurston's opposition to the Supreme Court's *Brown v. Board of Education* decision. Though she was roundly denounced for her stance, current political opinion finds itself in agreement with Zora Neale Hurston.

The very ideas, perspectives, stances, and actions for which Hurston was condemned during her lifetime are now praised as wise, enlightened, progressive, and "ahead of her time." A. Giselle Jones-Jones looks at Hurston's perspectives on race and race consciousness, and Joanne Braxton examines Hurston's configuration as a universalist who refused to invest in social and racial segregation, preferring the company of all her sistren and brethren. The new millennium requires it.

In a Time of Zora

After the terribleness—
we survived and learned to call ourselves
Count and Duke. This was after the lash
and Douglass. It was a time when Harlem
was on our minds and our souls prayed
their way into Amen Corners. One could
overhear Zora telling stories. She was
fabulous and gave the world its glitter

—E. Ethelbert Miller

To Paint a Woman Black and Female at the Turn of the 20th Century

Zora Neale Hurston: A Black White-Collar Working Woman

Piper G. Huguley-Riggins

Zora Neale Hurston is one of the primary black woman writers of the 20th century, rescued from oblivion and her books rescued from out-of-print status more than 30 years ago, to receive recognition as an important voice in American literary history. Her most famous work, *Their Eyes Were Watching God*, is acclaimed as part of the established canon of American literature; her anthropological work is used more widely now than before; and more recently because of the films she produced while conducting her anthropological work, she is regarded as a visionary in media, being one of the first black female directors of documentary films in the United States.

Of those works that have been reprinted and reevaluated, Hurston's autobiography, *Dust Tracks on a Road*, published in 1942, continues to be overlooked or underappreciated.[1] The narrative discusses and follows the development of Hurston's careers as an anthropologist and writer. Because the work does not directly focus on issues of race and racism as expected, *Dust Tracks* has been discounted as inauthentic. Alice Walker rejects *Dust Tracks* as "false," a rather harsh term applied to a book that is intended to be the depiction of a life story.[2] Only recently has *Dust Tracks*, as one of the few autobiographies by a black female of her time period, come to be seen as a carefully controlled production of Hurston's public and private images.[3] In Hurston's autobiography, she "privileges herself" as a writer and insists on asserting her right to self-definition of her career life.[4]

In the United States, black women have always had mixed feelings about work. The second wave of feminism that began stirring in the post-World War II period was designed to give white women an opportunity for white-collar work in the larger society. However, black women did not see white-collar work as a means to resist the tyranny of white patriarchy or as opportunities for freedom from gender role oppression in the domestic sphere. Black women wanted relief from being limited to menial jobs and fair compensation for their work. Even in the mid-20th century, the notion of being professionals with professional careers and appropriate compensation was a distant dream for the majority of black women. By the beginning of the 20th century, black women who were part of the black middle class could anticipate becoming professionals. Anna Julia Cooper and Sadie Turner, for example, were models of black womanhood that suggested that black women's abilities were not limited to domestic work.[5] However, little credit is given to an influential black writer like Zora Neale Hurston, who, in *Dust Tracks*, crafted a personal narrative like no other that had been written before. Hurston used the space of her life story to shape a vision of her working life—an independent life that had begun with domestic work then transitioned into the work of a professional in the white-collar world. I argue that Hurston's work in general, and her self-portrayal in *Dust Tracks on a Road* in particular, encouraged women of various racial identities to begin to perceive their possibilities as professionals in post-World War II American society. Hurston's voice was part of the growing chorus of voices that contributed to women's ability to re-envision themselves and to demand more of a share of the labor "pie."

The tensions between Euro-American and African American cultures characterize analyses of Zora Neale Hurston's life, language, and work. W.E.B. Du Bois articulated this sometimes overwhelming duality as the "double-consciousness" of the black American.[6] This tension can be seen as an important key to understanding Hurston's expression of her recreated self in an autobiographical work that she was asked to write and for which she anticipated compensation. Robert Hemenway believed that Hurston developed a "vocational schizophrenia," because she was part artist and part social scientist.[7] Perhaps Hemenway did not consider to what extent Du Bois's notion of "double-consciousness" expressed itself in Hurston's life in many ways. Yet, for as much as the Duboisian double-consciousness or double-bind may have affected Hurston, it neither repressed nor limited her creativity and productivity. Karla F.C. Holloway applauds Hurston's complex career aspirations and lauds Hurston as someone who paved the way for black women.[8] She was someone who was ahead of her time with multiple careers and was far from "schizophrenic."

Her posture as a developing woman writer and anthropologist is outlined defiantly in "Research," chapter ten of *Dust Tracks*: "I needed my Barnard education to help me see my people as they really are. But I found that it did not do to be too detached as I stepped aside to study them. I had to go back, dress as they did, talk as they did, live their life, so that I could get into my stories the world I knew as a child."[9] Even as Hurston was assessing her approach to her anthropological fieldwork and discerning its effectiveness, she was also learning about the dynamic socio-linguistic expression that would inform her writing. Hurston's acquisition of the clothes, lifestyle, and language of her Barnard college education was a point of dislocation from her past. As she joined her formally educated, professional self within her identify as one of the folk, she created a persona that allowed her easy access into the communities she studied. The self Hurston created not only allowed her access into folk communities, but it also allowed her access into white and upper-class institutions and social circles that typically excluded black people.

Hurston's genius emerges when she crafts her own unique blend of the languages of the two different worlds in which she operated. Her relatively detached and objective voice belongs to the realm of the social scientist, but her empathetic and intimate voice comes through in the engagement of the fiction writer. The lens of the cultural anthropologist and her knowledge of the folk meant that Hurston could create authentic characters and realistic plots and guide the action of her stories through a credible narrative voice. According to Hemenway, the pull between Hurston's two worlds or the tensions between Barnard and Eatonville prevented Hurston from becoming a social scientist of the first order:

Hurston never became a professional academic folklorist because such a vocation was alien to her exuberant sense of self, to her admittedly artistic, sometimes erratic temperament, and to her awareness of the aesthetic content of black folklore. If there is a single theme which emerges from her creative effort during the thirties . . . it is that eventually immediate experience takes precedence over analysis, emotion over reason, the personal over the theoretical.[10]

Hemenway's assumption of the lesser importance of anthropology in Hurston's life is debatable. Hurston used anthropology to nourish and augment her writing, and used her writing to advance her anthropological objectives. Rather than commit herself to one career path, she elected to pursue all paths that allowed her to exercise her creative self. She intended to "jump at de sun," as she was encouraged to do by her mother. Hurston also resisted succumbing to the dictates and expectations of the Black Intelligentsia.

Hurston assumed academic positions from time to time, but her tenure was always short-lived. And though she would never settle into a career as a professional academic folklorist, her academic background and experiences were essential to her growth and development. Her studies at Barnard College and Columbia University led to her work with "Papa" Franz Boas, the father of American Anthropology, as well as other giants in the field like Ruth Benedict, Gladys Reichard, and Melville Herskovitz. Her work with these mentors was foundational in terms of Hurston's academic achievements and her induction into various anthropological societies. Her success and recognition in the field was critical to her professional integrity. Validated by academic and scientific communities, Hurston's work met with positive reception, particularly during the early part of her career. Her achievements gave her the confidence to continue to write and to write her own life story with a new approach.

Hurston would have appreciated Sharon Harley's title of her summation regarding the development of a working-class consciousness in black women of the Progressive Era: "When Your Work Is Not Who You Are."[11] In Hurston's *Dust Tracks on a Road*, she writes from the perspective of her own labor experiences. Even as her work as a maid had some privileges, she writes of her drive to keep moving from one job to the next in search of what spoke to her inner light. Hurston lived during a time wherein occupations for black women were limited and not infrequently dehumanizing. Yet, Hurston insisted on casting a wider net. Her thought and her written expression represent bold acts of resistance that require careful investigation, so that we not only better understand Hurston, but so we also glean from her work that which may be instructive to women in contemporary society. Crispin Sartwell puts it well: "Zora Neale Hurston's work stands as a monument of resistance to all impositions of specific forms of visibility."[12] Laura Hapke confirms this view by saying that in *Dust Tracks*, Hurston's treatment of all her working opportunities was like a "writer's laboratory" of experiences.[13]

Part of Virginia Woolf's argument in *A Room of One's Own* is that money makes a difference in determining which writers are heard.[14] It is no coincidence that fiscal concerns are a recurring theme in *Dust Tracks*. In her foreword to Hemenway's *Zora Neale Hurston: A Literary Biography*, Alice Walker makes plain another of the lessons that Zora Neale Hurston's life teaches: "*Being broke made all the difference*. Without money of one's own in a capitalist society, there is no such thing as independence. This is one of the clearest lessons of Hurston's life and why I consider the telling of her life a 'cautionary tale.' We must learn from it what we can."[15] Some of the harshness and economic poverty of Hurston's life put her in touch with cultural realities that informed her work, but in the end, her penurious situation compromised her writing energy. The patronage she received undermined her self-esteem and professional independence—the situation that gave rise to Alice Walker's "cautionary tale." Hemenway describes her attitude at the end of her life: "What ate away at the 'delirium of joy' [that Zora reflected about while living in Eau Gallie, Florida] was the absence of cash." Hemenway recounts from an interview with Hurston's literary agent that Hurston could write "like an angel" but like many authors, from Poe and Melville to Faulkner and Fitzgerald, she could not write as well when she felt financial pressure.[16] In a vicious cycle, she was hard pressed to write publishable material when she needed money; and yet in order to make money, she had to write saleable work. What one might call the "Virginia Woolf problem" was decidedly Hurston's.

Hurston's ultimate need to resort to domestic work later on in life—one of the few professions consistently open to black women—is a tragic comment on her times. She explained her resumption of maid's work as a working vacation: "You can only use your mind for so long," she said. She was temporarily "written out."[17] Really, Hurston's work as a maid in a Florida home was a bizarre twist of fate for someone who had once written for *The Saturday Evening Post*, a popular journal among middle-class subscribers. James Lyons, the *Post* writer who exposed Hurston, was obviously ignorant of the truths of a serious writer's life, particularly a writer who was a "double minority."[18] Hardships never kept Hurston down. She strove to make the best of her life, whatever the circumstances. Her return to work as a maid (and the eventual relief from it when publishers read the Lyons article and offered her writing jobs), represented what Oprah Winfrey calls a "full circle moment."[19] Just as Hurston talks about her position as a domestic in several guises in *Dust Tracks* during her adolescent years, she talks about her work as a domestic during the later years of her life.

As part of the careerist reach that she crafts in her autobiographical work, she positions domestic work as a positive space because it allowed her the opportunity to be involved with activities that were pleasant to her and that spoke to her soul: "I did very badly because I was interested in the front of the house, not the back. No matter how I resolved, I'd get tangled up with their reading matter, and lose my job."[20] No matter how hard she tried to focus on her work, Hurston here was purposely, and to some extent out of necessity, positioning herself as someone whose work was not who she is, to paraphrase Sharon Harley's title. This positioning and use of a controlled guise in the presentation of events in her life can be considered a factor in the poor reception of this rather important literary work that also contains aspects of social documentation—though of a nature critics tend to overlook.

Like her life and her literary objectives, *Dust Tracks on a Road* was increasingly misunderstood. Up until the 1990s, the assessment of *Dust Tracks* was generally negative. As it is critical to understand this poor reception of Hurston's autobiography, it is also critical to consider alternative readings of *Dust Tracks*. For an appreciation of the career paths, as Hurston delineates them in her text, is insightful and instructive. Alice Walker, her most famous adherent and literary daughter, is disappointed in *Dust Tracks*: "For me, the most unfortunate thing Zora ever wrote is her autobiography. After the first several chapters, it rings false. One begins to hear the voice of someone whose life required the assistance of too many transitory 'friends.'"[21] Seeing Hurston as a literary foremother, Walker appears to have so much invested in Hurston that she apparently finds the book's style and substance disturbing and, worse yet, false. Walker completely overlooks Hurston's discourse on work and career paths, which actually anticipates Walker's essays on work and writing in *In Search of Our Mother's Gardens*. The apparently fragmented structure of *Dust Tracks* itself is also a testament to Hurston's resistance against the structure of conventional autobiography. This is one reason, among others, why there is much more in Hurston's text to be appreciated than what Walker and other critics perceive.

Hurston's refusal to live the conventional life expected of a black woman in early 20th-century America correlates with her refusal to write in the conventional style of black autobiography. The rules she broke to transcend social barriers can be compared with the rules she broke in not adhering to the literary expectations of black writers. It is clear that Hurston intended to write a compendium of the cumulative effect of certain forces on particular portions of her working life and not a synthesis of her life experiences. Deborah Plant echoes this sentiment in assessing Hurston's chapter titled "Love" in *Dust Tracks*, which she describes as a discussion of Hurston's work life and an accounting of Hurston as a professional woman who must guard her career.[22] Hurston writes in this chapter, "Don't look for me to call a string of names and point out chapter and verse. Ladies do not kiss and tell any more than gentlemen do."[23] This quaint-sounding Victorian remark originating from the usually "in-your-face" Zora Neale Hurston is pure resistance and a key to unlocking an understanding of her autobiographical writing. This is not a "tell-all" book about a woman's everyday existence or her bohemian life. It is Hurston's vision of the important events that created her own career and led to her writing an account of her life. In this creation, Hurston was not concerned with the "facts" of her life. The inconsistencies about her birth year were reconciled long after her death, but the facts of her life and her account of them are criticized precisely because she took the common liberties of a fiction writer and applied them to the "truth" of her life. *Dust Tracks* is the imaginative version of Hurston's life that reveals how selected events and personalities contributed to the writer she eventually became.

As *Dust Tracks on a Road* was criticized because Hurston did not meet the expectations set for a black writer, it was also criticized because she did not meet the expectations set for a black *female* writer. It is important to remember that this autobiography was published a scant two years after Hattie McDaniel tearfully stated in her Oscar acceptance speech that she wanted to be "a credit to her race." This was the same actress who was also assertive in justifying her work and the roles she played. Many blacks criticized McDaniel for accepting the role of a maid throughout her career. McDaniel responded that she would rather play a maid than be one—another example of claiming the domestic space as a positive and creative one.[24] McDaniel's awareness of her choice and its significance to her bespeaks a profound understanding of the self. Hurston also understood something about her life that her critics missed—that in works such as *Dust Tracks*, authors are seeking an understanding of themselves as artists, as writers, and will be selective about what details are included in and excluded from their text. In *Writing a Woman's Life*, Carolyn Heilbrun references the illustrious French theorist Roland Barthes to illustrate this point: "biography is a novel that dare not speak its name."[25] This understanding is applicable to autobiography as well. The construction of such texts requires that the writer select an appropriate presentation of details to arrive at an understanding of the subject, which in Hurston's case is not a pedestrian factual account of her existence, but an impression of how she came to be the writer composing the book that the reader holds. The biography, though heavily influenced by which details the author can find to create a portrait of the subject, is filtered through the understanding of the biographer. The "biographer," too, is a novelist, a fiction writer, and one can often tell just as much about the author of the biography as the "life" of the subject of the biography.

In her autobiography, the "biographer" and the "subject" are one and the same. The "author" of these works, who presumably knows everything about her subject—herself—in any event will select, arrange, and compress as well as compose and invent. Autobiographical writing is always subject to question in terms of the absolute "truth" of a life. Hurston worked especially hard throughout her life to subvert those expectations of what she *should* reveal about herself. Robert Hemenway discusses Hurston's notorious bent to protect her private life: "She had told neither of her sponsors about [her] marriage, maintaining closeness about her private affairs that she would persist in all her life."[26] Even Hurston's own relatives did not know much about the turbulence of her life. To the end of her life, Hurston maintained her own privacy, and the privacy she maintained in life was transmitted to the written pages of her biographical narrative. But privacy is perhaps not the issue here. The writer of fiction not only purposefully confuses fact with invention but also truly has a special story to tell about the creative and imaginative life. These are the central tasks of a good fiction writer. This capability would inevitably carry over to Hurston's re-creation of her life story and, I assert, is part of her strategy of resistance that is manifested in her determination to tell her own life story in her way.

Cheryl Wall argues that sometime in the 1950s, as Hurston's career went into deep decline, one of the many texts that Hurston was beginning to write was a sequel to *Dust Tracks*.[27] However, because she had published only one novel after *Dust Tracks* was written, she perhaps felt she had nothing laudatory to say. She might have elaborated on how she had struggled to continue writing despite the hostility shown to her by reviewers and the black literati—finding piecemeal work in the black press, offering books and stories that were rejected by supposedly "friendly" publishers—and then, how she had to work as a maid, substitute teacher, and librarian just to keep food on the table. That story might have been a little too much truth for her audience and was certainly not in keeping with Hurston's spunky worldview. She was much more optimistic than pessimistic and would have found it difficult to write a story of failure and decline. Other scholars point to the 1948 false accusation of child molestation as a turning point that changed her view of telling the rest of her life story. Other authors of her time, like Anzia Yezierska, incorporated the harsh costs of the writer's life in her own biographical narrative. But there still must be triumph. Hurston felt the same too. Thus, *Dust Tracks on a Road* is what we have, and it is, I maintain, primarily and firmly a positive account of her struggle to attain and maintain a career, rather than a "job."

Hurston's refusal to adhere to autobiographical convention allowed her mostly generous biographer, Robert Hemenway, to call *Dust Tracks* "a discomforting book [which] has probably harmed Hurston's reputation."[28] However, Hemenway is overlooking the ways in which Hurston subverted the conventional approaches that were usually made in autobiographical writing. Probably looking for patterns of continuity, Hemenway sees that the two halves of *Dust Tracks* prove Hurston's failure to reconcile her child world of Eatonville with her education at Barnard: "Did she become successful by rising above Eatonville or by digging into its very soul? She found herself in the uncomfortable position of mediating between two spheres of experience, searching for an interpretive voice that would authenticate both Eatonville and Bar-nard."[29] Though an astute observer in most regards, Hemenway never once considers that African Americans, as indicated by the typically hyphenated name by which her racial group is now called, have had to become masters at duplicity in order to achieve clandestine goals. The fact that Hurston succeeded in this twofold mastery is reflective of this reality.

Francoise Lionnet regards the style of *Dust Tracks* as "self-conscious" and argues, "*Dust Tracks* does not seek to legitimate itself through appeal to what William L. Andrews has called 'a powerful source of authoriza-tion,' such as religion or another organized system of belief. It is in that sense that *Dust Tracks* is a powerfully anarchic work, not anchored in any original and originating story of racial or sexual difference."[30] This seems rather wrongheaded, given Hurston's focus on the importance of her hometown of Eatonville as a crucial place, and the authenticity of folk voices as a contrast to the new urban sophistication and intellectualism of the "New Negro." Hurston brings both instinct and modern anthropol-ogy to bear in her development of a new kind of careerist guideline. Indeed, she is creating her own mythology and method of telling stories. Lionnet's idea of *Dust Tracks* as an "anarchic" work—meaning that the book does not fit in with any of the expectations of the genre of autobiogra-phy—only serves to heighten the fact that Hurston had done something unprecedented in this genre. The fact that she had deviated from a linear type of narrative does not mean that her work should be disregarded. Rather, readers and critics might benefit from an examination that is guided by an attempt to understand what she did produce.

Hurston's inclusion of her encounters with famous writer Fannie Hurst in *Dust Tracks* point to her various work postures. She is hired as Hurst's "secretary" and later earns Hurst's respect and trust as a writer. Though Hurston was required to assume an inferior position *vis-à-vis* Hurst, Zora Neale Hurston was Hurst's professional equal, and one who would, in later years, far surpass her employer in literary approbation. The inclusion of the Hurst events in *Dust Tracks* point to the reality of Hurston's life as a black woman in the first half of the 20th century, a social reality wherein Hurston was well used to having to posture. Her various career guises as a "fake" maid, writer, anthro-pologist, and Barnard graduate are all expressive of a free spirit in a restraining world who, through another willful pose, documents her life events, selectively, as she wishes to convey them.

With the restoration of the censored material, a full and complete picture of *Dust Tracks on a Road* is available, and present-day readers can make their own assessments. Rather than reflecting on *Dust Tracks* as evasive, disoriented, or silent, it is time to see it from this black woman writer's point of view. Mae Henderson argues that for too long "black women have been discounted or unaccounted for in the 'traditions' of black, women's, and American literature as well as in the contemporary literary-critical dialogue . . . [B]lack women writers have begun to receive token recognition as they are subsumed under the category of woman in the feminist critique and the category of black in the racial critique."[31] Cheryl Wall acknowledges this as well in her discussion of the utter difficulty in being a black woman writer in the early part of the 20th century: "What makes Hurston's life so problematic is the capacity for self-invention . . . at a time when the terms 'black,' 'woman,' and 'artist' were never complementary."[32]

Dust Tracks gives us a rare look into the unique self-invention of and the inner life of a "Genius of the South," as Alice Walker called Hurston.[33] As Henderson notes, both self-invention and a specific approach to craft are perhaps still required by black women writers to carry out "the dialogue between self and society and between self and psyche . . . 'a unique form of collaboration'" that Hurston explores in her text and that literally represents a privileged space in the structure of *Dust Tracks on a Road*.[34] James Olney adds something to the concept of this privileged space in his assessment of the "schizophrenic" artist-scientist Montaigne, whom he quotes: "'I study myself,' he proclaims, 'That is my metaphysics, that is my physics.'"[35] For all these reasons, Kelly Anne Mechling appropriately characterizes *Dust Tracks on a Road* as a "mother text"[36] because of its groundbreaking approach to an autobiography, written by a woman about her working life who had the courage to strive to do the work that was herself.

NOTES

1. Zora Neale Hurston, *Dust Tracks on a Road* (1942; repr., New York: Harper Perennial Modern Classics, 2006).

2. Alice Walker, "Zora Neale Hurston: A Cautionary Tale and a Partisan View," in *In Search of Our Mothers' Gardens: Womanist Prose* (San Diego: Harcourt Brace Jovanovich Publishers, 1983), 91.

3. Karla F.C. Holloway, *The Character of the Word: The Texts of Zora Neale Hurston* (Westport, CT: Greenwood Press, 1987).

4. Mae Gwendolyn Henderson, "Speaking in Tongues: Dialogics, Dialectics, and the Black Woman Writer's Literary Tradition," in *Women, Autobiography, Theory: A Reader*, ed. Sidonie Smith and Julia Watson (Madison: The University of Wisconsin Press, 1998), 343.

5. Sharon Harley, "When Your Work Is Not Who You Are: The Development of a Working-Class Consciousness Among Afro-American Women," in *Gender, Class, Race, and Reform in the Progressive Era*, ed. Noralee Frankel and Nancy S. Dye (Lexington: University Press of Kentucky, 1991), 49.

6. W.E.B. Du Bois, *The Souls of Black Folk* (1903; repr., New York: Signet, 1969), 45.

7. Robert Hemenway, *Zora Neale Hurston: A Literary Biography* (Urbana: University of Illinois Press, 1977), 70.

8. Holloway, *The Character of the Word*, 2.

9. Hurston, *Dust Tracks on a Road*, 196.

10. Hemenway, *Zora Neale Hurston*, 213.

11. Harley, 46.

12. Crispin Sartwell, *Act Like You Know* (Chicago: The University of Chicago Press, 1998), 123.

13. Laura Hapke, *Daughters of the Great Depression: Women, Work, and Fiction in the American 1930s* (Athens: University of Georgia Press, 1995), 135.

14. Virginia Woolf, *A Room of One's Own* (1929; repr., New York: Harcourt, Brace, Jovanovich, 1991), 54.

15. Alice Walker, "Foreword," in *Zora Neale Hurston: A Literary Biography*, by Robert Hemenway (Urbana: University of Illinois Press, 1977), xvi.

16. Hemenway, *Zora Neale Hurston*, 341.

17. Cheryl A. Wall, *Women of the Harlem Renaissance* (Bloomington: Indiana University Press, 1995), 200.

18. Ibid.

19. Joe Ruggeri, *A Full Circle Moment*, http://www.afullcirclemoment.com/index.htm.

20. Wall, *Women of the Harlem Renaissance*, 201.

21. Walker, "Foreword," xvii.

22. Deborah G. Plant, *Every Tub Must Sit on Its Own Bottom: The Philosophy and Politics of Zora Neale Hurston* (Urbana: University of Illinois Press, 1995), 26.

23. Hurston, *Dust Tracks on a Road*, 203.

24. Carlton Jackson, *Hattie: The Life of Hattie McDaniel* (Lanham: Madison Books, 1990).

25. Carolyn G. Heilbrun, *Writing a Woman's Life* (London: Women's Press, 1989), 12.

26. Hemenway, *Zora Neale Hurston*, 93.

27. Wall, *Women of the Harlem Renaissance*, 972.

28. Hemenway, *Zora Neale Hurston*, 276.

29. Ibid., 279.

30. Francoise Lionnet, "Autoethnography: The An-Archic Style of *Dust Tracks on a Road*," in *African-American Autobiography: A Collection of Critical Essays* (Englewood Cliffs: Prentice-Hall Inc., 1993), 113–137.

31. Henderson, "Speaking in Tongues," 343–351.

32. Wall, *Women of the Harlem Renaissance*, 201.

33. Alice Walker, "Looking for Zora," in *In Search of Our Mothers' Gardens: Womanist Prose* (New York: Harvest Books, 2003), 105.

34. Henderson, "Speaking in Tongues," 345.

35. James Olney, *Metaphors of the Self: The Meaning of Autobiography* (Princeton: Princeton University Press, 1972), 9.

36. Kelly Anne Mechling, "Creative Dimensions in Autobiographies of Selected Twentieth-Century American Women Writers" (Dissertation, Indiana University of Pennsylvania, 1996), 293.

Zora Neale Hurston:
Pioneering Social Scientist

Lucy Anne Hurston

"What Do the Simple Folk Do?" is a query posed in the title and lyrics of a song from the musical "Camelot."[1] This song tells the tale of the quest undertaken by Arthur and Guinevere to understand "the other."

Arthur, King of Camelot, and Queen Guinevere ponder how the simple folk deal with culturally universal problems that have been investigated by many since the early formations of human social structures. As King Arthur and Queen Guinevere ponder "the other"—"the simple folk"—they are engaging in observation, which is one component of the scientific method. As royalty whose time period precedes the establishment of anthropology as a social science, we can assume that they are without the benefit of formalized training. Nonetheless, they turn a critical eye to the question of the simple folk and proffer a description and explanation of perceived social problems within the larger community and among its members. The validity of their hypothesis and eventual conclusions is undermined by their lack of awareness of their positionality as privileged "other" within the social system and by the absence of any experimentation or actual fieldwork—as all their evidence is guesswork and hearsay. They might be considered armchair anthropologists, and yet, even though they fail to engage in authentic research and they never acknowledge their privileged positions and social biases, to some extent, the understanding they reach about their world has some plausibility. What the royals find is some measure of commonality in what is defined as a social problem: unhappiness in many forms—depression, overwhelming grief, frustration, disappointment, and despair. What is uncovered is that humans will question and resolve similar problems in different ways.

If we engaged in a bit of astral projection into early 20th-century America and replaced Guinevere and Arthur with Zora Neale Hurston, we would have a more enlightening method of inquiry and informed response. Still, the same quest persists, but the framework has changed: Hurston is the consummate investigator, unrestrained by social status to practice the science and art of a social scientist. And rather than a legendary Medieval English castle and countryside, Hurston is peering into the actual culture and society of the black folk. Hurston devised her own unique ways of studying and understanding the culture of African American folk. She combined the skills of a social scientist with her literary and theatrical abilities to collect the lore of the folk and to (re)present the folk. To sum it up, "Research is formalized curiosity. It is poking and prying with a purpose. It is a seeking that he who wishes may know the cosmic secrets of the world and they that dwell within."[2]

A social scientist may ask: "What do the simple folk do?" And indeed Hurston built an illustrious, professional, multifaceted career capturing and building a body of work that explored, documented, and extended the general base of knowledge in response to this inquiry as it pertained to the non-material, cultural elements of people of African descent. The purpose of the social sciences is specifically to report on the development and behavior of social groups. Using scientific methodology, the social sciences describe, and in the very best case scenarios, predict or generalize about the social world they study.

Zora Neale Hurston lived during a time in American history wherein the perceived inferiority of people of African descent was woven into the fabric of American social institutions. She worked tirelessly through a myriad of methods (scientific, literary, musical, poetic, and dramatic) to document and illustrate just the opposite. She steadfastly plied her efforts during a time, with few exceptions, when the data she collected about the African American folk was unappreciated and, in some circles, unwanted. Nevertheless, with anticipation of a future when the humanity of the African would be more fully recognized, Hurston documented and preserved the non-material cultural elements of the black folk. Her meticulous collection of data was a major contribution, not only to African American culture, but also to human culture. Her work, in effect, emphasized the importance, overall, of the study of the social life of human groups in general.

As a cultural anthropologist, Hurston concentrated her focus on people of African descent and articulated her understanding of the inter-section of the historical legacy of Africana peoples in the Americas with the oppressive political and social structures that generated the narrative of their lives. She facilitated this through cultural immersion, and the collection, documentation, interpretation, discussion, and analysis of the non-material elements of the culture. The non-material cultural elements—the symbols, beliefs, values, attitudes, and norms—of African Americans were what Hurston tirelessly sought to document, preserve, and reveal. Her inquiries were many, and they addressed a variety of topics. But through every venue in which she worked, she continuously posed her hypothetical question: "What do the simple folk do?"

In her approach to understanding the question and the search for a response, Hurston utilized the tenets of the theory of cultural relativity. She examined the culturally universal practices that exhibited "sameness" among people, while simultaneously recognizing and documenting the "differences." Hurston was brilliant in that way. She could see the many hats on one head. An inveterate multiculturalist, Hurston believed that different cultures could and should co-exist with equanimity.

Human social activity is consistent across cultures. For example, all human populations have established rituals for the disposal of the physical remains of members of the social group, that is, all groups have processes for handling the deceased. Hurston researched the rituals of death in the American South, especially Louisiana, and in the Bahamas, Jamaica and Haiti. Pair bonding—love, marriage, and family issues—is another transcultural social imperative and was one of the themes Hurston often examined in her work as social scientist as well as in her work as a fiction writer. Consider her best-known novel, *Their Eyes Were Watching God*, or her short stories such as "The Gilded Six-Bits," "Sweat," and "Spunk" that treat and question the strengths and limitations of heterosexual relationships. Repeatedly, Hurston created independent female characters who subtly or aggressively responded to the gender repression inherent in their social environments and the patriarchal domination of their male partners. Janie, the protagonist from *Their Eyes Were Watching God*, is one of the most well-known characters Hurston created that embodies the ideals of the feminist-womanist.

Hurston was quite successful at doing immersion work—placing herself within the environment that she studied. She was adept in her abilities to conduct this work. Using the participant-observant technique, she was able to absorb the information she sought for investigation. Among the first social scientists to employ this technique, Hurston used the participant-observation approach, as it provided an unprecedented depth of information by direct contact between the researcher and the subject. As Janie said to Phoebe in *Their Eyes Were Watching God*, "It is a known fact, Phoebe, you got tuh go there tuh know there."[3] Hurston left indications in her collected data and in her publications about her fieldwork techniques. One such source is *Mules and Men*, a 1935 collection of African American folk stories and practices gathered from her years of traveling the American South, living among sharecroppers and itinerant workers. It is also evident in *Tell My Horse*, a collection of folklore from Jamaica and Haiti that highlights the religion of Vodou. Hurston's field research across the American South and the Black Atlantic speaks to her insatiable curiosity about the "simple folk."

In these works, we see how Hurston, through the approach of the participant-observer, embodied the cultural explorations of the field anthropologist as she participated in performative events studied in context of the customs and social lives of the groups in their natural environments. The folklore Hurston collected was a natural database of demographic information yielding insights relevant to gender, class, family, age, status, employment, and other indices. The showcasing of folk song and folk narrative emphasized oral tradition as the predominant mode of cultural transmission. In the Florida Folklife collection of the Works Progress Administration (WPA) are 26 songs collected by Hurston. Embedded in these recordings is Hurston's process of capturing and presenting oral expressions, significantly highlighting Hurston's ability to meld the worlds of science and art.[4]

Hurston was most adept at bringing a lens to the everyday life of black folk and presenting their world through the vernacular of authentic storytellers and actors. In 1931, she penned a play titled "Forty Yards," one of four sketches she wrote for the revue *Fast and Furious*.[5] The play dramatizes a football game between the two historically black universities, Howard and Lincoln, and the antics of both the players and their fans. Her summary conclusion to the play reflects various aspects of black folk tradition—song, dance, spirituality, and community:

As the ball is caught and when the player who is carrying the ball plunges, followed by his team, the Lincoln players fall on their knees and begin to sing "I Couldn't Hear Nobody Pray." The Howard team charges down shouting "Joshua fit de battle of Jericho." Whenever there is a player tackled, there is a duet of dancing. Every step is a dance.[6]

Hurston captured in this dramatic sketch a dynamic of African American cultural life that continues into the 21st century. Contemporary African American football players are well known for their dance moves on the football field after tackles, field goals, and touchdowns.

Hurston was proficient at emphasizing the importance of language as she reported on African American culture. Social scientists believe that language is the most important element of culture in that it facilitates the sharing and interpretation of abstract concepts among its members.

This communication, in turn, functions to create the reality of the group. This critical element of culture, its varied and complex processes, is what distinguishes humans from all other species and is the foundation of every cultural group.

As Hurston learned from her mentor, Franz Boas, the language of people studied was to be transcribed with the utmost precision. The transcription process was to be void of any embellishment. The "story" of a people was unique and the social scientist was compelled to document that story in the original vernacular of the group. Folklore collections such as *Go Gator and Muddy the Water* and *Every Tongue Got to Confess: Negro Folk-Tales from the Gulf States* are primary examples of Hurston's beliefs and methods.[7] Her use of the black vernacular to record the expressions of black folk and to represent black folk and folk culture on stage or in her fiction served as a window into the world of people little known and much misunderstood. Language functions as a cultural gatekeeper. As it is open to some, it can also exclude others. Much of Hurston's efforts focused on the presentation of authentic black folk expression in contexts that would allow those unfamiliar with the culture to appreciate it. Thus, in spite of criticism, she not only included dialect in her folklore publications, but she also incorporated dialect in her musical productions, plays, and fiction.

The use of black Southern dialect in *Their Eyes Were Watching God* brings the characters to life, and the narrative voice interprets the dialogue and action of the characters, allowing readers to relate to and understand them. The fashion in which the story unfolds between Janie and Phoebe mimics the intimate chat that Hurston has with the reader, as Hurston shares an event through dialogue, then explains it through the narration. Her work contributes to our understanding of the social life of the Southern black population from an insider's perspective. Hurston's experience of growing up in Eatonville, Florida, and her explorations throughout the deep South made her an expert on black culture. As an "insider," she was better positioned to translate, and therefore, interpret black culture. Further, Hurston took the important position of taking control of the scientific and popular definitions of black folk and black folk culture rather than allowing perceptions of those external to the group to define the folk and their culture, and impose those definitions on the group while also transmitting them to the larger society. Her more authentic portrayal contradicted the simplistic, ill-conceived, and often dehumanizing portrayals of African Americans. This "insider's" perspective allows for authenticity and accuracy in the documentation of and the reporting about the culture.

Hurston worked diligently at gaining access to this cultural community—the community of her childhood—for the necessary field work that solidified all of her work. As a matter of strategy, she designed a persona that would facilitate her research. She explained this in the introduction to *Mules and Men*:

Folklore is not as easy to collect as it sounds. The best source is where there are the least outside influences, and these people, being usually underprivileged, are the shyest. They are most reluctant at times to reveal that which the soul lives by. And the Negro, in spite of his open-faced laughter, his seeming acquiescence, is particularly evasive. You see we are a polite people, and we do not say to our questioner, "Get out of here!" We smile and tell him or her something that satisfies the white person because, knowing so little about us, he doesn't know what he is missing. The Indian resists curiosity by a stony silence. The Negro offers a feather bed resistance, that is, we let the probe enter, but it never comes out. It gets smothered under a lot of laughter and pleasantries.[8]

When I was asked in an interview what I wanted to impress on this generation and generations to come, my response seems in line with what Hurston attempted to do with her entire career and was the impetus for her work:

An understanding that there is more than one way of being and doing in this world. An expansion of an appreciation for the diversity of ways of being, be they along color lines, gender lines, be it about same-sex, interracial or interfaith marriage, other ways of being and doing in communities of existence. And we don't have to convert or agree, but we must respect ways of being as social groups and we must respect the life of people.[9]

I would surmise that Hurston's response might be consistent with my own, in light of this statement that she made:

National coherence and solidarity is implicit in a thorough understanding of the various groups within a nation, and this lack of knowledge about the internal emotions and behavior of the minorities cannot fail to bar out understanding. Man, like all the other animals, fears and is repelled by that which he does not understand, and mere difference is apt to connote something malign.[10]

So it behooves us to be inquisitive and curious. The accomplished social scientist, Hurston would look back with immense pride on her anthropological repertoire framed around the question of "What do the simple folk do?", and know that she demonstrated the value of investigating cultural groups, in general, and in researching the life and lore of African Americans in particular.

NOTES

1. Alan Jay Lerner and Frederick Loewe, "What Do the Simple Folk Do?" in *Camelot*. Book and Lyrics for "Camelot" (New York: Chappell and Company, Alfred Productions, 1960).

2. Zora Neale Hurston, *Dust Tracks on a Road* (1942; repr., Urbana: University of Illinois, 1984), 174.

3. Zora Neale Hurston, *Their Eyes Were Watching God* (1937; repr., Urbana: University of Illinois Press, 1978), 285.

4. A sampling of the collected songs can be heard on the audio CD included in the volume of writing and memorabilia compiled by Lucy Anne Hurston in *Speak So You Can Speak Again: The Life of Zora Neale Hurston* (New York: Doubleday, 2004).

5. "Forty Yards" in *Zora Neale Hurston: Collected Plays*, ed. Jean Lee Cole and Charles Mitchell (1931; repr., New Brunswick, NJ: Rutgers University Press, 2008).

6. Ibid., 216.

7. Zora Neale Hurston, *Writings by Zora Neale Hurston from the Federal Writers' Project: Go Gator and Muddy the Water*, ed. Pamela Bordelon (New York: Norton, 1999); Zora Neale Hurston, *Every Tongue Got to Confess: Negro Folk-Tales from the Gulf States*, ed. Carla Kaplan (New York: Perennial, 2001).

8. Zora Neale Hurston, *Mules and Men* (1935; repr., Bloomington: Indiana University Press, 1978), 4.

9. Deborah G. Plant, *Zora Neale Hurston: A Biography of the Spirit* (Westport, CT: Praeger, 2007), 174.

10. Zora Neale Hurston, "What White Publishers Won't Print," in *I Love Myself When I'm Laughing, and Then Again When I'm Looking Mean and Impressive*, ed. Alice Walker (New York: The Feminist Press, 1979), 169.

Masculinity in Hurston's Texts

Kersuze Simeon-Jones

Ole Maker . . . Ah ast you *please* to give me mo' strength than dat woman you give me, so Ah kin make her mind.
—Zora Neale Hurston, *Mules and Men*[1]

. . . Mah wife don't know nothin' bout no speech-makin'. Ah never married her for nothin' lak dat. She's uh woman and her place is in de home.
—Zora Neale Hurston, *Their Eyes Were Watching God*[2]

In *Mules and Men* and *Their Eyes Were Watching God*, Zora Neale Hurston examines and challenges the notion of masculinity in correlation to the concept of femininity. Together, the texts illustrate the interrelations between myths and stereotypes as well as the socially constructed realities of prescribed gender identities and roles. An analysis of the narratives and actions in Hurston's novel and the folktales she collected demonstrates the extent to which the folk in Eatonville—and Hurston herself—attempt to decipher the source of distinctive gender attributes and roles through the conjectures they refer to as tales and through everyday discourse.

One of the central themes of *Mules and Men* and *the* focus of *Their Eyes Were Watching God* is female empowerment. By extension, embedded in Hurston's depiction of women's emotional and psychological strength, as well as their contribution to society, is the examination of masculinity as it was performed in 20th-century America and as it continues well into the 21st century. The stories told in *Mules and Men* and *Their Eyes Were Watching God* reveal female contention of assumed male rights and privileges. Within the context of female underprivileged condition and debasement are the following points to consider throughout the analysis of the texts: the meaning of maleness for black men, during a period when they are neither regarded nor treated as humans; the ways in which they express their idea of maleness; the significance of privately and publicly displaying their masculinity; and the extent to which black men use black women to assert their notion of maleness and perpetuate an image of male reality.

In "Folk Tales," chapter seven of *Mules and Men*, the dispute between Big Sweet and Joe Willard exposes differing expectations and perspectives regarding gender roles, even in relation to leisure activities. Joe Willard, for instance, assumes that his day off is his opportunity to engage in hobbies with his fellows without the women "dragging" behind them. For him, the day provides the luxury of being away from work, and, most importantly, the absence of Big Sweet. On the other hand, Big Sweet would rather share the time participating in his activities. Joe's reprimand to what he views as Big Sweet's conspicuous behavior did not dissuade her from the intention of going along. "See dat?" Joe frustratingly points out, "We git a day off and figger we kin ketch some fish and enjoy ourselves, but naw, some wimmins got to drag behind us, even to de lake." Resolutely, Big Sweet retorts: "You didn't figger Ah was draggin' behind you when you was bringin' dat Sears and Roebuck catalogue over to my house and beggin' me to choose my ruthers? Lemme tell *you* something, *any* time Ah shack up wid any man Ah gives myself de privilege to go wherever he might be, night or day. Ah got de law in my mouth."[3] The affirmation "Ah gives myself de privilege" is telling; it demonstrates Big Sweet's acknowledgment of her own power over herself to go where she chooses to go and when. It further shows the importance she accords to her voice, and the conviction of expressing herself. Big Sweet follows the rules she judges appropriate for her life, for she "got de law in [her] mouth."

Joe's comrades, Richardson and Jim Allen, perceive Big Sweet as the recalcitrant voice leading their women into disobedience. "Oh, Big Sweet does dat," comments Richardson, "Ah knowed she had somethin' up her sleeve when she got Lucy and come along." Jim Allen adds, "Well, you know what they say—a man can cackerlate his life till he git mixed up wid a woman or git straddle of a cow."[4] Here, the male reaction underscores the complexity of gender dynamics. Foremost, Allen reminds Richardson and Willard that a relationship with a woman is inevitably an encumbering entanglement. The underlying understanding is that if men claim specific rights and privileges, they must not be challenged by the women in their lives. The man who encounters resistance from his female counterpart is regarded as a victim. Here, Joe Willard is presented as a man trapped within the web of an overpowering, omnipresent, and controlling woman. The woman who is seen as disrupting the order of gender relations is often characterized as irregular. Ultimately, what Hurston lays bare in the presentation of the story is the tradition of male entitlement to a particular way of life. When the claimed privileges are challenged, the men are immediately viewed as the unfortunate victims of their nonconforming women.

In the tale, "Why Women Always Take Advantage of Men," Hurston presents a story on the origin of physical and psychological gender hierarchy. The story poses this fundamental question: Who holds the ultimate power, men or women? The answer is elucidated in a sort of historical account where one learns that men initially were stronger but, subsequently, women received from God the three keys to female strengths and male weaknesses. The tale is a conjectural explanation of the genesis of men's physical control over women. It begins with the explanation that, one day, a man goes to heaven to ask God for superior strength in order to dominate *his* woman:

Ah ast you *please* to give mo' strength than dat woman you give me, so Ah kin make her mind. Ah know you don't want to be always comin' down way past de moon and stars to be straightenin' her out and its got to be done. So give me a li'l mo' strength, Ole Maker, and Ah'll do it."[5]

Upon his return, the man boasts, "Woman! Here's yo' boss, God done tole me to handle you in which ever way Ah please. Ah'm yo' boss." According to the story, since that day men had complete physical control over women and could make them do anything they desired. "Long as you obey me, Ah'll be good to yuh," he proudly warns her, "but every time yuh rear up, Ah'm gointer put plenty wood on yo' back and plenty water in yo' eyes."[6] The abuse remained constant until the devil told the woman about the keys in heaven. God gave the woman the keys and the devil taught her how to use them:

See dese three keys? They got mo' power in 'em than all de strength de man kin ever git if you handle 'em right. Now dis first big key is de do' of de kitchen, and you know a man always favors his stomach. Dis second one is de key to de bedroom and he don't like to be shut out from dat neither and dis last key is de key to de cradle and he don't want to be cut off from his generations at all. So now you take dese keys and go lock up everything and wait till he come to you. Then don't you unlock nothin' until he use his strength for yo' benefit and yo' desires.[7]

The first observation is the devil's presence in the process of the woman reclaiming control over her being and acquiring lasting power. The reason behind the inclusion of the devil is not clear, except to say that it is in accordance with the Bible's account of the genesis of humans in the story of Adam, Eve, God, the devil, and the apple. Without digressing into a religious analysis, it is worth pondering the significance of the devil in "Why Women Always Take Advantage of Men." The folktale goes a bit further than the Adam and Eve story perhaps to suggest that it required the devil's instruction to counteract the man's clever deceit and to keep the woman from falling back under his abuse and manipulation: "Jus' one mo' thing: don't go home braggin' 'about yo' keys," admonishes the devil. "Jus' lock up everything and say nothin' until you git asked. And then don't talk too much." Realizing the magnitude of the woman's might—which transcends the physical—the man attempts to trick her into exchanging and dividing their respective gifts: "Ah'll give you half of my strength if you lemme hold de keys in my hands."[8] Because the devil cautions the woman of such a proposition from the man, she is aware of his desire to regain power over her, so she declines his offer. Since then, as recounted in the tale, women are the ones who possess the *real* or ultimate power. As one of the women storytellers in *Mules and Men* concludes, "you men is still braggin' bout yo' strength and de women is sittin' on de keys and lettin' you blow off till she git ready to put de bridle on you."[9]

Based on the presentation of similar tales of female strength in Hurston's texts, one can read the subtext as the narration of the female quest for empowerment. *Mules and Men* is the text that preceded and prepared Hurston's audience for a blatant feminist text, *Their Eyes Were Watching God*. Hurston's now-classic novel set a trend in the literary world with its presentation of the protagonist, Janie Crawford. Through this character, Hurston articulates a new definition of black womanness in the context of and in relation to society's conception of maleness. As the narrative unfolds, Janie Crawford evolves from a naïve girl to a woman who has "been to the horizon and back."[10] Janie's second husband, Joe Starks, whom she married after she left her first husband while still very young, became the mayor of Eatonville.[11] As a public figure, Joe Starks is proud of his accomplishments and his wife, whom he treats as an *emblem* of his success. He believes his wife should be the epitome of elitism and feminine decorum, according to the standard of the society within which they live.

During his opening speech as the mayor and in response to the townsfolk's suggestion that his wife take the floor, Joe Starks replies: "Thank yuh fuh yo' compliments, but mah wife don't know nothin' bout no speech-makin'. Ah never married her for nothin' lak dat. She's uh woman and her place is in de home." Following Joe's comment, the narrator describes Janie's mental disposition and disguised physical state:

Janie made her face laugh after a short pause, but it wasn't too easy. She had never thought of making a speech, and didn't know if she cared to make one at all. It must have been the way Joe spoke out without giving her a chance to say anything one way or another that took the bloom off of things. But anyway, she went down the road behind him that night feeling cold. He strode along invested with his new dignity, thought and planned out loud, unconscious of her thoughts.[12]

The notions of the silenced voice and suppressed desires pervade the story. Throughout the novel, however, Janie gradually finds her voice and uses it publicly. One of the male townsfolk observes and compliments the mayor on his wife's oratorical ability: "Yo wife is uh born orator, Starks. Us never knowed dat befo'. She put jus' de right words tuh our thoughts."[13] Apparently intended as praise to Joe and his wife, Joe Starks received the statement as an insult to his manhood. If his wife is regarded as a gifted orator who dared to speak publicly, the implication is that he has not accomplished his manly duty of keeping her in her place. Correspondingly, the day Janie took a stand and countered Joe's verbal assault on her age and looks with a verbal attack on his masculinity was the day Joe disowned her as a wife until his death. Over a period of two decades Janie "clerked" in Joe's store while being the constant target of his ridicule and vitriol. But on one day, Janie retaliated in kind. Joe Starks derides Janie's ability to properly cut a piece of chewing tobacco. In the process, he calls her an old woman "wid yo' rump hangin' nearly to yo' knees!" He further tells her that she need not feel insulted since she is no longer a "young gal," and "nobody in heah ain't lookin' for no wife outa yuh. Old as you is." Janie fires back:

Naw, Ah ain't no young gal no mo', but den Ah ain't no old woman neither. Ah reckon Ah looks mah age too. But Ah'm uh woman every inch of me, and Ah know it. Dat's uh whole lot more'n *you* kin say. You big-bellies round here and put out a lot of brag, but 'tain't nothin' to it but yo' big voice. Humph! Talkin' 'bout *me* lookin' old! When you pull down yo' britches, you look lak de change uh life.[14]

In her riposte, Janie openly challenges the long-standing discrimination against the aging woman in comparison to the acceptance of her male counterpart. Her response clearly shows that she does not subscribe to the widespread belief—accepted as reality—that a man's masculinity defies age and physical desirability while a woman's femininity and physical attractiveness is diminished in direct proportion to her progress in years. Janie denounces the marginalization of women as old hags. Like Big Sweet, she straightforwardly, clearly, and publicly uttered the words that expressed the feelings of many women of her era. The narrator intervenes to interpret the significance of Janie's retort and its impact on Joe Starks:

Then Joe Starks realized all the meanings and his vanity bled like a flood. Janie robbed him of his illusion of irresistible maleness that all men cherish, which was terrible. The thing that Saul's daughter had done to David. But Janie had done worse, she had cast down his empty armor before men and they had laughed, would keep on laughing. . . . Joe Starks didn't know the words for all this, but he knew the feeling. So he struck Janie with all his might and drove her from the store.[15]

The physical blow was Joe's attempt to reclaim his definition of maleness. Like the man in "Why Women Always Take Advantage of Men," Joe Starks is inclined to use his strength to subdue Janie and "make her mind." Essentially, Joe wants to preserve the image of the mighty and commanding masculinity that has been transmitted generationally, an image he accepts and with which he identifies. As a man thus conceived, Joe assumes the responsibility of maintaining a social order that perpetuates male dominance and female subjugation—economically, socially, politically, physically, emotionally, and psychologically. As a leader among men, Joe Starks must model the appropriate manly behavior, as he is keenly aware that other men observe his actions. Since the day of the open confrontation with Joe Starks in the store, Janie kept her found voice; hence, the subsequent death of Joe Starks symbolized her complete freedom. The night after the burial, she burned all head rags that Joe had forced her to wear in perpetuity and "went about the house next morning with her hair in one thick braid swinging well below her waist. . . . She would have the rest of her life to do as she pleased."[16]

Both *Mules and Men* and *Their Eyes Were Watching God* illustrate the mythology of a divinely ordained and heritable masculine entitlement. They also illustrate the female will to resist subjugation and pursue her quest for self-empowerment and freedom. Hurston's life and her life work are major influences on black women writers of the latter part of the 20th century and at the outset of the 21st century. Notwithstanding personal and professional challenges, Hurston's life story and writings have cleared a path for a new generation of black women writers and black female representation. In *The Character of the Word: The Texts of Zora Neale Hurston*, Karla F.C. Holloway observes that later generations of scholars, black women writers in particular, "look at writers like Hurston within a black aesthetic because she is mother to a tradition and has given voice to a generation of black women's concern that may otherwise have been lost."[17] In her texts, Hurston becomes/is the griot and orator of black folktales and black female thought. Though *Mules and Men* is a transcription of folktales, Hurston creates the context within which each story is told in order to establish a certain critical framework and a particular social and philosophical analysis. Holloway rightly suggests that one can symbolically view Hurston as "both a foremother and a child not yet conceived."[18] The apparent "foremother" attribute is just as pertinent to Hurston as that of a "child not yet conceived," for even though Hurston wrote these texts in the first half of the 20th century, they did not take full life until the second half of the century—the late 1970s. Their birth, or rebirth, as one may call it, did not occur until the new generation of black women writers gave them life. Today, the generation of writers of the 21st century continues to bring Hurston's work to life. Hence, Hurston "gave voice to a generation of black women and left legacies for generations to follow."[19]

The scrutiny of masculinity in Hurston's texts offers insight to 21st-century writers and women in general. In situating the genesis of gender politics within a mythico-historical framework—albeit through the conjectures of the folk—Hurston reminds her readers of the long-standing dynamic of male and female relationships. In 2005, Oprah Winfrey revived Hurston's social preoccupations through the television adaptation of *Their Eyes Were Watching God*. The movie inspired readers to revisit the novel and reassess Hurston's depiction of masculinity in the context of the changing conception of masculinity in the 21st century. The male characters Logan Killicks, Joe Starks, and Vergible Woods (Tea Cake) illustrate the different aspects of male psychology and behavior. Janie's first husband, Logan, wanted to keep her in subjugation by inculcating a belief of helplessness. His repeated remarks about the 60 acres of land and a house are used to remind Janie of his material power. Because Logan does not have much to offer, as an aging man who is insinuated to be impotent, his symbol of power and maleness becomes the land and the house. Most importantly, his objective is that Janie internalizes the thought that she cannot survive without his possessions. In essence, Logan treats Janie like a slave who is responsible for every aspect of house work and farm work. The observation the ethnologist, Jean Price-Mars, made in the early 1900s in reference to the condition of Haitian women of the masses (both rural and urban) is comparable to Janie's situation. In 1919, he wrote that for her man, the woman is the most effective work tool and machine; she is also a working farm animal—a donkey. The man is the boss, the master, and the god.[20]

If Janie is a work tool for Logan, she is an object of display for Joe Starks. If Logan affirms his masculinity by overworking his object of submission, Joe asserts his by exhibiting her as a symbol of social status. Joe views his position as the mayor of Eatonville as holding the ultimate social and political authority over the townsfolk and his wife. To maintain *dominion* over his wife, Joe keeps her sequestered: away from any male glance, away from fun activities with the townswomen. He not only controls her social interactions, but also regulates her wardrobe, her speech, her behavior, and tries to dominate her thoughts and beliefs. The severance of Janie's familiar relations with the townspeople is crucial to Joe, for her image plays an important role in his concept of masculinity. As a symbol of accomplishment, Janie is equivalent to his fancy house, his car, and his business suits. Similar to Logan, Joe also employs psychological manipulation to keep Janie in subjugation. While Logan often refers to his 60 acres and the house, Joe attempts to destroy the foundation of her being and crush her self-worth with the consistent repetition that she is no longer a young woman, and no other man would marry her. In both cases, the ultimate goal is to erase Janie's self-esteem and *rewire* her thoughts into beliefs of helplessness and dependency. However, such ploys, particularly the need for the erasure of Janie's character, speak to the insecurities of both men.

Tea Cake is a more complex character within the context of performing masculinity. Where Logan and Joe command Janie to tend the house, the farm, and the store, Tea Cake works with her. Where Logan mistreats her through excessive labor and Joe through insults, labor, and physical abuse, Tea Cake protects and provides for her without blatant and condescending domination. At first glance, Tea Cake is the illustration of disinterested love and respect. One could argue that Tea Cake, as the youngest man, is Hurston's visionary image of the 21st-century male. His dilemma is both internal and external. As such, he struggles between the desire to treat Janie as an equal and the desire to dominate her. He struggles between the effort to respect her empowerment and the desire to subdue her. He takes money from her purse without her permission and spends it, with a promise to win it back by gambling. And his jealousy compels him to emotionally and physically abuse Janie privately and publicly. Like Joe Starks, Tea Cake strikes Janie. His action was to prove to the prying Mrs. Turner— who wanted Janie to leave Tea Cake for her brother—that *he* is in charge, "he *is* the man" (in contemporary parlance). Stated differently, Tea Cake's performance was to assert his maleness in the presence of Mrs. Turner.

Both Joe Starks and Tea Cake follow the example of the black man who publicly displays his image of maleness through the physical abuse of the black woman. It has been theorized that in a society where the black man has been disenfranchised and robbed of meaningful social authority, the black woman becomes the victim of his anger and frustration. To the extent that such male psychology and performance is historical and generational, Hurston's 1937 novel remains pertinent today. If Janie represents the black woman's quest for freedom, self-assertiveness, and empowerment, Tea Cake's behavior is reflective of the black male's social, emotional, and psychological dilemma. Hurston's presentation of both the image and reality of maleness in the early 20th century offers the 21st-century scholar, and society in general, a paradigm with which to rethink and redefine the concept of masculinity, particularly as it relates to female survival in terms of her physical, emotional, and psychological health.

NOTES

1. Zora Neale Hurston, *Mules and Men* (1935; repr., New York: Harper Perennial, 1990), 31.

2. Zora Neale Hurston, *Their Eyes Were Watching God* (1937; repr., New York: HarperCollins Publishers, 2000), 51.

3. Hurston, *Mules and Men*, 124.

4. Ibid., 124.

5. Ibid., 31.

6. Ibid., 32.

7. Ibid., 33.

8. Ibid., 34.

9. Ibid., 33.

10. Hurston, *Their Eyes*, 225.

11. Janie's first marriage was a loveless one of convenience arranged by her grandmother. Before her final days, the grandmother wanted to be certain that Janie was married and living a respectable life.

12. Hurston, *Their Eyes*, 51.

13. Ibid., 69.

14. Ibid., 94.

15. Ibid., 95.

16. Ibid., 106.

17. Karla F.C. Holloway, *The Character of the Word: The Texts of Zora Neale Hurston* (Westport: Greenwood Press, 1987), 10.

18. Ibid., 16.

19. Ibid., 17.

20. Jean Price-Mars, *La Vocation de L'Elite* (Port-au-Prince: Imprimerie Edmond Chenet, 1919), 97. This passage is a translation by the author. The passage in its original expression was written as follows:

La paysanne est pour son homme le meilleur et le plus excellent outil de travail dont il ait le maniement . . . Où le paysan est métayer et petit propriétaire, la bête de ferme est d'abord et surtout *la femme* . . . L'homme, le patron, le maître et seigneur . . .

Hollywood Wants a Cracker: Zora Neale Hurston and Studio Narrative Culture*

Elizabeth Binggeli

What has Zora Neale Hurston, matriarch of 20th-century African American literature, to do with studio era Hollywood—purveyor of mass media hokum? The answer is, in short, a good deal more than one might initially expect. I offer here a brief sketch of the impression Hurston made on the Hollywood film industry of the 1930s and 1940s, and the impression that the industry, in turn, made on her.

"A TINY WEDGE IN HOLLYWOOD"

An early association with the author Fannie Hurst may have inspired Hurston to see her works adapted to film. In 1923, Hurston worked as chauffeur and secretary to Hurst, whose fiction was then being adapted to silent film and would soon be adapted to talkies. Universal Pictures twice adapted Hurst's 1933 novel, *Imitation of Life,* the melodramatic story of a white, upwardly mobile "new woman," and a young "tragic mulatta" attempting to pass for white. In 1934, the same year the first of the *Imitation of Life* films was released, Hurston's literary agent, Ann Watkins, submitted Hurston's first novel, *Jonah's Gourd Vine* (1934), to Hollywood studios for review.[1] Bertram Lippincott, Hurston's editor, imagined Paul Robeson cast as the lead in a potential adaptation.[2]

*First published as the article "The Unadapted: Warner Bros. Reads Zora Neale Hurston," by Elizabeth Binggeli, from *Cinema Journal*, Volume 48, Issue 3, pp. 1–15. Copyright © 2009 by the University of Texas Press. All rights reserved.

The ambitions of Hurston's agent and editor were not unreasonably optimistic. While it is common knowledge that Hollywood narrative production in the studio era was conservative, particularly in regard to race, Hollywood narrative consumption was strikingly liberal. Box office booms of the mid-1930s and early 1940s, together with the advent of double features in the box office slump of the Depression, necessitated intense studio story searches. Tino Balio estimates that by 1934, some 700 features were needed per year to "feed the maw of exhibition."[3] There was, naturally, a corresponding "maw of production," and indeed the narrative appetite of Hollywood story departments during the studio era had no rival among cultural institutions. In a single week beginning July 24, 1934, for example, the story analysts at Universal Pictures Corporation read and reviewed twenty-two published novels, twelve novel galleys, four novel manuscripts, two novel page-proofs, thirty-one original manuscripts, twelve play scripts, two screenplays, four individual magazine stories, and six magazines in their entirety.[4] Even after production abated in the 1950s, Warner Brothers boasted about reviewing over 5,000 submissions per year. The lofty goal of story departments was, in Janet Staiger's words, nothing less than "complete coverage of worldwide publishing."[5]

So it would be wrong to assume that the studios didn't bother to consider for adaptation stories by African American writers or stories featuring controversial racial content, including stories about miscegenation, "mixed blood" characters, interracial rape, lynching, and race wars. The fact is that the studios were then considering every scrap of narrative they could get their hands on. Hollywood did review the majority of works by prominent black writers of the day, including Arna Bontemps, Jessie Fauset, Chester Himes, Langston Hughes, Claude McKay, Jean Toomer, and Richard Wright, and prepared reports on such diverse texts as Toomer's radical collection of stories and poems *Cane* (1923) and Bontemps's novel of Haitian slave insurrection, *Drums at Dusk* (1939). Though these works were never adapted, it is important to recognize that the industry was intimately familiar with the literature of the prominent black writers of the day, including Hurston. While artists, intellectuals, and patrons of the Harlem Renaissance struggled with the aesthetic and political question of who would stand in the position of "the New Negro," Hollywood was asking an economic question: What black stories can we sell?

Jonah was reviewed but rejected by studio story editors. In 1937, however, Hollywood considered Hurston's work again. *Their Eyes Were Watching God* was reviewed nearly two months before its publication. It was not unusual for story editors to receive novels in galley form; fierce industry competition encouraged studios to gamble on novels the public had yet to approve.

Warner Brothers prepared a report on the novel featuring "Josette—a romantic, idealistic young Florida negress."[6] Either Hurston's most famous protagonist was given a different name in this particular galley version, or this slip from "Janie" to "Josette" gives us an indication of the hastiness of this synopsis. The report details Josette's relationships with Logan, "a much older man whom she doesn't love," Jody, "a dominating city negro [. . .] who thirsts for, and seems created for, power"; and Tea Cake, "a younger negro, a vital, romantic vagabond who plays the guitar and the dice with equal ease." The reader's concluding comment, where she is expected to endorse or reject the story, is succinct: "Quite charmingly written in spots . . . but obviously not for the screen" [ellipses in original].

What was "obvious" to Goldberg we can only guess. But if the problem was an all-black cast, it should be remembered that just the previous year, in 1936, Warner had released *The Green Pastures,* one of the top money-making films of the year. Adapted from white writer Marc Connelly's Pulitzer prize-winning play—itself based on the tales of Roark Bradford—the film, starring Rex Ingram as "De Lawd," depicted biblical stories through the eyes of Southern black children and included the famous "fish fry in heaven" scene. Warner paid Connelly $100,000—at the time the highest price ever paid—for screen rights.[7] The studio likely felt safe in its investment: musicals were money in the bank in the emerging sound era, and there were no big star salaries to inflate the budget. Donald Bogle considers *The Green Pastures* to be one of the three important features spotlighting black casts to emerge from the 1930s, together with Universal's *Imitation of Life* and MGM's *Gone With the Wind* (1939).[8] In addition to *Imitation's* tragic mulatta, each of these films relied heavily on black stock characters including *Gone With the Wind's* loyal slaves, and *Pasture's* contribution, what Bogle describes as "the liveliest collection of agreeable toms, uncle remuses, aunt jemimas and corn-patch pickaninnies ever assembled in one motion picture."[9] The studio of *The Green Pastures* was unwelcoming to the likes of "Josette" Crawford, a black woman of restless independence and sexuality, who strongly resists these narrative stereotypes.

Four years after the studios reviewed *Their Eyes,* in the spring of 1941, Hurston moved to Southern California. While she writes in her autobiography *Dust Tracks on a Road* (1942) that she "did not come [to California] to get into the movies," Hurston was briefly employed by Paramount Studios as a writer and technical advisor.[10] "This job here at the studio is not the end of things for me," Hurston wrote. "It is a means."[11] Her contract with Paramount indicates that her $150-per-week position lasted scarcely two months, ending in December of 1941. The bombing of Pearl Harbor suspended many Hollywood productions at this time, and it is possible that the unknown Paramount project with which Hurston was involved was tabled for more topical films. That same year, the studios reviewed and rejected Hurston's *The Man of the Mountain* (presumably *Moses, Man of the Mountain,* or a version of it) and, the following year, reviewed Hurston's autobiography *Dust Tracks.*

The story department at Warner Brothers analyzed *Dust Tracks* more thoroughly than any other Hurston work to that point. The Warner Brothers reader writes in his coverage of the autobiography that "from her earliest days, Zora Neale Hurston realized there was something extraordinary about herself and her family."[12] This exceptional quality, the reader explains, had something to do "with Eatonville itself, an incorporated town run wholly by and for Negroes." The reader describes Zora's visions, her childhood play, and the death of her mother, who was the "mainspring of her father's life." After "beat[ing] the stuffing" out of her stepmother, Zora leaves home and gets her "first real break" as a lady's maid for an opera singer. Eventually, she is, in the reader's words, "befriended by influential Negroes and whites," and launches her writing and academic careers. "At last," the reader writes, "she began to use the material stored up in her for novels, which immediately caught on." The reader notes that although Hurston's love life has been rather spotty [. . .], Zora's belief in her exceptionalism has come true, and she has found the second woman friend to bring her peace: Ethyl Waters.

It is interesting that the Warner Brothers reader should present as the climax of Hurston's autobiography her friendship with one of Hollywood's better-known black celebrities; at the time of the reader's report, Waters was set to begin work on MGM's *Cabin in the Sky* (1943). The reader's final comments on *Dust Tracks* are worth quoting in full:

The flavor of this interesting autobiography cannot be caught in a one page summary. Zora Hurston has an extraordinarily vivid style and sense of imagery; she writes with power and simplicity and humor. Her viewpoint of the Negro people is so complicated and confused that it would require a thesis to disentangle; she has contempt for a large portion of her race.

The reader's appreciation for Hurston's style and complexity seems almost reverent when compared to the opinions of many literary reviewers of the day. Just a few days before the Warner Brothers reader wrote his coverage, the *Saturday Review* declared, that *Dust Tracks* was

told in exactly the right manner, simply and with candor, with a seasoning—not overdone—of the marvelous locutions of the imaginative field nigger. [. . .] It is a fine, rich autobiography, and heartening to anyone, white, black, or tan.[13]

The Warner Brothers reader does not make this kind of patronizing gesture in his report. He concludes his coverage with the statement that "of course the theme rules this out for a picture." His "of course" rings like Goldberg's "obviously"—an insider's nod to another insider of the thing so evident it need not be spoken. While still in Los Angeles in late 1942, Hurston wrote to her friend Carl Van Vechten, confiding:

I have a tiny wedge in Hollywood, and I have hopes of breaking that old silly rule about Negroes not writing about white people. In fact, I have a sort of commitment from a producer at RKO that he will help me do it. I am working on the story now.

At this point, Hurston's hopes for a project with RKO were directly linked to a decision to "write about white people." If the project to which Hurston refers is an early version of *Seraph on the Suwanee*, as Claudia Tate has suggested, the novel should be read as a story not merely influenced by, but first conceived for, studio production.[14]

HURSTON AND MARJORIE KINNAN RAWLINGS

For those primarily familiar with *Their Eyes*, however, *Seraph* can come as something of a shock. Literary critics have called *Seraph* "implausible," "ludicrous," "schizophrenic," and "bewildering," and generally attribute the novel's failures to Hurston's decision to focus on white characters, effectively "turn[ing] her back" on black cultural traditions.[15] *Seraph*'s neurotic protagonist, Arvay Henson, is a wretchedly insecure Southern white woman in a masochistic marriage. Any reader hoping for a female liberation epiphany *à la Their Eyes Were Watching God* will be disappointed by *Seraph*—Arvay finds fulfillment only when she realizes that she was "meant to serve" her abusive husband Jim. For many Hurston readers, *Seraph* is a confused, embarrassing aberration amidst the author's otherwise distinguished and innovative work.

But Hurston's "failure" of a novel is much more understandable when considered in terms of her desire to court Hollywood studios and, in particular, her perception of the industry's appetite for a particular kind of white character: the Southern cracker.

While Hurston's first three novels and autobiography had failed to tempt the studios, a white writer specializing in rural Floridian life was quickly becoming a Hollywood darling. In 1938, Marjorie Kinnan Rawlings sold the rights of her Pulitzer prize-winning novel *The Yearling* (1938) to Metro-Goldwyn-Mayer for $30,000. Director Clarence Brown's lush adaptation, released in 1946, was a critical and box-office smash. Rawlings would see further success in Hollywood with MGM's purchase of her stories "A Mother in Mannville" (1936) and "Mountain Prelude"

(1947), which together became the film *The Sun Comes Up* in 1949, directed by Richard Thorpe. It may have rankled Hurston that Rawlings, a Northerner by birth, was quickly becoming recognized as America's ambassador to the rural South, in both literature and film. In order to understand Hollywood's influence on *Seraph*, it is necessary to delve into Rawlings's studio-friendly fiction, that fiction's racial preoccupations, and the complicated relationship the two authors had with each other.

Rawlings herself described her work as "true sketches of the Cracker folk in the still pioneer heart of Florida."[16] Her embrace of the term "cracker" is significant. Originally a Scots-Irish term for "boaster," by the mid-nineteenth century the term "cracker" came to signify poor white farmers (or "corn-crackers") and itinerant white cattle herders (or "whip-crackers") of the American Southeast. Rawlings used the term to mean those who were white, poor, rural, and Southern. But among black people, the term was associated with the whipping of black slaves and had the connotation of "overt white racist."[17] For its part, Hollywood's run of crackerphilia began in force in 1941, with John Ford's *Tobacco Road* at Twentieth Century-Fox, and continued well into the 1950s with Universal's long-running Ma and Pa Kettle series. Rawlings's work was a perfect fit for this narrative niche.

Hurston was paying attention to Rawlings's fame. She "carefully and prayerfully" read Rawlings's depictions of both white and black Floridians, then wrote to the author with her praise. Of the quasi-autobiographical collection of stories, *Cross Creek*, Hurston told Rawlings that she had "written the best thing on Negroes of any white writer who has ever lived," adding, "Maybe you have bettered me."[18]

To contextualize Hurston's praise of *Cross Creek*, it should be pointed out that black people are largely represented in this work as the girls and young women whom Rawlings attempts to train as housekeepers. Rawlings describes this training as a kind of "taming." In the chapter entitled "Catching One Young," Rawlings relates:

I bought Georgia of her father for five dollars. The surest way to keep a maid at the Creek, my new friends told me, was to take over a very young Negro girl and train her in my ways. She should be preferably without home ties so that she should become attached to me. [. . .] It is possible that in catching one young, I had picked too early a litter.[19]

The unsuitability of a string of black housekeepers is presented as a running joke, and Rawlings casts herself as a kind of mother to her charges, calling one servant her "changeling child." Overall, *Cross Creek* suggests that "mothering the other" is a project that is doomed to failure. While there are no black characters in either Rawlings's Pulitzer prize-winning novel *The Yearling* or MGM's adaptation of it, the coming-of-age tale is marked by similar racial tropes.

The novel, *The Yearling*, tells the story of Jody, a dirt-poor pioneer boy who adopts a wild deer as a beloved pet but must eventually kill that deer when it threatens to drive the pioneer Baxter family to starvation. Jody's journey to manhood is linked to his ability to accept the death of his fawn, Flag, for the sake of the family. The text of *The Yearling* most known today is expurgated: in the first edition, the edition that was read by MGM's story department, Rawlings included many metaphorical references to black people: a raccoon's paws are likened to a "nigger baby's hands"; the family's hunting dogs are compared to "nigger dogs" chasing escaped slaves; the dreaded bear, Slewfoot, hunted throughout the text is called "the black gentleman"; the family patriarch sings that he "would rather be a nigger than a poor white man" (which is particularly odd because the character *is* a poor white man). Even with the expurgations, however, Rawlings's novel persistently casts the tale of the Baxters as a kind of white national origin myth. MGM's adaptation, while eliminating the racial epithets that would run it afoul of the Production Code, bolsters such a reading. The studio saw fit to add a written preface to the film:

We dedicate this picture to those who came to our land long ago and made it their home—and our inheritance! For us they faced the unknown. For us they hungered and toiled, their endurance is our prosperity: their struggle is our freedom: their dawn is our day. From their dust we spring; and, reaping the great harvest of their lives and works, we remember them with blessings.[20]

The preface, created wholecloth by the studio, tells "us"—a presumed if not actual homogenously white audience—that the people represented in the film we are about to see are our national, economic, and even genetic forebears; people whose existence provides an authentic history for, and thus a justification of, our own existence. Crackers as an American Adam and Eve.

And this Adam and Eve must patrol the garden for serpents; or for, as it turns out, cuddly deer. The overarching narrative question of *The Yearling* is asked by Jody: "Kin you tame 'em, do you get 'em young?"[21] Is it safe to bring the alien into the family circle? In the film, Jody promises to pen and whip his pet in order to train it to stop stealing food. But his efforts fail miserably. While Rawlings's failure to train domestics in *Cross Creek* is meant as a mere crisis in housekeeping, Jody's attempts to tame the deer, Flag, prove catastrophic. *The Yearling* suggests that maturation is linked to a serious understanding of what can and cannot be a "pet," and what can and cannot be "tamed."

In both *Cross Creek* and *The Yearling*, Rawlings plays with the literary trope Werner Sollors identifies as *Natus Æthiopus*: the birth of a black child to a white mother.[22] Sollors also describes this trope's mirror, *Natus Albus:* the birth of a white child to a black mother. In narrative, the *Natus Æthiopus/Natus Albus* child is born to expose a mother's once hidden inter-racial history—either as a person of "mixed blood" (the tragic mulatta) or as a person guilty of miscegenation. The idea that "blood will tell" can be a comforting fiction in environments where the purported "purity" of white identity is perceived as under threat. The jokes that Rawlings makes about her incorrigible black "changeling children" function to underscore her difference from them, and thus her own identity as white.

After receiving Hurston's letter, Rawlings invited her to the famous Cross Creek residence, where the two authors chatted over whisky long into the night, but where Hurston was eventually escorted to sleep in the tenant house with the black servants.[23]

If it is difficult to understand why Hurston stood for this treatment, it is almost impossible to imagine her reaction to a 1943 letter in which Rawlings hinted that she—Rawlings—needed housekeeping help in order for her to finish a book.[24] Hurston agreed, and returned to Cross Creek for ten days to help make Rawlings "comfortable."

Just a few months earlier, Hurston's essay, "The 'Pet Negro' System," appeared in *The American Mercury.* In it, Hurston outlines the system that "symbolizes the web of feelings and mutual dependencies" of Southern race relations. The "pet negro" system, Hurston argues, assures that white affection for individual black "pets" will always be regarded as exceptional, and will "in no way extend to black folk in general."[25] Indeed, the trouble of finding a deserving "pet," as narrated by Rawlings in "Catching One Young," works to underscore both the exceptionalism of the black person who can merit such a status and the white person's gracious whiteness in bestowing the title at all. But Hurston reminds us that Negroes, too, "have their pet whites."

It is amusing to see a Negro servant chasing the madam or the boss back on his or her pedestal when they behave in an unbecoming manner. Thereby he is to a certain extent preserving his own prestige, derived from association with that family.[26]

The Negro servant Hurston describes is a stock character of the plantation novel tradition: the newly-freed slave who longs for the security of servitude in the family of his master. But this character could also describe the predicament of black authors of Hurston's day who had to carefully cultivate their own "pet whites" in order to advance in a racist publishing world, as Hurston had done with Carl Van Vechten and her wealthy patron Charlotte Osgood Mason.

We cannot know whether Hurston offered to act as Rawlings's house-keeper out of genuine friendship or in an effort to preserve a prestigious association. If Hurston was currying favor with a literary star and Hollywood darling, she was certainly in need of it at the time. After *Dust Tracks*, Hurston's writing career had hit a slump. J.B. Lippincott, her long-time publisher, passed on her plans for two novels with black protagonists. Fortunately, Rawlings began to use her influence on Hurston's behalf with her own publisher, Scribner's, which agreed to publish Hurston's *Seraph on the Suwanee*.

To Rawlings, Hurston described *Seraph on the Suwanee* as "an attempt at an answer to your kind and loving letter of last Spring," which had advised Hurston "to take care and do [her] best."[27] While composing *Seraph*, Hurston wrote that she was careful to avoid what "might be considered coarse" out of fear that her agent would "not try to sell it to the movies."[28] When published in 1948, copies of *Seraph on the Suwanee* were sent, at Hurston's expense, to Berg-Allenberg, a Hollywood agency associated with a "motion picture offer."[29] Phil Berg was a well-known talent agent representing the likes of Clark Gable, Judy Garland, and Joan Crawford. He is credited with devising the "package deal" where script, actors, and director are assembled by the agent and sold together to a producer.[30] Whitney Darrow of Scribner's also attempted to interest MGM, the studio of *The Yearling*, in screen rights.[31] Hurston's first book in six years, and only published novel with white protagonists, was dedicated to Marjorie Kinnan Rawlings.[32]

"NEGROES . . . WRITING ABOUT WHITE PEOPLE"

As a black-authored work of fiction about white characters, *Seraph on the Suwanee* is certainly not alone. It must be considered alongside Wallace Thurman's *The Interne* (1932); William Attaway's *Let Me Breathe Thunder* (1939); Frank Yerby's *The Foxes of Harrow* (1946); Willard Motley's *Knock on Any Door* (1947); Ann Petry's *Country Place* (1947); Richard Wright's *Savage Holiday* (1954); and James Baldwin's *Giovanni's Room* (1956). It is striking how many of these authors, like Hurston, had strong affiliations with Hollywood. Thurman wrote two screenplays, *Tomorrow's Children* and *High School Girl*, for the production company of Brian Foy, head of the Warner Brothers "B" picture unit in the mid-1930s.[33] Yerby's *The Foxes of Harrow* was adapted by 20th Century Fox in 1947; his novels *The Golden Hawk* (1948) and *The Saracen Blade* (1952) were adapted by Columbia in 1952 and 1954. Motley's *Knock on Any Door* was purchased by Humphrey Bogart's production company Santana Pictures, directed by Nicholas Ray, and distributed by Columbia in 1949. Columbia also made Motley's *Let No Man Write My Epitaph* (1958) in

1960.[34] Petry wrote a screenplay, *That Hill Girl,* for Columbia in 1958, as a potential vehicle for Kim Novak.[35] Attaway wrote for both film and television, including adaptations of Irving Wallace's *The Man* (1964) and Bruce Bahrenburg's *My Little Brother's Coming Tomorrow* (1971).[36]

The decision of black authors to write about white characters and to court Hollywood may be read as merely a regrettable—if pragmatic—capitulation to white narrative consumption. That their creative output was constrained by the racism of the publishing world and Hollywood is without doubt. But capitulation or not, by presuming to narrate whiteness Hurston and her contemporaries posed a significant challenge to an entrenched narrative code that granted only white authors the privilege of writing beyond their own racial identity.

Like much of Rawlings's work, *Seraph* focuses on Floridian crackers. But rather than create a folksy and uplifting frontier origin myth that bolsters white identity on the back of black caricature, Hurston introduces us to Arvay Henson, a beautiful blue-eyed cracker who lives a life that is tormented by self-loathing, paranoia, and masochism.

The very first lines of Hurston's *Seraph on the Suwanee* raise this question of the racialization of narrative authority:

Sawley, the town, is in west Florida, on the famous Suwanee River. It is flanked on the south by the curving course of the river which Stephen Foster made famous without ever having looked upon its waters [. . .].

Hurston of course refers to Foster's "Old Folks at Home: Ethiopian Melody." Opening with the familiar "Way down upon de Swanee ribber, far, far away," the immensely popular minstrel standard was put into the mouth of Uncle Tom in Harriet Beecher Stowe's *The Christian Slave* in 1855 and proclaimed the State Song of Florida in 1935. The racial origin of the tune itself was a familiar point of dispute. W.E.B. Du Bois contended that it was "distinctively influenced" by slave songs, though a song of "white America."[37]

Hurston thus decides to open her only novel focusing on white experience by quickly evoking a Northern white writer's culturally granted authority over Southern black experience. She is careful to point out Stephen Foster's lack of presence on the banks of the Suwanee. His text is granted narrative authority without "bodily" authority. In fact, the real power of Foster's nostalgic idyll lay in its ability to narrate the South from a location "far, far away."

What Hurston undoubtedly knew is that this ability to narrate beyond the body is a cultural privilege often tethered to whiteness. As Richard Dyer and others have argued, the hegemony of whiteness in Western culture relies on its configuration as spirit able to "master and transcend the white body."[38] Foster's lack of presence at the site of his story is not only a privilege of white narrativity then, but the very condition that maintains narrativity as white. White writers are able to produce "just fiction" rather than "white fiction," precisely because white narrativity, like white subjectivity, is granted the privileged position of transcending bodily presence.

With *Seraph on the Suwanee,* Hurston set this narrative economy on its head. Readers have seen in the Meserve, or "Me-serve," surname of *Seraph*'s protagonists an indictment of the self-centeredness of Arvay's husband, Jim.[39] But what if we read this as a dictum of the author—that the "Me-serve" family is there, as fictional creations, to serve Hurston herself? Some critics maintain that the whiteness of Seraph's characters is superficial—a joke played with black characters in whiteface.[40] But what if Hurston wrote about white characters specifically because she wanted to say something about the psychological effects of claiming whiteness?

The very title *Seraph on the Suwanee* neatly encapsulates Arvay's problem. She is the angelic "seraph" of the story. But what does it mean, the title asks, for a cracker to occupy a space of celestial whiteness, to be a pure spirit and to eat the clay of the land? How can an angel be so rooted in the mud of the Suwanee—not the idyllic Suwanee of Stephen Foster's imaginings, but the "poor and shabby and mean" Sawley, infested with roaches and bedbugs, driven by lust and gossip and petty rivalries? *Angel in the Bed,* an early rejected title of *Seraph,* suggests that Arvay's spiritualized whiteness is directly at odds with her sexuality. "To ensure the survival of the race," Dyer reminds us, white people "have to have sex—but having sex, and sexual desire, are not very white: the means of reproducing whiteness are not themselves pure white."[41] Hurston portrays Arvay's psychological suffering as arising from a lifelong attempt to maintain spiritualized white identity, particularly in the face of rape and pregnancy. Arvay's psychology throughout the novel is more understandable if she is read, as the tragic mulatta is read, as anxiously *passing* for white, and in constant fear of exposure. *Seraph* is indeed a critique of the masochism of erotic love, as Claudia Tate argues, but it is more accurately a critique of the masochism of erotic love in whiteness.

In Arvay, Hurston created a twist on the trope of the tragic mulatta: a "tragic cracker." As Hortense Spillers argues, the tragic mulatta should be recognized not as a historical subject position but as a "stage prop of the literary"—a light-skinned character of both black and white ancestry who, by virtue of internal or external conflict, is plotted to narrative doom.[42] Like the tragic mulatta, the cracker figure owes its deployment to cultural anxieties about the stability of racial identity. Both the cracker and the mulatta are positioned on the boundary of whiteness and blackness. Because the mulatta's racial liminality is linked explicitly with blood and racist conceptions of blood quantum, blackness is assigned as her identity; because the cracker's racial liminality is linked with "mere" acculturation—class, dialect, geographical location—whiteness is assigned as her identity. Like *The Yearling's* matriarch Ora Baxter, Hurston's Arvay must work to support the civilized "white" identity of herself and her family. But because whiteness is linked to sexuality and the body, and white women are positioned as the sexual property of white men, Hurston portrays the maintenance of white female identity as a losing battle.

SERAPH IN HOLLYWOOD

While Hollywood studios were not interested in symbolic critiques of race, they could hardly get enough domestic melodramas starring self-sacrificing, masochistic white women.

The story department at Warner Brothers reviewed *Seraph* in galleys, which had been "submitted thru J.W."—either Jack Warner, vice-president in charge of production, or writer-turned-producer Jerry Wald. Wald, screenwriter and Warners' top producer at the time, helped to shape the studio's signature gritty style, including the Cagney film *The Roaring Twenties*, the George Raft film *They Drive by Night*, and the Humphrey Bogart films *High Sierra* and *Casablanca*. It was Wald who convinced Jack Warner to purchase the screen rights to the pulp novel *Mildred Pierce* by James M. Cain and the stage play *Key Largo* by Maxwell Anderson.

Working out of the Warner Brothers New York office, a studio reader provided the eastern story editor with a 22-page summary of *Seraph* and a paragraph of comments which recommended the novel for executive attention.[43] The length of the report suggests it was not the first summary to be produced by the studio: an earlier favorable report likely prompted the close attention represented in this summary. The dialect of Hurston's crackers seems to rub off on the reader in her coverage: describing Arvay's guilt for her psychic "affair" with Carl, the reader writes that "people would have thought she was clean out of her head if they had known." Other commentary is infused with the voices of Jim and Arvay:

Arvay and her mother are like to die of embarrassment. Not so Jim, fall right in with the old man, he does, laughing at his jokes, and then tells him right out straight, he means to marry Miss Arvay if she will have him.[44]

A summary of the problematic rape scene falls back, nearly word-for-word, on Hurston's ambivalent abstractions:

Her skirts are jerked roughly upwards and Jim is fumbling wildly at her thighs. Arvay opens her mouth to scream, but no sound emerges. Her mouth is closed by Jim's passionate kisses, and in a moment, despite her struggles, Arvay knows a pain remorseless sweet.[45]

Occasionally the combination of homespun talk and critic-speak collide in a single sentence, as in "She just doesn't feel fitten for him and never realizes how her contradictory behavior worries the man."[46]

The reader cautiously begins her comments section on *Seraph:* "Make no mistake about it, SERAPH ON THE SUWANEE is no first-rate novel." She finds the conflict between Arvay and Jim "trumped up" and the love scenes "faintly ridiculous." Despite these reservations, however, she does recommend Hurston's novel for studio purchase. The reader praises *Seraph*'s "tried and true elements which have proved successful on the screen before," including the rags-to-riches story, the authentically rendered locales, and the "married love still going hot and strong, after twenty years."[47] Here, the reader clearly situates a potential adaptation within the long-standing tradition of the "woman's film" or "weeper"—at Warner Brothers—often starring Bette Davis or Joan Crawford. One of the prominent themes of the woman's film "was the innocent girl betrayed into sin" who brought "disaster on herself, through sheer naiveté."[48] Arvay might certainly be read as one of these victims waiting to happen. The reader concludes with the assertion that the story "of a domestic nature" would be "dear to the heart of women" and "should not be expensive to film."[49]

After receiving the summary and comment from the reader, the eastern story editor sent an inter office memo describing the novel as "fairly good" to the head story analyst and to the assistant story editor on the west coast. The head story analyst describes the novel:

based on one emotional problem: the almost life-long misunderstanding between a complex, introverted 'cracker' wife and her Black Irish, tempestuous, driving husband.[50]

The analyst recommends that this misunderstanding be specified: "What is needed for screen purposes is a definite incident which would make the situation sharper." She rounds out her memo by referring to the "sex scenes" as "lending library fare" and declaring that he doesn't "find [the story] good enough for us to revamp."[51]

Despite the lukewarm recommendation from the eastern story editor and the rebuff from the head story analyst, the assistant story editor on the west coast saw a particular potential for *Seraph*. In a memo to producer Jerry Wald, this editor, while acknowledging that the story needed "dramatic sharpening" and would likely have "censorship problems," recommended *Seraph* as a "stunning vehicle for Jane Wyman if it were felt that we could duplicate the same sort of background as *The Yearling*."[52]

At the time of this memo, Wald was working with Wyman on *Johnny Belinda* (1948), a "weeper" if there ever was one. In *Johnny Belinda*, Wyman plays a sweet deaf-mute girl living in remote Nova Scotia who bears the child of the man who rapes her and must suffer a court battle and public shame to keep that child from being taken away. Two years earlier, Wyman had starred opposite Gregory Peck in MGM's *The Yearling*.

Riding on the coattails of a rival studio's success was, of course, a common practice. To Chapman, Wyman as the cracker Ora Baxter at MGM could easily become Wyman as the cracker Arvay Henson at Warner Brothers. Chapman also tried to convince *The Green Pastures* producer Henry Blanke of the merits of *Seraph* as a Warner Brothers version of *The Yearling*. Hurston's novel had managed to strongly evoke the Hollywood-friendly cracker world of Rawlings's novel in the end. But Chapman's enthusiasm, ultimately, was not enough. Neither Wald nor Blanke asked the studio to purchase *Seraph on the Suwanee*, and the story was rejected by senior story editor Ellingwood Kay on January 10, 1949.

Though *Seraph on the Suwanee* was never produced, Hurston's desire to see her fiction adapted to film would continue throughout her life, and undoubtedly influenced her writing. In 1949, her editor Burroughs Mitchell was "kind of surprised" to discover that the white protagonist of her new book manuscript "The Lives of Barney Turk," "winds up as a Hollywood glamour boy."[53] In 1953, Hurston wrote to Mitchell about her plans for yet another book, this one based on Herod the Great. "Not only a swell book is inherent in the theme," Hurston promised, "but a most magnificent movie."[54] Cheryl A. Wall links the Herod project directly to Hurston's desire to court the famed director of biblical epics Cecil B. DeMille.[55] Neither "The Lives of Barney Turk" nor the Herod project was ever published, nor did any Hollywood studio, as far as it is known, ever see the manuscripts.

Seraph on the Suwanee's current critical status may be at least in part a textual case of *Natus Albus*: an inscrutable birth of a white story from a black author. Hurston successfully positioned Rawlings as a surrogate cracker "mother" for *Seraph* at the studios. While the tragic cracker Arvay Henson is a character who has repelled generations of literary critics, she nearly succeeded in beguiling Hollywood.

NOTES

1. "Writer's Card" of Zora Neale Hurston, entries from October 30, 1934, to January 28, 1960. Warner Brothers Story Department Files, University of

Southern California Cinematic Arts Library, Los Angeles, California. Unless otherwise noted, all quoted studio reader's reports, writer's cards, and story department communications are from this collection. Since I first examined these materials, the Story Department Files were reacquired by the corporate archive of Warner Brothers Studio in Burbank, California, and are currently housed there. While Warner Brothers was not the only studio to consider Hurston's fiction, its exceptionally complete story department archive provides a glimpse into industry-wide source acquisition practices.

2. Valerie Boyd, *Wrapped in Rainbows* (New York: Scribner, 2002), 257.

3. Tino Balio, *Grand Design: Hollywood as a Modern Business Enterprise, 1930-1939* (Berkeley: University of California Press, 1993), 73.

4. Universal Story Bulletin Collection. American Film Institute's Louis B. Mayer Library, Los Angeles, California. The covered magazines were *Colliers, Liberty, Saturday Evening Post, McCall's, Redbook*, and *Ladies' Home Journal*.

5. Janet Staiger, "The Producer-Unit System: Management and Specialization After 1931," in *The Classical Hollywood Cinema: Film Style and Mode of Production to 1960*, ed. David Bordwell, Janet Staiger, and Kristen Thompson (New York: Columbia University Press, 1985), 322.

6. Alice Goldberg, Coverage of Zora Neale Hurston's *Their Eyes Were Watching God*, August 5, 1937.

7. Alan Gevinson, ed., *Within Our Gates: Ethnicity in American Feature Films, 1911–1960* (Berkeley: University of California Press, 1997), 418.

8. Donald Bogle, *Toms, Coons, Mulattoes, Mammies and Buck: An Interpretive History of Blacks in American Films*, New Expanded Edition (New York: Continuum, 1989), 86.

9. Ibid. 67.

10. "Brief Sheet" of Zora Neale Hurston's contract with Paramount Pictures. Paramount Archive. Academy of Motion Picture Arts and Sciences Center for Motion Picture Study, Margaret Herrick Library, Beverly Hills, California.

11. Zora Neale Hurston to Edwin Osgood Grover, December 30, 1941, in *Zora Neale Hurston: A Life in Letters*, ed. Carla Kaplan (New York: Doubleday, 2002), 463.

12. Tom Chapman, Reader's Report on Zora Neale Hurston's *Dust Tracks on a Road*, December 1, 1942.

13. Phil Strong, review of *Dust Tracks on a Road, by Zora Neale Hurston, Saturday Review* (November 28, 1942), 6.

14. Zora Neale Hurston to Carl Van Vechten, November 2, 1942, *Zora Neale Hurston: A Life in Letters*, ed. Carla Kaplan, 467; Claudia Tate, *Psychoanalysis and Black Novels: Desire and the Protocols of Race* (New York: Oxford University Press, 1998), 210.

15. Ann Rayson, "The Novels of Zora Neale Hurston," *Studies in Black Literature*, 5 (Winter 1974), 1–11; Janet St. Clair, "The Courageous Undertow of Zora Neale Hurston's *Seraph on the Suwanee*," *Modern Language Quarterly* 50, No. 1 (March 1989), 40; Robert E. Hemenway, *Zora Neale Hurston: A Literary Biography* (Urbana and Chicago: University of Illinois Press, 1977), 307–310.

16. Elizabeth Silverthorne, *Marjorie Kinnan Rawlings: Sojourner at Cross Creek* (Woodstock, NY: Overlook Press, 1988), 59; Patricia Nassif Acton, *Invasion of*

Privacy: The Cross Creek Trial of Marjorie Kinnan Rawlings (Gainesville: University of Florida Press, 1988), 5.

17. John Solomon Otto, "Cracker: The History of a Southeastern Ethnic, Economic, and Racial Epithet," *Names: A Journal on Onomastics* 35, no. 1 (1987 March), 28–39.

18. Zora Neale Hurston to Marjorie Kinnan Rawlings, May 16, 1943, in *Zora Neale Hurston: A Life in Letters*, ed. Carla Kaplan, 486, 486–487.

19. Marjorie Kinnan Rawlings, *Cross Creek* (New York: Charles Scribner's Sons, 1942), 77–78.

20. Scrolling Preface to the MGM adaptation *The Yearling*.

21. Marjorie Kinnan Rawlings, *The Yearling* (New York: Charles Scribner's Sons, 1939), 84.

22. Werner Sollors, *Neither Black Nor White Yet Both: Thematic Explorations of Interracial Literature* (Cambridge: Harvard University Press, 1997), 242.

23. Idella Parker with Mary Keating. *Idella: Marjorie Rawlings' "Perfect Maid"* (Gainesville: University of Florida Press, 1992), 87.

24. Silverthorne, *Marjorie Kinnan Rawlings*, 233.

25. Zora Neale Hurston, "The Pet Negro System," in *The American Mercury.* May, 1943. Reprinted in *Zora Neale Hurston: Folklore, Memoirs, and Other Writings*, Cheryl A. Wall, ed. (New York: Library of America, 1995), 916.

26. Hurston, "The Pet Negro System," 916.

27. Zora Neale Hurston to Marjorie Kinnan Rawlings, Fall/Winter 1948, *Zora Neale Hurston: A Life in Letters*, ed. Carla Kaplan, 575.

28. Zora Neale Hurston to Burroughs Mitchell, October 1953, *Zora Neale Hurston: A Life in Letters*, ed. Carla Kaplan, 703.

29. Zora Neale Hurston, *Seraph on the Suwanee* (1948; repr., New York: HarperPerennial, 1991); Ann Watkins to Burroughs Mitchell, October 6, 1948, in The Archives of Charles Scribner's Sons. Princeton University Library, Manuscript Division, Department of Rare Books and Special Collections.

30. "Phil Berg, 80, Pioneered Movie Packages," in the *New York Times.* (February 4, 1983).

31. Kenneth MacKenna to Whitney Darrow, December 9, 1948, The Archives of Charles Scribner's Sons. Princeton University Library, Manuscript Division, Department of Rare Books and Special Collections.

32. Rawlings shares this dedication with Mrs. Spessard L. Holland.

33. Phyllis Klotman, "The Black Writer in Hollywood, Circa 1930: The Case of Wallace Thurman," in *Black American Cinema*, ed. Manthia Diawara (New York: Routledge, 1993), 80.

34. See Binggeli, "The Unadapted," *Cinema Journal*, 48:3, 1–15.

35. Hazel Arnett Ervin, *Ann Petry: A Bio-Bibliography* (New York: G.K. Hall & Co., 1993).

36. Richard Yarborough, Afterword to William Attaway's *Blood on the Forge* (New York: Monthly Review Press, 1987).

37. W.E.B. Du Bois, "The Sorrow Songs," *The Souls of Black Folk.* (1903; repr., New York: Modern Library: 2003), 540.

38. Richard Dyer, *White* (London and New York: Routledge, 1997), 30.

39. Carol P. Marsh-Lockett, "What Ever Happened to Jochebed? Motherhood as Marginality in Zora Neale Hurston's *Seraph on the Suwanee*," in *Southern Mothers: Fact and Fictions in Southern Women's Writing*, ed. Nagueyalti Warren and Sally Wolff (Baton Rouge: Louisiana State University Press, 1999), 102; Tate, *Psychoanalysis and Black Novels*, 151.

40. Tate, *Psychoanalysis and Black Novels*, 170.

41. Dyer, *White*, 26.

42. Hortense J. Spillers, "Peter's Pans: Eating in the Diaspora," in *Black, White, and In Color: Essays on American Literature and Culture* (Chicago: University of Chicago Press, 2003), 27.

43. Anna Silva, Memorandum to Don Moore Regarding *Seraph on the Suwanee*. July 30, 1948.

44. Anna Silva, Reader's Report on *Seraph on the Suwanee*, 29 July 1948.

45. Ibid.

46. Ibid.

47. Ibid.

48. Ted Sennett, *Warner Brothers Presents* (New Rochelle: Arlington House, 1971), 119.

49. Silva, Reader's Report on *Seraph*.

50. Kent Williamson, Memorandum to Tom Chapman Regarding *Seraph on the Suwanee*, August 5, 1948.

51. Ibid.

52. Tom Chapman, Memorandum to Jerry Wald regarding *Seraph on the Suwanee*, August 5, 1948.

53. Burroughs Mitchell to Zora Neale Hurston, October 10, 1949, The Archives of Charles Scribner's Sons. Princeton University Library, Manuscript Division, Department of Rare Books and Special Collections.

54. Zora Neale Hurston to Burroughs Mitchell, October 1953, in *Zora Neale Hurston: A Life in Letters*, ed. Carla Kaplan, 703.

55. Wall, ed., *Zora Neale Hurston: Folklore, Memoirs, and Other Writings*, 979.

A Renaissance Woman:
Poetics, Performance,
Photography, and Film

Zora Neale Hurston's Folk Choreography*

Anthea Kraut

On Sunday, January 10th, 1932, at the John Golden Theatre in New York, the African American artist Zora Neale Hurston premiered a concert of black folk ways based on the anthropological research she had conducted in the southern United States and the Bahamas during the late 1920s. Presented under the title *The Great Day* and billed as "A Program of Original Negro Folklore," Hurston's revue traced a single day in the life of a railroad work camp in Florida, from the waking of the camp at dawn to a climactic Bahamian Fire Dance cycle at midnight.[1] In between, the concert advanced from a scene in which men performed various work songs as they spiked and lined the rails to a series of movement-oriented children's games back at the camp. An animated open-air sermon and several rousing spirituals brought the first act to a close. After a brief intermission, the second act picked up the narrative in the interior of a Jook, where the adult camp members passed the nighttime hours playing card and dice games, singing the blues, and performing social dances to piano and guitar music. Finally, camp members retreated to the woods, where in ring formation, a group of Bahamian migrant workers sang West-Indian melodies and enacted the three-part Fire Dance as drummers provided dynamic rhythmic accompaniment.

*Originally published as Anthea Kraut, "Recovering Hurston, Reconsidering the Choreographer," *Women & Performance: A Journal of Feminist Theory* 16.1 (March 2006): 71–90. Reprinted by permission of the publisher, Taylor & Francis Ltd, http://www.tandf.co.uk/journals.

Hurston made no money on *The Great Day*, but the concert was well received, and she continued to stage versions of it in the next few years. Using the titles *From Sun to Sun*, *All De Live Long Day*, and *Singing Steel*, she mounted the revue at the New School for Social Research in New York in March of 1932, in a number of cities around Florida between 1933 and 1934, and in Chicago in November of 1934. Archival evidence suggests that she produced variants of the folk concert as late as 1952. While Hurston consistently reworked the program—inserting and removing certain scenes, accommodating different casts, and occasionally performing a dance solo herself—the basic structure of the concert and the Bahamian folk dance finale remained constant. Besides putting on these full-length productions, Hurston presented music and dance excerpts from the revue at several venues in New York, twice at the National Folk Festival (in St. Louis in 1934 and in Washington, D.C., in 1938), and under the auspices of the Florida Federal Writers' Project in Orlando. Along the way, her Bahamian dance material captured the interest of choral director Hall Johnson, Russian-born jazz dance promoter Mura Dehn, theatre director Irene Lewisohn, modern dance artists Ruth St. Denis, Doris Humphrey, and Helen Tamiris, and ballroom dance icon Irene Castle.[2]

Even as Hurston's writing has been the beneficiary of widespread scholarly and mainstream attention in the past two decades, her stage work, and her choreographic activity in particular, has continued to suffer from neglect. This essay aims to rectify that neglect by placing her folk choreography front and center. Though Hurston never pursued dance to the exclusion of other media, her staging of choreographed movement constituted a crucial aspect of her approach to representing the folk. In what follows, I will first describe the process by which she prepared the Bahamian Fire Dance for the New York theatre, arguing that her work in this capacity amounted to a kind of choreographic labor. Recognizing it as such demands that we not only broaden our understanding of Hurston but also deepen our understanding of the mediated nature of her relationship to the folk. I will then take a closer look at the function of dance within her revues to explore how the medium of live performance and the dynamics of embodiment enabled Hurston to put forth a nuanced view of black diasporic folk culture.

HURSTON AS CHOREOGRAPHER

Clearly, Hurston did not function as a choreographer in the conventional sense of composing new dances. The Bahamian Fire Dance that served as her concert's finale was a preexistent, communally created, and sustained folk form that was transported by African slaves to the

Caribbean, where it commingled with European practices. The archive, moreover, provides no evidence that Hurston ever referred to herself as a choreographer, nor did she ever use the related term "choreography" to describe her dance endeavors. It is worth bearing in mind, however, that in the 1920s and 1930s, terminology like "arranged," "staged," and "directed" was much more commonly used to recognize dance artists working on the theatrical stage. And indeed, the program for a 1939 exclusive presentation of the Fire Dance listed Hurston as "Dance Director."[3] Whereas she employed both a musical arranger and a chorus director to help train her singers for the New York debut of her concert, Hurston never sought any professional assistance with the movement numbers. Instead, she took on the responsibility for transforming the Fire Dance folk cycle from its Caribbean vernacular incarnation to its American theatrical manifestation.

Still, there were a number of reasons why the attribution "choreographer" was not available to Hurston at the time she staged the Bahamian Fire Dance. Chiefly among these was the perception that the dancing that appeared in her revue was unrehearsed, spontaneous expression—in other words, the opposite of choreographed. The critic Arthur Ruhl's testimonial that *The Great Day* embodied the ideal of "natural and unpremeditated art" epitomizes this view.[4] However much Hurston actively cultivated the impression of naturalness and used the semblance of spontaneity to her advantage, this discourse played into entrenched racist stereotypes about instinctive black performativity—stereotypes that left little if any room for the recognition of methodical black artistry. As a black woman working with "low art" black vernacular forms, Hurston faced a convergence of racial and artistic hierarchies that made it unthinkable for her to identify herself as a choreographer. Assigning Hurston a mantle she was not afforded in her own time, then, is a deliberate tactic, designed to grant her credit for the initiative and leadership she assumed in transferring the Bahamian dance cycle to her assembled cast and to acknowledge the labor involved in this activity.[5]

Hurston's first encounter with Caribbean dance occurred in the late 1920s, during an anthropological expedition to southern Florida. The dancing of a group of Bahamian migrant workers there struck Hurston as "so stirring and magnificent that I had to admit to myself that we had nothing in America to equal it."[6] The Fire Dance that she found so captivating was actually a cycle of three dances. In the first two, the Jumping Dance and Ring Play, a circle of players took turns in the center, stepping, leaping, and posing to the rhythms of an accompanying drum. In the subsequent Crow Dance, a soloist performed an imitation of a buzzard "flying and seeking food."[7] In October of 1929, Hurston traveled to Nassau to find out more about Bahamian music and dance. There, she not only took three reels of film footage of the dancing, she also "took pains," as she later reported in her autobiography, to learn the Fire Dance movements herself.[8]

Back in New York in the fall of 1931, as she fine-tuned the script for the production that would become *The Great Day*, Hurston took the initial step of assembling a "troup of sixteen Bahamans who could dance," as she explained in *Dust Tracks on a Road*.[9] Information about precisely who these dancers were, how Hurston recruited them, and what their dance backgrounds were is extremely sketchy. Among the known members of the troupe were Leonard Sturrup, also known as Motor Boat; Carolyne Rich; Alfred Strochan; John Dawson; Joseph Neely (or Nealy); William Polhamus; Reginald Alday; Lias Strawn; and Bruce (Mabel) Howard.[10] Despite Hurston's claim, it is next to certain that not all sixteen of her Fire Dancers were actually Bahamian natives.[11]

As Hurston began conducting rehearsals in her apartment on West 66th Street, and wherever she could find space, she discovered that her research footage could be put to a perhaps unanticipated use. In an October 15th letter to her white patron, Charlotte Osgood Mason, she made the following plea:

Godmother, may I show Mr. Colledge the fire-dance films from the Bahamas? . . . He wants to see first a sample of all the materials and while I am training the group it takes so long for the preliminary showing and that holds back definite arrangements. Then too, seeing the films would refresh *my* memory on details. Please, may I?[12]

Preparing to audition her concert material for a producer at the Steinway Theatre, Hurston gingerly requests permission to borrow back her own film footage. Her explanation of how she plans to use the films—as a concrete representation of what she intends to present on stage and as a visual reminder to herself of the folk dances—vividly demonstrates the interconnections between her anthropological and theatrical work. In transferring the Bahamian folk dance cycle to the stage, Hurston followed what VéVé Clark termed a "research-to-performance" method, translating her anthropological findings into a live presentation in the public theatre.[13] Yet crucially, Hurston's allusion to the "training" of her performers suggests how mediated this translation process was. While some of her cast members may have been familiar with the Fire Dance, clearly not all of them were. The Fire Dance that eventually appeared in *The Great Day* thus followed a circuitous path from Bahamian bodies to Hurston's body to film, back to Hurston's body, and finally to the 16 bodies of her ensemble. Attention to this sequence of interpolations seriously complicates the claims of naturalness that surrounded the Caribbean number.

Of course, Hurston's choreographic process included more than just teaching movement to her performers. As scholars of staged folk dance routinely point out, the process of adapting participatory dance forms for presentation on the proscenium stage involves any number of artistic choices. These range from the selection of movement material, to decisions about how much improvisation to permit on stage, to considerations of "time, space, and spectacle," all of which are constrained by Western theatrical conventions.[14] Hurston faced this same set of issues in readying the Fire Dance for her revue. After settling on which portions of the dance to stage and in what order, compressing and plotting their duration within her own concert must have been one of her foremost decisions. While it is impossible to determine how much improvisational freedom Hurston allowed her dancers and drummers, certain concessions to the proscenium stage were conspicuous, from forgoing the presence of a live fire, to arranging her dancers in a semi-circle rather than a closed ring, which would have obstructed the audience's view of the soloists. She may well have also coached her dancers on the precise spacing, degree of virtuosity, and movement scale for each section of the Fire Dance cycle.

At the same time, it is clear that much of Hurston's choreographic labor involved masking the various capitulations she made to the Western theatrical stage. Determined to present black expressive practices in a way that bore a closer resemblance to the folk from whom she had collected her material than to the black artists and entertainers who populated the New York stage, Hurston purposely sought out cast members who did not fit the Broadway mold. This included darker-skinned performers with less experience in the professional theatre. In the same October 15th letter in which she requested use of her film footage, Hurston described to Charlotte Mason the "black" and "dark brown" singers she had assembled, concluding, "No mulattoes at all." Hurston also touted the "gawky" and "naïve" singer she had enlisted for *The Great Day*.[15] The fact that, according to Hurston, her concert was the first public performance for some of her Fire Dancers suggests she took a similar tack in recruiting dance performers.[16] Such casting decisions made it possible for her to contend that *The Great Day*'s dances had "not been influenced by Harlem or Broadway."[17]

Concomitantly, Hurston adopted performance conventions that diverged from the polished norms of the mainstream theatre. The best evidence of this can be found in the recommendations for improvement offered by Rollins College president Hamilton Holt in response to a 1933 production of *From Sun to Sun* in Florida. "They need to keep their eyes much more to the audience," he wrote of Hurston's performers, "and they need to do their swinging more in unison. Some did it from the right side and some from the left side."[18] The asymmetry and lack of self-consciousness that Holt objected to as amateur were, for Hurston, a closer approximation of the black folk aesthetic she embraced and endeavored to bring to the stage.

Hurston did not reject mainstream theatrical principles outright, however, and on several occasions, she referred expressly to the need to "polish" her troupe before presenting them.[19] One such reference came in her autobiography, in an account of a disturbance among her Bahamian dance troupe in 1932:

. . . one of the men, who was incidentally the poorest dancer of all, preached that I was an American exploiting them and they ought to go ahead under his guidance. Stew-Beef, Lias Strawn, and Motor-Boat pointed out to him that they had never dreamed of dancing in public until I had picked them up. I had rehearsed them for months, fed them and routined them into something.[20]

When she deemed it necessary, Hurston thus found ways to affirm her choreographic labor, even when it may have contradicted the professed naturalness of her folk revue. Subtly but surely here, she shores up her originality and authority by ventriloquizing the defense of her lead dancers. Not only do they verify that it was her idea in the first place to stage the Caribbean material, they also emphasize the work she undertook to discipline, finesse, and "routine" her dancers into "something" worthy of the public theatre.

Consideration of the choreographic process by which Hurston transformed the Bahamian Fire Dance for the stage thus offers fresh insight into the mediation that governed her relationship to the folk, notwithstanding the claims of authenticity that surrounded her concert and that have clung to her renderings of the folk more generally. No simple or straightforward operation, the transmission of movement material to her cast of performers and the cultivation of a performance aesthetic located somewhere between professionalism and amateurism demanded that Hurston make a series of careful calibrations in everything from casting to training to staging. Although her work in this capacity certainly didn't qualify her for choreographer status at the time, conceding the term to her today helps redress a historical blind spot by crediting her for the embodied work that underwrote and helped constitute her folk representations.

THE FIRE DANCE AND HURSTON'S EMBODIED THEORY OF DIASPORA

Attention to Hurston's choreographic labor also gives cause for revisiting her conceptualization of the folk, for the theory her concert advanced was not identical to that conveyed in her textual productions. Most significantly, Hurston enlisted dance to introduce a nuanced representation of the black diaspora, a "bodily writing" of what Paul Gilroy has termed the Black Atlantic.[21] To decipher this bodily writing, it is helpful to return to the structure and content of *The Great Day*.

As mentioned at the opening of this chapter, the concert depicted the daily activities of a railroad work camp community in Florida and was capped by a thrilling cycle of Bahamian songs and dances. In other words, after immersing her audience in the folkways of Southern black Americans, Hurston's stage narrative erupted into a display of a distinctly Caribbean dance form, thereby shifting the geographical terrain of the revue. While a bit of dialogue early in the program called attention to the presence of several Bahamians among the black workers, the dance enacted in the final section brought into the foreground and intensified the West Indian dimension just as the concert reached its conclusion.[22] In crowning her vision of African American folk culture with a number whose African origins she frequently underscored,[23] Hurston effectively charted the Middle Passage in reverse, staging a theory of African influences well before the concept of Afrocentricity entered popular or academic discourse. Just as crucially, she demonstrated how discrete diasporic expressive practices were transported to American shores on the bodies of Bahamian migrant workers.

Recounting the concert's finale in her autobiography, Hurston wrote, "As soon as the curtain went up on the Fire Dancers, their costuming got a hand."[24] A photograph taken by *Theatre Arts Monthly*, the sole surviving visual image of *The Great Day*, shows Hurston and 14 of her dancers arranged in a semi-circle, leaning in and clapping along as they intently observe a male and female dancer who perform in the center of the ring.[25] While the women all wear boldly patterned dresses, three of the men stand out for their extravagant head-pieces and feather-adorned robes. The male dancer in the center, meanwhile, wears only a snake-skin loin cloth, cape, and head-piece, leaving his legs and torso completely bare. Between the exotic costumes, exposed male body, insistent drum rhythms, vigorous leaping and dancing, and air of ceremonial ritual, the Fire Dance in performance must have more than fulfilled the publicity announcement's promise of a "primitive and exciting folk dance."[26]

Yet if the placement of the unfamiliar Fire Dance at the end of the concert traced a line of descent back toward the Caribbean and invoked African roots, the choreography that operated within this structure betrayed a more complex and heterogeneous vision of diaspora. Without question, the Bahamian number stood apart visually and kinesthetically from the expressive idioms featured earlier in the concert. But movement was not confined to the Fire Dance finale, and it is essential to keep in mind the other choreographic dimensions of the revue. One of the children's games, for example, involved wing-flapping and hopping motions that must have borne unmistakable affinities to the Crow Dance.[27] The Jook scene, meanwhile, featured versions of social dances that became popular in the North during the 1920s and 1930s, such as the Slow Drag, Black Bottom, and Buck and Wing. By dramatizing this spectrum of Southern rural children's games, urban black vernacular dances, and a Caribbean folk dance cycle—Hurston staged both the similarities and the differences between movement practices of the African diaspora. Worth noting too is Hurston's description of the middle section of the Fire Dance as "African rhythm with European borrowings," already hybrid in its West Indian incarnation.[28] This variegated vision of diaspora was one that Hurston held from early on. As she explained to her friend, Langston Hughes, in a 1929 letter from the field, she was interested in the Bahamian material for two fundamental reasons: "(1) There are so many of them in America that their folk lore definitely influences ours in South Florida. (2) For contrast with ours."[29] For Hurston, African surviv-als necessarily existed alongside revision and transformation, and the embodied cartography of her concert expressed just this multiplicity.

Seen in this light, Hurston's *The Great Day* anticipates and answers the concerns of more recent theorists of the black diaspora. In the 1990s, scholars like Paul Gilroy and James Clifford articulated provocative and influential formulations of diaspora that approached culture not as a fixed, bounded entity but rather as a category produced by movement and travel between places.[30] In particular, Gilroy's acclaimed 1993 book, *The Black Atlantic*, proposes that rather than perceiving identity as tied to "roots and rootedness," we should understand it "as a process of move-ment and mediation that is more appropriately approached via the homonym routes."[31] With its attention to cross-cultural exchange and transnational discontinuities, Hurston's concert represents an important early moment of diaspora consciousness, an enactment of the Black At-lantic that predates by decades Gilroy's coinage of the term. At the same time, her stagings complicate any *a priori* assumption that espousals of African roots and transatlantic routes are antithetical, showing them instead to be alternating and interlacing constituents of cultural identity.

Interestingly, in the months leading up to *The Great Day*'s premiere, Hurston experimented with the placement of the Fire Dance within her revue. An examination of extant playscript drafts reveals that in one early version, the dance was set to occur at the end of the first act, in the middle of the railroad camp workers' day. In this iteration, the per-formance of the dance was limited to the Bahamian migrants; this was a marked contrast to the version that was ultimately produced, in which the entire work camp gathered for the Caribbean ritual. In the earlier draft, after being taunted by their African American co-workers for not joining in the work songs, the Bahamians maintain that they have their "own songs and dances."[32] When the lunch whistle blows, they venture off alone to enact the Fire Dance. Though grouped together to perform the same manual labor, the Bahamian migrants preserve their ethnic and national difference by refusing to adopt wholly the ways of African American folk, and the Fire Dance serves as a kinesthetic display of this difference.

The location of the Fire Dance, then, had real repercussions for Hurston's depiction of intra-racial relations among the folk. While no re-cord of the dialogue used in *The Great Day* survives, Hurston's resolution to place the Fire Dance at the end of the second act is telling. If she once considered presenting a program that depicted an uneasy coexistence between Bahamians and African Americans, with the dance cycle func-tioning as a break in the work day and a rupture between the two groups, the version she finally adopted presented the Caribbean number as a force that united the heterogeneous folk communities of the railroad work camp by involving the entire cast. Situated at the close of the narra-tive, enlisting universal participation, the Fire Dance helped bridge national differences introduced during the work day. In the end, Hurston used the kinesthetic distinctiveness of the Fire Dance to broach intra-racial tensions without letting them become divisive.

Performed rather than written, Hurston's delineation of diaspora played a more forceful role in her stage concert than in her literature. Live theatre not only allowed Hurston to illustrate the physicality of black folk culture in general, but also to spotlight the corporeal power of the Fire Dance in particular. Certainly, Hurston continued to explore the relations between Caribbean and African American practices in other media, and Africanist dance scenes appear in both *Jonah's Gourd Vine* and *Their Eyes Were Watching God*.[33] Yet the prominence of the Bahamian dance cycle in *The Great Day*—its position as the climactic finale of the production and its sheer intensity when performed live—undeniably amplified its import to Hurston's presentation of the folk. In fact, I would argue, Hurston took advantage of the theatrical arena to put forward a complex vision of harmonious heterogeneity among the folk without having to enunciate it explicitly. By representing the Fire Dance as a unifying force, Hurston held up to her audience a model of black diasporic solidarity. This was not necessarily a solidarity that Hurston encountered off-stage.[34] Yet in the space of performance, Hurston demonstrated the possibility of a folk collectivity forged in and through dance. Requiring physical labor, aesthetic choices, and a sensi-tivity to the dynamics of live performance, choreography was central, not incidental, to Hurston's theory of diasporic folk culture. As schol-ars and fans continue to recover and reassess Hurston's life and legacy, we can no longer afford to overlook the embodied dimensions of her work.

NOTES

1. Program, *The Great Day*, 10 January 1932, John Golden Theatre, Prentiss Taylor Papers, Archives of American Art, Smithsonian Institution.

2. See my book *Choreographing the Folk: The Dance Stagings of Zora Neale Hurston* (Minneapolis: University of Minnesota Press, 2008) for a full account of Hurston's theatrical productions throughout the 1930s and the attention they garnered from various well-known artists.

3. Program, *The Fire Dance*, January 25, 1939, New Auditorium, Orlando, Florida, Department of Special Collections, George A. Smathers Libraries, University of Florida.

4. Arthur Ruhl, "Second Nights," review of *The Great Day*, *New York Herald Tribune*, 17 January 1932, 11.

5. See Kraut, *Choreographing the Folk*, 53–89, for a lengthier discussion of the politics inherent in the label "choreographer."

6. Zora Neale Hurston, *Dust Tracks on a Road* (1942; repr., New York: HarperPerennial, 1996), 281.

7. Program, *The Fire Dance*, January 25, 1939.

8. Hurston, *Dust Tracks*, 281. While several films taken by Hurston are currently held in the Motion Picture Division of the Library of Congress, I have been unable to locate the Fire Dance footage Hurston made while in the Bahamas.

9. Hurston, *Dust Tracks*, 281.

10. The names I list here are derived from various archival sources, including a comparison of multiple programs for performances of the Fire Dance throughout the 1930s. See Kraut, *Choreographing the Folk*, for more information about the Bahamian dancers.

11. According to a 1947 *Crisis* article, for example, Howard was from New Rochelle, New York, not the Bahamas. John Lovell, Jr., "Democracy in a Hit Revue," *Crisis* 54, n. 3 (March 1947): 76.

12. Zora Neale Hurston to Charlotte Osgood Mason, October 15, 1931, Alain Locke Papers, Manuscript Division, Moorland Spingarn Research Center, Howard University.

13. VéVé Clark, "Performing the Memory of Difference in Afro-Caribbean Dance: Katherine Dunham's Choreography, 1938–87," in *History and Memory in African-American Culture*, ed. Geneviève Fabre and Robert O'Meally (New York: Oxford University Press, 1994), 188–204.

14. Kate Ramsey, "Vodou, Nationalism, and Performance: The Staging of Folklore in Mid-Twentieth-Century Haiti," in *Meaning in Motion: New Cultural Studies of Dance*, ed. Jane Desmond (Durham, NC: Duke University Press, 1997), 363.

15. Hurston to Mason, October 15, 1931.

16. Hurston, *Dust Tracks*, 284.

17. "Announcing 'Great Day,'" program announcement, James Weldon Johnson Collection, Beinecke Rare Book and Manuscript Library, Yale University.

18. Hamilton Holt to Robert Wunsch, 29 January 1933, Rollins College Archives.

19. Hurston to Edwin Grover, 1 February 1933, Department of Special Collections, George A. Smathers Libraries, University of Florida.

20. Hurston, *Dust Tracks*, 284.

21. On "bodily writing," see Susan Leigh Foster, "Choreographing History," in *Choreographing History*, ed. Susan Leigh Foster (Bloomington: Indiana University Press, 1995), 3. See Paul Gilroy, *The Black Atlantic: Modernity and Double Consciousness* (Cambridge: Harvard University Press, 1993).

22. "The Passing of a Day," typescript, Alain Locke Papers, Manuscript Division, Moorland Spingarn Research Center, Howard University.

23. In her 1930 article "Dance Songs and Tales from the Bahamas" (*Journal of American Folklore* 43, no. 169 [July–October 1930]), for example, Hurston characterized the Fire Dance as an "exceedingly African folk dance" (294).

24. Hurston, *Dust Tracks*, 283–284.

25. "Bahaman Dance," photo, *Theatre Arts Monthly* 16.4 (1932): 263.

26. "Announcing 'Great Day,'" program announcement.

27. Research footage that Hurston took of "Chick-Mah-Chick," in which children assume the roles of a crow, a hen, and a band of chicks, is available in the Margaret Mead Collection in the Motion Picture, Broadcasting, and Recorded Sound Division of the Library of Congress.

28. Hurston, "The Fire Dance," in *Go Gator and Muddy the Water: Writings by Zora Neale Hurston from the Federal Writers' Project*, ed. Pamela Bordelon (New York: W.W. Norton & Company, 1999), 55.

29. Hurston to Hughes, 15 October 1929, James Weldon Johnson Collection, Beinecke Rare Book and Manuscript Library, Yale University.

30. See Gilroy, *The Black Atlantic*; James Clifford, "Traveling Cultures," in *Cultural Studies*, ed. Laurence Grossberg, Cary Nelson, and Paula Treichler (London: Routledge, 1992), 96–116; James Clifford, "Diasporas," in *Routes: Travel and Translation in the Late Twentieth Century* (Cambridge: Harvard University Press, 1997), 244–277.

31. Gilroy, *The Black Atlantic*, 9.

32. Hurston, "From Sun to Sun," typescript, Alain Locke Papers, Manuscript Division, Moorland Spingarn Research Center, Howard University.

33. See Zora Neale Hurston, *Jonah's Gourd Vine* (1934; repr., London: Virago Press, 1987), 58–62; and Hurston, *Their Eyes Were Watching God* (1937; repr., New York: Harper & Row, 1990), 133, 146, 147.

34. In her autobiography, Hurston details a clash between her troupe of Bahamian dancers and choral director Hall Johnson's African American singers, who ridiculed the Bahamians as "monkey chasers" (*Dust Tracks*, 281–282).

Modernist Visions of "Self" within Community: Zora Neale Hurston's *Their Eyes Were Watching God* and James Van Der Zee's Home in Harlem Photographs*

Emily M. Hinnov

Modernist images created by African Americans—and those seeking to represent them—oscillate between the emphasis on poverty and unemployment in the black community and the embodiment of the uplifted, dignified "New Negro" comfortable within the context of strong family and community. Modernist artists such as Zora Neale Hurston and James Van Der Zee also mediate between representations of African American characters that might invite readers to objectify them and straight-on views that allow agency and the often unsettling "look back" from the subject.[1] These complex concepts of vision and the intersubjective encounter contribute to the performance and realization of self in these Harlem Renaissance texts, produced once, many have argued, that the New Negro movement had crumbled in disappointment.[2] In this chapter, I explore the topic of African Americans' modernist representations of selfhood and community in the era of the Harlem Renaissance as I look more closely at Hurston's *Their Eyes Were Watching God* (1937) alongside contemporary photographic images by Van Der Zee. Here I will show how Hurston's novel and Van Der Zee's photographs represent a supreme affirmation of interconnective communal identity.

Janie Crawford begins *Their Eyes Were Watching God* without being able to recognize herself in a photograph, and she soon finds a full realization

*Parts of this chapter discussing Hurston and *Their Eyes Were Watching God* were published in my book, *Encountering Choran Community: Literary Modernism, Visual Culture and Political Aesthetics in the Interwar Years* (Susquehanna University Press, 2009).

of self within community. Through the course of Hurston's novel, however, Janie moves away from her outsider status toward a heterosexual
relationship of intersubjectivity with her lover, Tea Cake. In their
longing to coexist with each other, Janie and Tea Cake seem to experience a matrixial, spiritual, and physical connection that allows Janie to
fully reveal herself as complete within the context of community.
Finally content in herself and her story told by the novel's end, Janie
gazes out at the horizon in a culminating moment of future possibility, where she finds a wholeness of self within the wide world. Photographic images created by James Van Der Zee in 1920s and 1930s
Harlem, much like Hurston's novel, proclaim that the black community has a strong, autonomous sense of self. He consistently places his
subjects within the context of family, while his photos look at a community seen through an insider's eyes. Transforming stereotypical
images of blackness, Van Der Zee was a visionary and optimistic early
20th-century American photographer, depicting his people with a cos-
mopolitan style that suggests progress and the successful establishment and expansion of African American identity.

I am interested in how Hurston and Van Der Zee's self-conscious
knowingness—signaling a performativity of identity—exploits the ideal
of utopian wholeness as a means to poke fun at the concept of an
"essential" self. When comparing Hurston's horizon imagery and Van
Der Zee's visual compendium of racial uplift, I find that each suggests
a new, physically embodied gazer whose outward look suggests futurity and openness to the larger world beyond the view of the horizon.
Each of these artists negotiate W.E.B. Du Bois's legacy of African
Americans' "double-consciousness" through the ways in which their
characters and subjects inhabit multiple roles at once while engaging
with shifting interior and exterior perspectives of the self. Edward
Pavlić connects the Janus-faced process of coming to identity with Du
Bois's idea of the double-consciousness, the essential "interracial anxiety of two-ness, and the intraracial communion in multiplicity" of the
African American's experience.[3] The African American self holds together against the forces of racism and the Veil, and "fluidly disperses
through communal, cultural forms of contestation and affirmation."
This "plural, socially constructed self provides the basis for modernist
communions as well as fractures," culminating, as I argue, in the concept of a performative and communal identity. Could Hurston and
Van Der Zee, then, be intentionally staging seemingly utopian moments
of intersubjectivity between self and other to reveal their ironic play with
social conventions in their texts?

My understanding of these modernist texts as inflected with a communal spirit would not exist without our recognition of art's redemptive force once it gets into the hands, hearts, and minds of open

audiences. Carla Kaplan's work is instructive in defining how literary scholars might realize Hurston's success, in particular:

By including oneself in Hurston's blanket indictment, assuming that one is, for whatever reason, a different reader than Hurston's idealized, eroticized, and romanticized projection, one can learn to listen, to listen differently, and to help, thereby, create the very conditions under which black female longing for narration and self-revelation might, someday, be satisfied.[4]

By recognizing, through our reading/viewing practices, the organic whole that is present in our own communities, we might then change our daily interfaces with difference. We are the scholars who can benefit from Hurston's (and Van Der Zee's) potentially transformative vision of interconnective community.

REVISIONING SELF AND OTHER IN *THEIR EYES WERE WATCHING GOD*

The significance of reimaginary vision, particularly in the context of a natural landscape, is paramount in Janie Crawford's full self-discovery and affirmation of common humanity in *Their Eyes Were Watching God*. It is important that the novel begins with the nonlinear, interior dream world of women against man's wish to dominate the outer, visible world. In an image of a ship on a perpetually linear horizon, "never out of sight, never landing,"[5] men's "dreams [are] mocked to death by Time." At first, Janie too is entrapped by this sense of outer visibility. Except for her friendship with Phoeby, Janie remains an outsider in a society that privileges outer appearances as indicators of self. As a result, Janie is "full of that oldest human longing—self-revelation."[6] Here I will show that Hurston transforms this linear view of the horizon into an all-encompassing nexus of interconnective community.

Significantly, in the photo of her family, Janie misrecognizes herself as white: "Ah couldn't recognize dat dark chile as me. So Ah ast, 'where is me? Ah don't see me.'. . . 'Dat's you, Alphabet, don't you know yo' ownself?' . . . 'Aw, aw! Ah'm colored! . . . Ah thought Ah wuz just like de rest.'"[7] Hurston's Janie represents the doubly positioned experience of a young African American girl in the early 20th-century Southland. Janie's sexual awakening to an originary, interior self in the midst of the pear tree denotes her evolving consciousness of her own authenticity and a communal reconnection with her originary self:

She saw a dust-bearing bee sink into the sanctum of a bloom; the thousand sister calyxes arch to meet the love embrace and the ecstatic shiver of the tree from the tiniest branch creaming in every blossom and frothing with delight. So this was marriage! She had been summoned to behold a revelation . . . She was seeking confirmation of the voice and vision, and everywhere she found and acknowledged answers.[8]

Here Janie seeks confirmation of herself as complete, and she receives it in flashes of fleshly ecstasy. Again, Janie is exiled in her grandmother's house, but her gaze remains set on the future, anticipating the wholeness she will find there as much like the illuminated moment experienced under the pear tree.

When Janie longs for a joyful marriage with Logan Killicks, her first husband—"Ah wants things sweet wid mah marriage lak when you sit under a pear tree and think"[9]—Nanny responds, "Wait awhile baby. Yo' mind will change." As Janie connects her romanticized view of marriage with her blissful moment under the pear tree, Nanny warns her against such a utopian vision. Once Nanny has passed away, Janie's recommunion with "the words of the trees and the wind"[10] once again reminds her of her true self. Now realizing Nanny's truth that "marriage did not make love,"[11] Janie comes closer to recognizing the whole, autonomous, independent woman she always already is.

Nevertheless, immediately once Janie finds her voice with second husband Joe Starks—she declares, "women folks thinks sometimes too!"[12]—she is stifled. As a result, their marriage disintegrates and Janie no longer has any sexual desire for her husband: "She wasn't petal-open anymore with him." Once Joe begins physically abusing her, Janie retreats further into herself: "She stood there until something fell off the shelf inside her." Janie can no longer live in the internal dream world embodied by the pear tree: "She had no more blossomy openings dusting pollen over her man . . . She was saving up feelings for some man she had never seen. She had an inside and an outside and suddenly knew how not to mix them."[13] Out of the need to care for her total self, Janie compartmentalizes herself in a gesture of self-preservation. Yet despite the debilitation of a passionless, airless marriage, Janie does not completely lose her sense of self. In a significant moment just after his death, she looks at herself in the mirror, takes down her hair, and sees that "[t]he young girl was gone, but a handsome woman had taken her place . . . the glory was there."[14] What Janie still must countenance is the fact that she does not need a man's approval of her sexuality to create coherence of self. She will not find this kind of wholeness until the death of her third husband, Vergible "Tea Cake" Woods.

After Joe's death, Janie's initially intersubjective relationship with Tea Cake is associated as well with the pivotal moment under the pear tree. Tea Cake appears to Janie as a veritable forest of passion and possibility: "He looked like the love thoughts of women. He could be a bee to a blossom—a pear tree blossom in the spring . . . He was a glance from God."[15] She and Tea Cake are natural together from the beginning, and as their relationship blossoms, she appears self-aware. Janie resolves not to live without passion any longer. Tea Cake and Janie become acquainted with one another through formulation of a new kind of visceral language of body and mind: "So in the beginnin' new thoughts had tuh be thought and new words said . . . He done taught me de maiden language all over."[16]

Janie valorizes the connection she feels with Tea Cake, and, even though she might believe that her soul has been released in the process, her emotions are not entirely unproblematic. She "felt a self-crushing love. So her soul crawled out from its hiding place."[17] She may experience a brief glimpse of wholeness here, yet despite preliminary signs of another relationship that might impede and even devastate the self, Janie rather blindly continues her liaison with the young vagabond twelve years her junior: "They were doped with their own fumes and emanations . . . [he] held her there melting her resistance with the heat of his body, doing things with their bodies to express the inexpressible."[18] For Janie, the overpowering narcotic of Tea Cake's passionate desire provides both a return to the purely physical part of herself and an opportunity for total intersubjectivity with another. The noteworthy element of Janie and Tea Cake's convergence, however, is the fact that he is enacting much of the aggression in "melting her resistance."

Soon she finds that Tea Cake is certainly not so "sweet as all dat,"[19] as he begins to whip her to "show he is boss."[20] Although they do seem to share some joy living down in the "muck" of the Everglades, it is Tea Cake who maintains the upper hand. Once in Okeechobee, Janie fulfills her domestic role while Tea Cake works outside the home. Soon, however, they are shooting, dancing, and gathering together with the other workers to enjoy Tea Cake's guitar playing. But even in their leisure time, Tea Cake remains king of his castle: "Tea Cake's house was a magnet, the unauthorized center of the 'job.' "[21] Janie is quickly put in her place with Tea Cake's demand that "you betta come git uh job uh work out dere lak de rest uh de women"[22] because she does not work as much as the other women in the community. Janie becomes increasingly silent as a result of her relationship with Tea Cake, and finally, he whips her for no other reason than that "it relieved that awful fear inside him. Being able to whip her reassured him in possession."[23] Tea Cake, the once warm and loving bohemian who awakened the pear tree inside of her, has become just as harshly abusive and possessive as all the other men with whom Janie has aligned herself. Here Hurston warns her readers about the perils of misinterpreting intersubjectivity as too easy and utopian.

Janie's achingly painful, final response to Tea Cake's domination is to do something he taught her to do in fun—to shoot and kill with a rifle. Once Tea Cake contracts rabies from a stray dog in the overpowering hurricane and flood that rages through the town, he threatens

her life with a pistol and ravenously bites her arm. The narrator
describes this episode as "the meanest moment of eternity" and
uncovers a tragic and pathetic picture of Janie's mothering influence on
Tea Cake: "Janie held his head tightly to her breast and wept and
thanked him wordlessly for giving her the chance for loving service."[24]
I contend that, at this moment, Hurston is staging a consciously false
moment of utopian intersubjectivity, or, an ironic utopian moment. Her
tears and her insistence on rocking and holding Tea Cake to her breast
simultaneously mimics the life-giving flow of milk lovingly given by
mother to child and the drama of the inevitable moment of separation.
Yet the fact remains that Janie is often servile, blind, and delusional in
her love for Tea Cake. Taking altruism and nurturing sacrifice to the
level of self-destructive hyperbole, Janie actually looks at her own situation of cruel domestic violence as a "chance for loving service"! For
her role in Tea Cake's death, Janie is put on trial for murder and must
plead her case to an all-white, all-male jury. How, then, are we finally
to read the relationship between Tea Cake and Janie? Even after his
absolutely necessary death, Tea Cake and Janie experience spiritual
and physical connection: "Of course he wasn't dead. He could never
be dead until she herself had finished feeling and thinking."[25] Indeed,
Janie's intense abjection at returning to their home after his death is
palpable. The objects in their bedroom begin a kind of sympathetic call
and response: "[they] commenced to sing a sobbing sigh out of every
chair and thing. Commenced to sing, commenced to sob and sigh, singing and sobbing. Then Tea Cake came prancing around her where she
was and the song of the sigh flew out of the window and lit in the top
of the pine trees. Tea Cake, with the sun for a shawl."[26] The fact that
Tea Cake emerges from her imagination like some phantasmic god of
the sun further implicates Janie in her own misguidance; her misrecog-
nition leads her to view transcendent love as that she had shared with
a man who physically and emotionally abuses her.

Of course it is not until later, after Tea Cake has died and she is
recounting her story to Phoeby, that Janie fulfills her destiny of wholeness. The wrath of nature finally forces Janie to see her world anew.
The pattern of Janie's behavior and experience is irrevocably changed
by the storm; the shocking and disruptive experience of reacting to the
unexpected hurricane (a literal "bolt of lightning") puts Janie's full
transformation into motion. As a result, she is shaken out of her som-
nambulance and is awakened to her full potential—connecting inner
with outer identities, imagined to real experiences—culminating in her
realization of self within community.[27]

Janie finds herself out of the confines of a romantic heterosexual
relationship and instead in a recognition of her own inner resolve, and,
notably, her outer vision of connection with the rest of humanity.

Significantly, Janie returns to her community by the end of the novel in order to regale her audience with tales of her adventures. The shared story of the novel concludes with an affirmation of communal awareness as Janie gazes at the horizon, finally content in herself in a penultimate moment of interconnection and future possibility: "The kiss of his memory made pictures of love and light against the wall. Here was peace. She pulled in her horizon like a great fish-net. Pulled it from around the waist of the world and draped it over her shoulder. So much of life in its meshes! She called in her soul to come and see."[28] The memory of her over-romanticized love for Tea Cake connects them eternally. More importantly, however, Janie has found a new mode of being, which was always her most genuine self. Drawing it inward from the outer web of interconnection, releasing its grasp around the world, and placing it over the mantle of her shoulder in a gesture of self-acceptance, Janie appears as a newly reigning queen of her own best self. As readers, we finally witness her fully integrated body, mind, and soul, encompassing all the promise of the horizon; we too are absorbed into Janie's total vision of self within a shared community of which we become part.[29]

JAMES VAN DER ZEE'S VISUAL HOME IN HARLEM

Early 20th-century examples of similarly intersubjective moments revealing a mutual gaze, those which draw the reader into the narrative with "the look" that reveals the subject's essential self, are abundant in the work of James Van Der Zee in 1920s Harlem. Carol Shloss describes 20th-century photographer Henri Cartier-Bresson's idea of the "decisive moment" as a moment of complete reciprocity, the "simultaneous recognition in a fraction of a second"[30] of the unity of photographer and subject, the congruence of self-expression and revelation of both self and other in creating meaning. Van Der Zee's images "speak of the liveliness of the community and its capacity for renewal, its constant reinvention of itself, and its growth . . . [they] are about the connection between self and family and self and community."[31] His pictures signify the black middle class's strong, autonomous sense of self.

Van Der Zee opened his studio in Harlem in 1912 and attained a local reputation that lasted for two decades. After World War II his work went into an eclipse but became known to a wider audience through a controversial exhibition "Harlem on My Mind" at the MoMA in New York in 1969.[32] He had a sheltered childhood in Lenox, Massachusetts, yet a provocative confrontation with the Harlem Renaissance influenced his work. Van Der Zee consistently placed his subjects within the context of family and community; his photos look at a community seen through an insider's eyes. In countenancing his work, "we are privy to the joys of a new life, marriage, and accomplishment as well as the pain of loss; we learn who is important, who is fashionable, and who is powerful."[33] As a commercial and portrait photographer in the 1920s and 1930s, Van Der Zee created important and beautiful historical documents of and for Harlem's most distinguished residents: World War I heroes Henry Johnson and Needham Roberts; singers Mamie Smith, Hazel Scott, and Florence Mills; poet Countee Cullen; and boxer Joe Louis. Van Der Zee was also the official photographer for Marcus Garvey and the Universal Negro Improvement Association in 1924.[34]

Van Der Zee's "pictures of love and light"[35] represent a "sweeping survey of the most vital pre-World War II African American community existing in the United States," providing "an overt celebration of black middle-class life, and particularly family life." His small photography business reflects later 19th-century portraiture styles, but were created to value a client's "dignity, independence and comfort." There is always a sense of self-worth present in his images—they "define a people in the process of transformation and a culture in transition" and a growing sense of personal and national identity of African Americans.[36] Van Der Zee helped transform stereotypical images of blackness into that of Alain Locke's *New Negro*: educated, dignified, economically successful, tied with pride in family and race.

Two quintessential Van Der Zee images of racial uplift are contemporary with Hurston's novel: *A Harlem Couple Wearing Raccoon Coats Standing Next to a Cadillac on West 127th Street* (1932) and *Memories* (1938). The first image in particular reveals a feeling of dignity and success in upper middle-class black American selfhood at this time. A handsome man and woman pose triumphantly wearing their luxurious fur coats—the man is seated in the car while the woman leans beside the open door—to show off the shiny chrome finish of their luxury car, an emblem of the American Dream. They are posed in the street in front of the upper middle-class brownstones that most likely comprise their neighborhood, revealing a proud and economically healthy African American community.

The other image, *Memories*, falls in line with traditional domestic family portraiture. This photograph captures a domestic moment of repose: it pictures three adoring and attentive children circled around their father, who shows them a picture book. The small girl gently caresses her father's chin in a loving gesture that completes the triangulation of warm physical contact created by herself, her two brothers, and her father. The parlor in the background is richly decorated with flowers and tapestry-like wallpaper, suggesting the family's healthy, "Talented Tenth" economic status. Indeed the whiteness appearing in the dress and skin of those pictured, as well as the flowers boardering the image, suggest a kind of circle of whiteness which reveals the contemporary culture's proclivity for "whitening up" in order to rise

above past indignities and violence in a racist society. Another intrigu-
ing detail in this photograph is the cutout of the dog, which is made to
look like a three-dimensional member of the family. The dog cutout
adds to this image another dimension of performativity. Van Der Zee,
here, consciously crafts a kind of photomontage in order to illustrate
this emblem of a racially uplifted family—complete with mother,
father, children, and the family dog. But the most telling detail of their
interconnectivity is the shadow overhead of their deceased mother and
wife. As with Janie's evocation of the phantasmic Tea Cake, Van Der
Zee's photograph supposes that the memory of loved ones lives on in
our everyday lives—even that the spirits of the dead watch over and
guide us with benevolence and pride. In line with Hurston's novel,
they celebrate the powerful connection between a sense of fortified
self-identification and community.

These images, among Van Der Zee's others, suggest the waves of
African American immigration from the Caribbean and the migration
from the rural South to the cities of the North forever changed the visual self-image of the people who made the journey: they have been
metamorphosed into suave and aware big-city dwellers; the degradation of the past has been seemingly eliminated from their present
lives.[37]

His Harlem shows a healthy, diverse, spiritual, prosperous, and productive African American community, helping to create African American art and culture in Harlem—they are "visual embodiments of the
racial ideals promoted by such leading African American intellectuals
and writers of the era as W.E.B. Du Bois, Claude McKay, Alain Locke,
Langston Hughes, and Zora Neale Hurston in Locke's noted 1925 book
The New Negro."[38]

It is interesting to note that Van Der Zee often retouched his portraits
(as with the family dog previously mentioned) to fit this image and
staged spaces where his subjects "could expand spiritually, emotionally,
and symbolically." Like Hurston, he also poked fun at stereotypical
domestic situations, yet his powerful images of African American soldiers positioned them at the forefront of the struggle for democracy.
Most importantly, "the loving family is central to the life of the African
American community" for Van Der Zee. His positive images of Harlem
celebrate a sense of fortified self-identification and racial pride.[39] Much
like the image of Janie at the end of Hurston's novel, Van Der Zee's photographs "speak of the liveliness of the community and its capacity for
renewal, its constant reinvention of itself, and its growth . . . [They] are
about the connection between self and family and self and community."[40] Van Der Zee and Hurston share a concern for the communal
voice of black American consciousness in the age of Jim Crow, race riots,
and everyday lynchings. As Henry Louis Gates, Jr., points out, Hurston's

"authentic narrative voice that echoes and aspires to impersonality, ano-
nymity, and authority of the black vernacular tradition . . . [a] selfless
tradition, at once collective and compelling . . . the unwritten text of
common blackness"[41] could just as easily describe the multiple narrative
registers that Van Der Zee's images inhabit. Both modernist artists,
although speaking from different class positions, were actively engaged
in ways of storytelling that would negotiate the doubly conscious, possi-
bly shared voice of the African American community at this time in history. In the expansive horizon of futurity and wholeness, these African
American artists depict photographic and textual figures of healthy self-
development within the context of human interconnection.

THE LEGACY OF MODERNIST VISIONS OF COMMUNITY

The title of Hurston's novel finally offers a clue about her concept of
vision as a movement from optic vision (outer surveillance of inner
life) to the power of envisioning self within community. The obvious
truth is that you can't watch God, and the people in the muck only
stare into the darkness of the hurricane and flood that overtake many
of them. Yet, they can at one and the same time be overwhelmed by its
horror and reminded of the limited constructs of culture which that
dark void represents. Modernist women like Hurston knew that
the social order is limited, yet they are able to see beyond it and create
a counter-narrative to constrictive ideologies. Hurston's narrative
voice—both limited omniscient and first person, as well as lyrical and
mythical—is all-encompassing, inviting the reader into that intimate
communal space enacted by the living art of her novel. Through
Hurston's image of "the biggest thing God ever made, the horizon,"[42]
she confirms Janie's quest for wholeness of self within her community,
which by now extends to the reading audience: "She had been getting
ready for her great journey to the horizon in search of *people*; it was important to all the world that she should find them and they find
her."[43] Janie becomes a character in her own story and the omniscient
narrator of her own community, and potentially ours as well.[44]

Like Janie, who has found a home through her own reformed sense
of self within the context of a larger community, many feminist and
black readers, in an affective response to their shared feeling of community, could find a more complete representation of self in Hurston's
narrative. Moreover, as Cheryl Wall deftly sums up, Hurston strived to
"reconstruct a home in language that acknowledged but did not dwell
on the history of racial oppression, counted African-American creative expression as a powerful mode of resistance, and fostered the recognition of differences without and within oneself."[45] For Hurston, and
for Van Der Zee as well, the self can only play itself out within a

greater community of collaborators in identity-making. Hurston's novel represents a version of modernism that could be shared within the greater community; this novel enacts the call of community itself. Finally, then, Morrison's "dream and dreamer" can become one,[46] and African American artists such as Hurston and Van Der Zee can cross the divide between self and other, at least aesthetically.

NOTES

1. Hurston herself may not have been particularly interested in contemporary photographic theories, but images taken of her suggest her ability to play with both visual perceptions of herself and the camera itself. She regularly pretended to be younger than she was, and often dressed that way. For instance, when she arrived in Baltimore at the age of 26 in 1917, she easily passed herself off as 16 in order to qualify for free public schooling (Boyd). She also enjoyed wearing stylish coats, "chic hats, long dresses, and dramatic colors," as revealed in photographs of her during her years at Howard University. As she traveled through the south collecting folklore in 1927, she stopped to pose for a feisty shot, arms akimbo with a belt and pistol secured around her hips. A portrait of her taken by Carl Van Vechten in 1934 shows Hurston's more reserved side; here she appears like the serious writer she is, yet a slight turn of her head and a somewhat sly, side-long glance into the camera divulges her persistent playfulness. The variety of images of Hurston, available in Valerie Boyd's biography, *Wrapped in Rainbows: The Life of Zora Neale Hurston* (New York: Scribner, 2003), attest to the multiplicity of roles she was capable of playing, particularly as a photographic subject.

2. Edward Pavlíc, in *Crossroads Modernism: Descent and the Emergence of African American Literary Culture* (Minneapolis, MN: University of Minnesota Press, 2002), demonstrates the ways in which African American artists negotiated the intersection of high modernism in Europe and American discourse to fashion their own distinctive response to American modernity. His book re-envisions the potentials and dilemmas where the different traditions of modernism meet and firmly establishes African American modernism at this cultural crossroads.

3. Ibid., 7.

4. See Carla Kaplan's book, *The Erotics of Talk: Women's Writing and Feminist Paradigms* (New York: Oxford University Press, 1996), but in particular her chapter on Hurston entitled " 'That Oldest Human Longing' in *Their Eyes Were Watching God*" (99–122), 122.

5. Zora Neale Hurston, *Their Eyes Were Watching God*, Foreword by Mary Helen Washington and Afterword by Henry Louis Gates, Jr. (1937; repr., New York: Perennial Classics, 1990), 1.

6. Ibid., 6.

7. Ibid., 9.

8. Ibid., 10–11.

9. Ibid., 23.

10. Ibid., 23–24.
11. Ibid., 24.
12. Ibid., 67.
13. Ibid., 68.
14. Ibid., 83.
15. Ibid., 101–102.
16. Ibid., 108.
17. Ibid., 122.
18. Ibid., 132.
19. Ibid., 93.
20. Ibid., 140.
21. Ibid., 126.
22. Ibid., 127.
23. Ibid., 140.
24. Ibid., 175.
25. Ibid., 183.
26. Ibid., 183.

27. Janie's voice at the end of the novel has been read as communal by critics such as Nellie McKay, Robert Hemenway, and Barbara Christian. Yet according to Mary Helen Washington, Hurston's conclusion problematizes that reading:

Testifying to the limitations of voice and critiquing the culture that celebrates orality to the exclusion of inner growth. Her final speech to Phoeby at the end of *Their Eyes* actually casts doubt on the relevance of oral speech and supports Alice Walker's claim that women's silence can be intentional and useful.

Other critics, such as Carla Kaplan, similarly argue that the novel's end signals Hurston's indication of "the absence of any community" (*The Erotics of Talk*, 119). She writes that to read Hurston's story as a realization of redemptive community "through the positivity of love and voice occludes the ways in which Hurston's revision of the romance narrative . . . works to *deepen* rather than reduce the contradictions cutting across it" (121).

28. Hurston, *Their Eyes*, 183–184.

29. A number of critics have relevantly commented on the concluding image in the novel. Barbara Johnson argues that Janie triumphantly rediscovers "life in its meshes" in "a gesture of total recuperation and peace" ("Metaphor, Metonymy, and Voice in *Their Eyes Were Watching God*," ed. Cheryl A. Wall, *Zora Neale Hurston's Their Eyes Were Watching God: A Casebook* [Oxford and New York: Oxford University Press, 2000], 41–58, 50). I contend this perspective denotes a matrixial space of web-like, organic interconnectivity. Hers is, as Karla Holloway supports, "the language of community, the imagery of nature, and the symbol of the spirit" ("The Emergent Voice: The Word within Its Texts" in *Zora Neale Hurston: Critical Perspectives Past and Present*, ed. Henry Louis Gates, Jr., and K.A. Appiah [New York: Amistad, 1993], 67–75, 69). Mae Gwendolyn Henderson considers the horizon as well. For Henderson, Janie's calling in of her soul reveals "not [just] a unity of self" but a conquering "over the division between self and other" ("Speaking in Tongues: Dialogics and Dialectics and the Black Woman Writer's Literary Tradition," in *African*

American Literary Theory: A Reader, ed. Winston Napier [New York: New York University Press, 2000], 348–368, 363). Indeed, Janie Crawford achieves a fluent interpersonal web of perspectives and voices. She is finally capable of articulating the depths of her experience in interpersonal terms. As Cheryl A. Wall outlines, "the pear tree and the horizon . . . help unify the narrative. The first symbolizes organic union with another, the second, the individual experiences one must acquire to achieve selfhood" ("Zora Neale Hurston: Changing Her Own Words," in *Zora Neale Hurston: Critical Perspectives Past and Present*, ed. Henry Louis Gates, Jr., and K.A. Appiah [New York: Amistad, 1993], 76–97, 89). By the novel's end, Janie goes through this process of fortification of self and unity with other selves and community.

30. Carol Shloss, *In Visible Light: Photography and the American Writer, 1840–1940* (New York: Oxford University Press, 1987), 7.

31. Deborah Willis-Braithwaite, *Van Der Zee: Photographer, 1886–1983* (New York: Harry A. Abrams, Inc., 1993), 25.

32. This is according to Alan Fern, Director of the National Portrait Gallery.

33. Willis-Braithwaite, *Van Der Zee: Photographer*, 7.

34. Ibid., 8.

35. Hurston, *Their Eyes*, 184.

36. Willis-Braithwaite, *Van Der Zee: Photographer*, 10.

37. Ibid., 11.

38. Ibid., 13.

39. These images appear in contrast to the documentary photos of Aaron Siskind in the 1930s and 1940s, which depict oppression, poverty, and chaotic crowds.

40. Willis-Braithwaite, *Van Der Zee: Photographer*, 25.

41. Henry Louis Gates, Jr., *The Signifying Monkey: A Theory of Afro-American Literary Criticism* (New York: Oxford University Press, 1988), 183.

42. Ibid., 85.

43. Ibid., Hurston's emphasis.

44. Henry Louis Gates, Jr., argues that Hurston's text speaks of the search for identity and self-understanding and its connected themes of "discovery, rebirth and renewal" (*The Signifying Monkey* 185). Speaking to the full integrity Janie achieves, Edward Pavlíc concurs, arguing that "Hurston imagined a communal underground space that offered new possibilities for black encounters with American modernity as well as any modernist creative process" (176). Her diasporic modernism encompasses myth, West Africanist traditions of oral culture, a multiple understanding of the self, and an awareness of the way humor disrupts hierarchical relationships. Gates writes in his Afterword to Hurston's *Their Eyes Were Watching God,*

Part of Hurston's received heritage—and perhaps the paramount notion that links the novel of manners in the Harlem Renaissance, the social realism of the thirties, and the cultural nationalism of the Black Arts movement—was the idea that racism had reduced black people to mere ciphers, to beings who only react to an omnipresent racial oppression, whose culture is 'deprived' where different, and whose psyches are in the main "pathological." (Gates, 189)

Hurston found "this idea degrading, its propaganda a trap, and railed against it." Freedom, she wrote in *Moses, Man of the Mountain*, "was something internal . . . The man must make his own emancipation" (189).

45. Cheryl A. Wall, *Women of the Harlem Renaissance* (Bloomington: Indiana University Press, 1995), 32.

46. See Toni Morrison, *Playing in the Dark: Whiteness and the Literary Imagination* (Cambridge: Harvard University Press, 1992). In her discussion of the "surrogate" (26) blackness present in the development of modern American literature and identity, Toni Morrison writes, "the subject of the dream is the dreamer" (17) to emphasize the interdependency of black and white, self and other.

Hurston, Toomer, and the Dream of a Negro Theatre

John Lowe

Zora Neale Hurston (1891–1960) and Jean Toomer (1894–1967) are usually listed as leading lights of the Harlem Renaissance. Toomer, however, had written his major contribution to the Renaissance well before the other key players had even tuned their instruments, and Hurston's true literary masterworks only began to appear in the 1930s. Furthermore, although he had had extensive contact with many of the "New Negroes" before the publication of *Cane*, Toomer afterward played little role in the social scene, as he had shifted his interests to the mystic philosopher Gurdjieff and his circle as early as 1926. Similarly, although Hurston was a legendary participant in many "rent parties" and the early literary salons, she was often absent from the scene to work on her alternate career as student and innovative ethnologist. She devotes exactly one paragraph to the Harlem Renaissance in her autobiography, *Dust Tracks on a Road*, and she spent most of her later life back in Florida. As with Hurston, Toomer did not mention Harlem in his memoirs, although New York City plays a prominent role there. Both writers, however, stand out from the lists of Renaissance writers in that they knew the South firsthand, and saw nothing wrong with presenting the unadorned folk they knew there as living avatars of a precious cultural tradition. Worse, as far as critics were concerned, both scorned the idea of presenting correct "representatives" of the race in their fiction or in their authorial stance: as Hurston proclaimed, "every tub must sit on its own bottom."[1] As such, they proved to be Renaissance renegades, offending many of the "talented tenth" and urban writers who preferred either a more refined fictional palette or alternately, a more or less "white" language and style that could stand up to the scrutiny of white culture and criticism. Still others demanded overt social protest, which neither artist felt inclined to provide. This essay will examine the affinities and attitudes of Hurston and Toomer, situate their literary production during the Renaissance, particularly drama, and speculate on the lasting effects their dramatic works had during the "New Negro" period, and the possible ways in which these texts might affect their long-term literary reputations.

June Jordan has stated that "the affirmation of Black values and life-styles within the American context is, indeed, an act of protest."[2] This is a crucial distinction to bear in mind when examining not just Hurston's dramatic production, but that of all African Americans, particularly during and just after the age of minstrelsy (which David Krasner has done in his excellent study of early African American drama), but also during the age of the New Negro, when some racial barriers were falling, but others remained. Financial success in a white-run business like theatre (where most of the patrons of Broadway houses were white), dictated donning a minstrel-like mask, or even blackface. Well into the 20th century, blackface/minstrel traditions continued to appear, from the blackface performances of Shirley Temple to the minstrel antics of black actors who portrayed television's *Amos and Andy*. Consequently, the most popular forms of black entertainment for mass audiences were musicals and comedies.

Zora Neale Hurston, however, always felt that humor was one of the chief glories of her culture, and as I have demonstrated at some length, most of her work used subversive and folk-based humor to deconstruct racial pieties of all sorts, and her dramatic writing was no different.[3] The strictures of the American stage were for her an opportunity, for almost all of her plays were chock full of the magnificent folk culture she had been observing and then collecting. Then too, Hurston surely would have shared Jordan's belief that the affirmation of black culture was an act of protest, and she no doubt recognized how this had been accomplished in the first great manifestation of the Harlem Renaissance, Jean Toomer's *Cane*.[4] She would have also been keenly interested in how the complex narrative strands of that work culminated in a drama, "Kabnis." Hurston thought so much of Toomer that she and Langston Hughes visited Sparta (the actual setting for *Cane*) in 1927, on their long, leisurely motor trip from Mobile to New York. We have every reason to believe that she found Toomer's valorization and concurrent interrogation of African American life in the South encouraging and challenging.

Hurston's own book-length works, all set in the South or the Caribbean, did not begin to appear until 1934, with the publication of *Jonah's Gourd Vine*.[5] For much of the time between December 1927, when she signed a contract for the financial support of the white philanthropist Mrs. Osgood Mason, and 1933, Hurston was collecting and writing about folklore, partly in support of her attempt to earn a Ph.D. at Columbia University. During this time, she and Hughes collaborated on the ill-fated play *Mule-Bone,* which was never produced during their lifetime. Before their collaboration on the play, she had written Hughes in 1928 that she had discovered six "laws":

1. The Negro's outstanding characteristic is drama. That is why he appears so imitative. Drama is mimicry; note gesture is place of words. 2. Negro is lacking in reverence. Note number of stories in which God, church, and heaven are treated lightly. 3. *Angularity* in everything, sculpture, dancing, abrupt story telling. 4. Redundance. Examples: low-down, Cap'n high sheriff, top-superior, the number of times—usually three—that a feature is repeated in a story. Repetition of single simple strain in music. 5. Restrained ferocity in everything. There is a tense ferocity beneath the casual exterior that stirs the onlooker to hysteria, note effect of Negro music, dancing, gestures on the staid Nordic. 6. Some laws in dialect. The same form is not always used. Some syllables/words ["syllables" is written above "words"] are long before or after certain words and short in the same positions[.] Example: You as subject gets full value but is shortened to yuh as an object. Him in certain positions and 'im in others depending on the consonant preceding. Several laws of aspirate "H."[6]

A month later (May, 1928), she emphasized that her dream of a Negro theatre included him: "Of *course* you know I didn't dream of that theatre as a one-man stunt. I had you helping 50-50 from the start. . . . I *know* it is going to be *Glorious*! A really new departure in the drama."[7]

We now know, however, that she had had this preoccupation even before she met Hughes, and had been writing plays since the early 1920s. One of her several contributions to the "Harlem Renaissance," as it became known, was a play, *Color Struck*, which she submitted along with another play, *Spears*, to *Opportunity* magazine's annual literary contest. *Color Struck* won second prize, and was eventually published in a short-lived magazine, *Fire!!* (1926).[8] This four-scene melodrama initially depicts a group boarding a Jim Crow railway car en route to a cakewalk contest. The best performers quarrel because Emma, a dark woman, thinks brown-skinned John has been flirting with the mulatta, Effie. Throughout the play, Emma's jealousy and self-hatred keep her from accepting John's love, first at the cakewalk itself, and then after a 20-year separation. Recently widowed John says he chose a dark wife because he longed for Emma, and he teases her when he discovers her invalid teenage daughter is nearly white. He tells her he'll stay with the girl while Emma goes for a Doctor. Emma doubles back and accuses John of lust for her daughter. John departs and the daughter dies, leaving Emma hopeless and alone. The play's

melodrama makes it top-heavy, but it succeeds in suggesting the creativity and exuberance of African American culture in the highly animated cakewalk scenes, and in sketching in the parameters of color
prejudice within the race.[9] The play was one of the few she wrote that
was produced during her lifetime, when it was staged by the Negro
Art Theatre of Harlem.[10]

The next year, Hurston was asked to contribute a piece to Charles S.
Johnson's *Ebony and Topaz: A Collectanea*, an anthology of black writing.
The First One: A Play in One Act, was an imaginative retelling of the
story of Noah and his son, Ham, set in the Valley of Ararat three years
after the flood, featuring Noah, his wife, their sons Shem, Japheth, and
Ham; Eve (Ham's wife), and the sons' wives and children.[11] This play
could be considered a "pendent" to *Color Struck*, in that it offers a
comic rebuttal of the equation of blackness with a curse. *The First One*
was the first of several pieces Hurston would set in biblical times, frequently in black dialect. Here, however, Hurston uses standard speech.
As the play opens, Noah and everyone else stand fuming because
Ham, the wayward son, is once again late for the annual commemora-
tion of the delivery from the flood (a signification on the stereotype of
"C.P.T." or "colored people time"). Ham comes in playing a harp and
in dress that links him with both Orpheus and Bacchus. Mrs. Shem
criticizes Ham because he doesn't bring an offering and because, unlike
his brothers, who toil in the fields, he merely tends the flocks and
sings. Noah calls on Ham to play and sing to help them forget, while
he gets drunk to efface the image of the dead faces that floated by the
ark. When Ham, also inebriated, laughingly reports on his father's nak-
edness in the tent, Shem's jealous wife wakes Noah, reporting the deed
but not the identity of the perpetrator. Noah, enraged, roars that "His
skin shall be black . . . He and his seed forever. He shall serve his
brothers and they shall rule over him." All involved are appalled and
try to reverse the curse, but Ham comes in laughing, unaware that he
has been turned black. His son has changed color as well. Noah ban-
ishes them, fearing the contagion of blackness. Ham, rather than showing dismay, laughs cynically, saying, "Oh, remain with your flocks and
fields and vineyards, to covet, to sweat, to die and know no peace. I go
to the sun."[12]

Two things are worth noting here: first, a race begins because of its
founding father's joke; and secondly, the ending suggests that "The
First [black] One" surpasses whites by knowing how to lead a fully
imagined and creative life. As such, Hurston's playlet embraces and
inverts the traditional interpretation of the biblical passage, and contra-
dicts the sentiments of the tragic Emma of *Color Struck*. The story also
echoed the intraracial color issues Toomer raised in *Cane*, as in "Bona
and Paul."

Meanwhile, Hurston continued her education at Columbia University. Encouraged by Boas, she began a series of trips to Florida to gather folklore materials. This work was facilitated for years by the sponsorship of a wealthy white woman, Mrs. Charlotte Osgood Mason, who also supported the careers of Hurston's gifted friends, the writers Langston Hughes and Alain Locke, as well as the musician Hall Johnson, who was active in the Broadway theatre.

Hurston and Hughes became close friends, and became enthusiastic with the idea of founding a vernacular theatre and opera based on "*real* Negro" life. Over a period of months, they worked on a three-act play entitled *Mule-Bone*, which was based on a short story by Hurston.[13] Eventually, however, in a complicated series of events, the authors had a permanent "falling out" and the play was never published or produced during the authors' lifetimes.[14] In 1985, Henry Louis Gates, Jr., read the play at Yale, and began a campaign to get it produced. It almost didn't happen; a staged reading before 100 prominent black writers and theatre people in 1988 led over half of them to urge the project be shelved, partly because its humor seemed stereotypical: it made extensive use of racial humor and vernacular speech, including the word "nigger." Changes were duly made, and *Mule-Bone* was finally brought to the New York stage, opening at the Ethel Barrymore Theatre on February 14, 1991. The play as performed was edited and revised by George Houston Bass, Ann Cattaneo, Henry Louis Gates, Jr., Arnold Rampersad, and the director Michael Schultz. Taj Mahal provided the musical numbers, which included lyrics drawn from some poems by Hughes. Bass wrote a "frame" story involving Hurston herself, who pronounced to the audience that the evening's event was a result of her scientific folklore expeditions.

In both the original and revised versions, the plot stems from Hurston's unpublished short story, "The Bone of Contention," which detailed the falling out of two friends who quarrel over a turkey one of them has shot. In the three-act version, the two friends, Jim Weston, a musician, and Dave Carter, a dancer, form a musical team. They quarrel over a flirtatious local domestic worker, Daisy Taylor, who skillfully plays them off against each other. Eventually, Daisy chooses Jim, and demands he take a good job as the white folks' yardman. When Jim refuses, she sidles up to Dave, but he too rejects her, and the play ends with the two men back together, determined to make the town accept both of them.

Mule-Bone enjoyed only moderate success at the box office; it closed on April 14, 1991, after 27 previews and 67 performances. Although a few critics found it funny and historic (Kissel); an "exuberant" theatrical event (Beaufort); and a "wonderful piece of black theatre" (Barnes); it was deemed "an amiable curiosity" (Winer); "one of the American theatre's more tantalizing might-have-beens" (Rich); "pleasant but uneventful" (Wilson); and a "theatrical curio" (Watt) by other critics, who found it charming but dramatically deficient.[15]

In 1931, Hurston was hired to write some skits for a black musical review produced by Forbes Randolph, entitled *Fast and Furious*, which opened at the New York Theatre on September 15, 1931. She also appeared as a pom-pom girl in a football skit and helped direct the show, which folded after a week. Her next theatrical adventure was writing skits for the revue *Jungle Scandals* (1931), which also closed quickly. Hurston had nothing but scorn for the white-dominated "Negro" musicals being produced on Broadway. She saw an opportunity to correct their errors with a musical of her own. Accordingly, she sought out Hall Johnson, who had directed the chorus of the wildly successful *Green Pastures* (1931). Hurston thought that play, written by a white man, Marc Connelly, was a dreadful hash of black culture; conversely, she felt Johnson was master of his craft and could help her mount *authentic* folk narratives. She decided to set a single day in a railroad work camp to music. At first she thought of calling it *Spunk*, but settled on *The Great Day*. Johnson worked on the project desultorily, but finally withdrew, only to filch some of Hurston's material for his production, *Run Little Chillun*; it opened to favorable reviews in 1931. It is worth noting that both Hughes and Johnson were Hurston's rivals, in a sense, for they too were protégés of Mrs. Mason.

Hurston nevertheless persevered, pawning some of her possessions to raise funds, wheedling the final backing from Charlotte Mason. The musical was presented at New York's John Golden Theatre on January 10, 1932. It used a concert format, and Alain Locke wrote the program notes. In the first part, the audience saw workers arising and going to the job; singing work songs as they laid track; returning to their homes where their children play folk games; and listening to a preacher's sermon accompanied by spirituals. Part Two presented an evening's entertainment at the local "Jook" (nightclub), consisting mainly of blues songs, ending with half the cast doing a blues, half singing *Deep River*. As Hurston once stated, "The real Negro theatre is in the Jooks and the cabarets."[16] No theatrical producer came forward to offer an extended run, and the show lost money, even though it attracted a good crowd and favorable reviews. Mason refused to let Hurston stage the play again, and also forbade the theatrical use of other portions of "Mules and Men." Hurston did succeed in mounting an edited version of *The Great Day* at Manhattan's New School on March 29, 1932; a program survives, and *Theatre Arts* published a photo of the cast. Over the next decade Hurston would mount this production again in a variety of venues and with quite different casts. It was always, like the folklore she treasured, "still in the making."

Thanks to Anthea Kraut, we now know much more about this sequence of performances. Kraut's book on Hurston's role as choreographer sheds much ancillary light on her sense of theatre in general, and on her quite complex use of the concept of authenticity, which she used both to privilege her productions, her own expertise, through critiquing the contemporary *faux* representation of Africans and African Americans in popular entertainment, while at the same time using this supposed "untampered" material as a wedge for penetrating that very same market.[17] Importantly, the inclusion of Caribbean materials—especially the Bahamian fire dance which usually concluded the show—bore evidence of Hurston's determination to demonstrate the transnational nature of the African diaspora.

Repeating some of the things she had related to Hughes, Hurston said in "Characteristics of Negro Expression": "Every phase of Negro life is highly dramatized. No matter how joyful or how sad the case there is sufficient poise for drama. Everything is acted out. Unconsciously for the most part of course. There is an impromptu ceremony always ready for every hour of life. No little moment passes unadorned."[18] Toomer firmly situated himself in this tradition: "I am nothing if not a dramatist; and, together with everyone, I make drama of even the minute features and behavior of myself and others."[19] Like Hurston, he understood the dramatic quality of African American culture, and tried to make an impact in theatre throughout his career, not just in the inserted play of "Kabnis" in *Cane*. He might not have written *Cane* as he did, in fact, had he succeeded in the two years prior in getting "Kabnis" produced. But he had been writing drama before "Kabnis." As Darwin Turner noted, Toomer struggled for over ten years to become a playwright. Turner conjectures that in his attempt to dramatize man's desperate need for new spiritual resources in an age of increasingly oppressive and mechanical life, he turned to the model of the German expressionists.[20] His first play, 1922's *Natalie Mann*, combines a staid urban bourgeoisie, raffish nightclub denizens, and a hero, Nathan, whose free-thinking avant-garde persona dedicates himself to liberating the shackled but magnificent Natalie from her dictie background.[21] They live together despite their parents' objections, and at play's end Natalie's new-found "blackness" finds a benchmark in the sensual cabaret dancer Etta, who draws Nathan to the dance floor and a virtual dance of death that ironically signals spiritual rebirth. The play spins from imitations of Shaw to truly original impressionism. It is spoiled, however, by overt posturing, preaching, and a failure to develop characters. "Kabnis," however, would have been impossible without the experiment of *Natalie*, which similarly depicts a search for identity and salvation against a backdrop of racial repression, albeit an urban one.

Balo, a one-act sketch, was written before *Cane* was published and was included without Toomer's permission in a drama anthology by Alain Locke.[22] It was performed by the Howard players in 1924 and the only piece of his to be staged other than *Topsy and Eva*. *Balo*, set in a Georgia cane field during harvest, features Will Lee and his sons Tom and Balo, who are experiencing a bad crop. The white Jennings family nearby help out, but aren't really close friends. Guests arrive for a festival, including old Uncle Ned, who resembles Father John in "Kabnis" in his representation of slavery and old time religion, which hampers their card-playing and desire to party. Balo, filled with divine spirit, cries out to God, discomfiting the party, which is further muffled by Uncle Ned's sermonizing. Ned and the now "saved" Balo, having ended the party, embrace, as white Jennings tells Will that he heard Balo raving in the field, yelling "White folks ain't no more'n niggers when they gets ter heaven."[23] The impasse between Jennings and Will mirrors the divorce between industrializing society and the old time religion, a split that makes Ned and Balo pariahs. *Balo*, while clumsy, undoubtedly contributed to the powerful and successful playlet "Kabnis" that pulls the disparate parts of *Cane* into a terrible harmony. "Kabnis," impressionistic, yet as Barbara Foley has recently and completely demonstrated, realistically faithful to the smallest detail of the scene Toomer actually lived in Sparta, Georgia, partakes as Eugene O'Neill's plays often do of both mystical symbolism and naturalistic reality. The tale sketches in the terrors and precarious choices of the intellectual in the Jim Crow rural South, but also presents the audience/reader with a mythic display of the fissures within the black community as the modernist age dawns, replicating the scenario of *Balo* but considerably complicating it, especially in terms of the Dionysian drinking and sexuality and the body/soul split that is evoked through the contrast of the revelers with Carrie Kate and Father John, and in the fear of Kabnis which so resembles that of O'Neill's *Emperor Jones* (a play Toomer admired). Most importantly for African American fiction and drama, perhaps, the settings and movements of the play suggest the process of immersion and descent that Robert Stepto has identified as key aspects of African American art. As such, the playlet is strongly predictive, as many have argued, of the general pattern of Ellison's *Invisible Man*, although I would remind readers there was an intervening text, namely Richard Wright's surreal, comic, and chilling fable, "The Man Who Lived Underground" (1945).

Critics have often noted that Hurston's late works suffer from her decision to abandon African American folk culture as her subject. The same claim has been made for most of Toomer's work apart from *Cane*. Two other plays he wrote are of less interest here because they were not produced, led to no greater work, and have far less dramatic intensity because of his tendency to have characters lecture rather than dramatize. Still, *The Sacred Factory* of 1927 in some ways compares favorably to other expressionistic plays of the decade such as Elmer Rice's *The Adding Machine* (1923), one of the landmarks of the American theatre, and is surreal, abstract, and chilling in its indictment of modern life.[24] Toomer's didactic indictment of modern, urban, industrial life has little to do with African American culture or folklore. When *Cane* appeared, Toomer's friend, the white writer Waldo Frank, wrote the foreword, stating: "A poet has arisen in the land who writes, not as Southerner, not as a rebel against Southerners, not as a Negro, not as an apologist or priest or critic: who writes as a poet."[25] Except for a few eloquent outbursts, most of the characters in Toomer's plays are more concerned with preaching than poetry.

The Gallonwerps, Toomer's 1928 drama, was a satire designed to be staged with puppets; it was to dramatize the ego's rescue of the id from the superego.[26] Toomer would continue to try to write drama—notably a play about his later experiences in New Mexico—but nothing came of it, although his 1947 sketches about a man who falls in love with the robot he has for a maid might have worked in our day of R2D2. Set against the other expressionistic plays of the period, *The Sacred Factory* could conceivably find a new audience as well, but it is unlikely that Toomer will find a dramatic audience save for "Kabnis," which still exerts a dramatic intensity unlike any other drama of the Harlem Renaissance, for it speaks for the moment itself, despite its deep-south setting, just as Hurston's Eatonville narratives—especially the novels—seem the very keystone of the new age of African American expression.

Ten of Hurston's previously unknown plays were found in 1997 at the Library of Congress. I would now like to turn to some of those efforts in an attempt to connect Toomer and Hurston and their concurrent dream of a Negro theatre. The earliest of the three-act plays collected in the new anthology from the Library of Congress cache, *Meet the Mamma* (1925)[27] offers a fascinating collection of sketches and a play within the play, all strung on a thin narrative line about a young couple traveling to Africa to fetch home the husband's uncle, who has become rich in the diamond trade. *Meet the Mamma*'s broadly satirical portrayal of Africa mocks popular stereotypes but also deconstructs the romanticism of "back to Africa" schemes such as Garvey's, as Kurt Eisen has shown in his consideration of theatrical ethnography and modernist primitivism in O'Neill and Hurston.[28]

One of the most delightful of the new finds is *Cold Keener*, a 1930, nine-skit work that begins at a filling station on the Georgia-Alabama line. Very much like one of the comedy skits in the fabled Rabbit Foot Circuit that toured the South, *Keener* features a series of jokes loosely strung together around slip-shop service at the station. The state line setting permits verbal dueling between Alabama and Georgia residents.

Many of the jokes echo the old duels between slaves who bragged on how good their masters were, but as they extend into a debate about the merits of Fords and Chevrolets they perhaps gave the audience a source of pride, since both combatants own cars.[29] The tale seems meant for a black audience in the South, and it never sags. It shows Hurston at her signifying best, knitting together bits and pieces of African American humor, some topical, some classic, all of it demonstrating the man of words thinking on his feet to beat the band.

Hurston's final three-act play, *Polk County* (1944, co-written with Dorothy Waring),[30] lacks a compelling story line, but demonstrates that she never gave up trying to achieve her dream of the "real Negro theatre" she had outlined to Hughes in 1928. Like *Mule-Bone* before it, *Polk County* attempts to meet this goal with a combination of humor, folklore, and music, and a large cast—sixteen named characters and many others play parts. Hurston, obviously profiting from her experiences with *From Sun to Sun*, included 27 vocal and instrumental numbers. The first act provides exposition, first by using song and ritual to demonstrate the breaking of day in the camp, including a conversation between a rooster and his hens. Virtually all the human characters reprise roles they played in Hurston's book of folklore, *Mules and Men* (1934),[31] and thus are presumably based in fact. The simple story line centers on a mulatta girl, Leafy Lee, who has wandered down from New York hoping to learn the blues; this device runs throughout the play, and provides the rationale for the insertion of most of the musical numbers. Big Sweet, the dominant character in the camp, befriends Leafy, using her fists and knife to protect her, and to maintain order when the white Bossman isn't around. Like Ike in "The Fiery Chariot," she finds inspiration in the example of the legendary hero, High John de Conquer. Although she can physically dispatch any enemy, her arsenal of verbal taunts makes her truly formidable and entertaining, and the comic dynamo of the play.

Big Sweet's man Lonnie, "friends" with My Honey, a guitar player sought after by Dicey, a sour, scheming, dark-complexioned woman. Significantly, her plans find temporary success only when she can involve the white Quarters Boss. Despite her role as villain, Dicey resembles the despairing Emma of *Color-Struck* in her bitterness over color.

When Dicey's plot to set the other characters against each other fails, Leafy and My Honey marry, setting a new standard the other characters intend to follow. Their courtship throughout the play has a communal dimension, affording much commentary from the cast on the nature of love. Leafy, as initiatee into the community's lore, parallels the role Zora herself played in Polk County in *Mules and Men*.

As in *Mule-Bone*, children play typical African American games, as part of the display of everyday life in the Quarters, and central scenes are communal. While *Mule-Bone* focuses on the Methodist/Baptist quarrel that accompanies Jim's "trial," here the chief battles take place in the Quarters' jook, which Hurston describes elaborately, and in the woods, where Ella Wall's hoodoo fails to conjure Leafy and My Honey's marriage. Amazingly, the generally realistic play ends expressionistically; a huge rainbow descends and all get on board, plates in hand, with Lonnie singing "I ride the rainbow, when I see Jesus." The curtain falls as the rainbow ascends.

Especially with this startling and surreal ending, *Polk County* demonstrates Hurston once again working her conjuror's roots, reshaping earlier material into a new form. The comedy is far less realistic than its earlier manifestation in *Mules and Men* and *Dust Tracks* and clearly shows Hurston gravitating toward the patterns traced by other semi-mystical folk musicals popular on Broadway such as *Oklahoma!* and *Cabin in the Sky* (both 1943), a trend continued a few years later with *Finian's Rainbow* and *Brigadoon* (both 1947). All of these shows, including *Polk County*, integrated story and song seamlessly and led to a new direction in American musical theatre. Unfortunately, Hurston was unable to penetrate this realm, even though she continued to enjoy connections with theatrical figures in New York, such as *Cabin*'s star Ethel Waters.

Polk County was finally produced in 2002 by Washington's prestigious Arena Stage Company. A gifted quartet operated on stage, and critics were lavish in their praise of the performers, particularly Harriett D. Foy, who played Big Sweet. The *New York Times* asserted that the Arena "has given the theater world a gift. 'Polk County' is not only a significant contribution to dramatic literature; it brings a new musical sound to the theater and welcome opportunities for black actors." The critic, Bruce Webber, also suggested that other companies should mount the play, and several have, including the Matthews Theater in Princeton and the Berkeley Repertory Theatre.[32]

I have tried to shape here the parallel interests and methods of two great American writers who had much to do with shaping both the Harlem Renaissance and African American and American modernism. Toomer differed from Hurston, however, in that although both were modernists, he far more than she shared the "lost generation" conception of post-World War I America as a wasteland of sterile materialism, a view strengthened by his concurrent associations with Waldo Frank and his school, which excoriated their America, which they believed had wandered from enduring values and traditions. Further, we also know how Toomer and his first wife, the writer Margery Latimer, turned to mysticism and the religious philosophy of Gurdjieff as an antidote to the moral void of 1920s America. Later still, he and his second wife, Marjorie Content, would find an alternate religious haven in the Society of Friends. Toomer's second marriage made him financially independent. Hurston, however, had to scramble for a living, and thought the theatre could provide it. Lucre, however, was only part of the equation. Hurston always felt that the performative aspects of African American culture was one of its chief glories, and could profoundly function as a bridge across the racial divide. Then too, writing plays was another way of preserving a precious culture that both Toomer and Hurston feared was evaporating under the pressures of modernism, industrialization, and Northern migration. Eventually, however, Hurston came to see this threat differently, as she began to conceptualize culture as a dynamic process, understanding that her culture—in both its Southern and Northern arenas—was still "in the making," and that the new forms in effect preserved the old ones.

There are many affinities between Hurston and Toomer. Their literary work and their aesthetic, social, and philosophical announcements suggest so, but perhaps the following remarks he made in a 1922 letter to Sherwood Anderson gives a truer indication of possible affirmation of his stance: "The mass of Negroes, like peasants, like the mass of Russians or Jews or Irish or what not, are too instinctive to be anything but themselves. Here and there one finds a high type Negro who shares this virtue with his primitive brothers . . . I feel that in time, in its social phase, my art will aid in giving the Negro to himself."[33] Setting Hurston's and Toomer's plays side by side shows each writer strove to create an African American theater along modernist lines, yet one that would find a way to include and valorize the race's Southern past. These plays failed to find an immediate audience, but we see their fertilizing effect on virtually every page of *Cane* and Hurston's masterworks of the thirties, abundant proof of the virtues of "acting out."

In all their dramas, however successful we might judge them today, both writers operated on the cutting edge of modernism; aware of the seismic shifts after World War I in gender roles, racial mobility, immigration, and the adoption at home and abroad of African artistic traditions. They embraced experimentalism, refused to respect old definitions of genre, and in their best efforts—as in "Kabnis," *Cold Keener*, and *Polk County*—sought to show how African American culture, always dynamic and creative, was at the heart of the new age.

NOTES

1. Zora Neale Hurston, *Dust Tracks on a Road*, 2nd edition, ed. Robert Hemenway (1942; repr., Urbana: University of Illinois Press, 1984), 325.

2. June Jordan, "On Richard Wright and Zora Neale Hurston: Notes Toward a Balancing of Love and Hatred," *Black World* 23 (August 1974), 5.

3. See John Lowe, *Jump at the Sun: Zora Neale Hurston's Cosmic Comedy* (Urbana: University of Illinois Press, 1994).

4. Jean Toomer, *Cane* (1923; repr., New York: Liveright, 1974).

5. Zora Neale Hurston, *Jonah's Gourd Vine* (1934; repr., New York: Harper, 1990).

6. Carla Kaplan, *Zora Neale Hurston: A Life in Letters* (New York: Doubleday, 2002), 115.

7. Ibid., 117.

8. Zora Neale Hurston, *Color Struck* in *Zora Neale Hurston: Collected Plays*, ed. Jean Lee Cole and Charles Mitchell (New Brunswick, NJ: Rutgers University Press, 2008), 35–50. Originally published in *Fire!!*, 1 (November 1926). *Spears* in *Zora Neale Hurston: Collected Plays*, 52–62.

9. David Krasner (2001) has made a strong case for the significance of this early play, both in terms of the Harlem Renaissance in particular, and African American theatre history in general. See David Krasner, *Resistance Parody, and Double Consciousness in African American Theatre, 1895–1910* (New York: St. Martin's Press, 1997).

10. Barbara Speisman, "From *Spears* to *The Great Day*: Zora Neale Hurston's Vision of a Real Negro Theater," *Southern Quarterly* 36.3 (1998), 37.

11. Zora Neale Hurston, *The First One: A Play* in *Ebony and Topaz: A Collectanea*, ed. Charles S. Johnson (New York: National Urban League, 1927), 53–57.

12. This play, too, has drawn a variety of responses. Robert Hemenway suggests that "the play pokes fun at all those who take seriously the biblical sanction for racial separation" (68), but Werner Sollors fears that the script inadvertently provided "a belated literary support to the central racial transformation of the biblical story" (108). Hemenway, *Zora Neale Hurston: A Literary Biography* (Urbana: University of Illinois Press, 1977). Sollors, *Neither White nor Black But Both: Thematic Explorations of Interracial Literature* (Cambridge: Harvard University Press, 1977).

13. Zora Neale Hurston and Langston Hughes, *Mule-Bone: A Comedy of Negro Life*, ed. George Bass and Henry Louis Gates, Jr. (New York: Harper, 1991).

14. A full discussion of this literary saga has been provided by George Houston Bass and Henry Louis Gates, Jr. in their edition of the play, along with supporting documents. Rachael Rosenberg has provided an excellent and careful reconstruction of the actual composition of the various drafts.

15. These newspaper reviews were culled from the 1991 edition of the *New York Theatre Critics' Reviews* including comments from John Beaufort, "Mule-Bone Debuts After 60 Years," *The Christian Science Monitor* (26 Feb. 1991); Clive Barnes, "'Mule-Bone' connected to Funny Bone," *New York Post* (15 Feb. 1991); Frank Rich, "A Difficult Birth for 'Mule-Bone,'" *New York Times* (15 Feb. 1991); Doug Watt, "Second Thoughts on First Nights," *New York Daily News* (22 Feb. 1991); Edwin Wilson, "Fireworks," *Wall Street Journal* (27 Feb. 1991); Linda Winer, "A Precious Peek at a Lively Legend," *New York Newsday* (15 Feb. 1991).

16. Zora Neale Hurston, "Characteristics of Negro Expression," in *Within the Circle: An Anthology of African American Literary Criticism from the Harlem Renaissance to Present*, ed. Angelyn Mitchell (1934; repr., Durham, NC: Duke University Press, 1994), 93.

17. Anthea Kraut, *Choreographing the Folk: The Dance Stagings of Zora Neale Hurston* (Minneapolis: University of Minnesota Press, 2008).

18. Hurston, "Characteristics of Negro Expression," 49.

19. Jean Toomer, "Reflections of an Earth Being," *The Wayward and the Seeking: A Collection of Writings by Jean Toomer*, ed. Darwin T. Turner (Washington, D.C.: Howard University Press, 1982), 16.

20. Darwin Turner, ed., "Introduction," in *The Wayward and the Seeking*, 1–8.

21. Jean Toomer, *Natalie Mann: A Play in three Acts*, in *The Wayward and the Seeking*, 243–325.

22. Jean Toomer, *Balo*, in *Black Folk Plays of the 1920s*, ed. Alain Locke (1927; repr., Westport, CT: Greenwood Press, 1971), 219–224.

23. Ibid., 277.

24. Jean Toomer, *The Sacred Factory: A Religious Drama of Today*, in *The Wayward and the Seeking*, 327–410.

25. Waldo Frank, "Foreword," in *Cane*, by Jean Toomer (New York: Liveright, 1923), ii.

26. See *African-American Dramatists: An A–Z Guide*, ed. Emmanuel Nelson (Westport, CT: Greenwood Press, 2004), 447.

27. Zora Neale Hurston, *Meet the Mama*, in *Collected Plays*, 2–31.

28. Eisen in particular dissects *The Emperor Jones*, and of course Hurston uses a character by that name in her sketch "Bahamas," indicating she knew O'Neill's work. Like Cayer, Eisen notes Hurston's seeming disdain for elements of the well-made play (which would include a strong plot line); both seem to approve of this gambit and Eisen persuasively demonstrates that many of the aspects of the new ten plays reveal Hurston as a forerunner of postmodern theatre, and as a fellow traveler of Brecht's. While this may indeed be the case, I still maintain (despite Cayer's demurrer) that the weak plots of Hurston's plays apparently still represent a barrier to future productions, and that this problem led to the abbreviated run of *Mule-Bone* and to the limited appeal (thus far) of *Polk County*. *Spunk*, however (which Eisen and Cayer both largely ignore), may eventually find an audience, partly because it features a strong and dramatic plot, convincing central characters, a choral set of secondary figures, and abundant doses of folk dialect and folklore. Finally, both Cayer and Eisen largely ignore the crucial comic aspect of these plays, which in fact ties in closely with their postmodern affinities (pastiche, parody, non-linear structure, subversion, inversion).

29. Zora Neale Hurston, *Cold Keener*, in *Collected Plays*, 77–129.

30. Zora Neale Hurston, *Polk County*, in *Collected Plays*, 271–362.

31. Zora Neale Hurston, *Mules and Men* (1934; repr., Bloomington: Indiana University Press, 1978).

32. Bruce Weber, "Critic's Notebook; Joy and Blues in Florida's Piney Woods," April 25, 2002, http://Theater.nytimes.com/mem/theater/treview.html?res=9905E2D7173EF936A15757C0A9649C8863.

33. Fredrik L. Rusch, ed., *A Jean Toomer Reader: Selected Unpublished Writings* (New York: Oxford University Press, 1993), 85.

Zora Neale Hurston and the Possibility of Poetry

Phyllis McEwen

Of course she wrote poetry. It would have been very unlikely that such a wordsmith would not ever write poetry. Poetry was a rich, full presence in the linguistic air she breathed from her time as a child in Eatonville, Florida, where she declared she was born "headfirst" into the Missionary Baptist Church, an institution famed for its poetic treasures in liturgy and song. Then later, during her association with the Harlem Renaissance, poetry was like a signature genre of the time, and Hurston appeared to have embraced it warmly, in several ways.

The question has been posed: Do we label Hurston as poet? From time to time in Hurston Studies, one encounters descriptions and introductions of her as "anthropologist, novelist, folklorist, and poet" or some other type of cataloging. When asked to quote or even read one Hurston poem, most people cannot—either because they have never seen a Hurston poem or because they cannot remember having read one. It is an assumption that many make about famous writers who work in various forms as Hurston did, that poetry should be thrown in there somewhere, if even just for good measure, or perhaps to simply "cover all the bases." But she did write poetry and even published it, too.

As has been the material nature of Hurston Studies, one never knows—much to the delight of the Zora Neale Hurston admirer—what will turn up and be recovered from year to year and decade to decade. At present we have at least the following poems: "O Night" published in the May 1921 issue of *Stylus* (Howard University's Literary Club Annual Publication);[1] "Poem" published in *The Howard University Record*, February 1922;[2] "Night," "Journey's End," and "Passion"—all three published in 1922 in Marcus Garvey's *Negro World*, the official publication of the Universal Negro Improvement Association.[3]

Additionally, Professor Lucy Anne Hurston, Zora Neale Hurston's only surviving niece, has provided us with other poems, not previously published, in her unique and engaging 2004 Hurston biography *Speak, So You Can Speak Again*. Lucy Hurston has collected and reproduced facsimiles of her famous aunt's poetry and published them as attachments on authentically reconstructed stationery, complete with Hurston's comments, scribbles, and notes (pure aphrodisiac for the true Zora Head!). The collected poems include the following: "Maine" (1918); "Love" (1918); "Contentment"; "Twas the Night After Lobster—"; "Oh! My Love Is a Strong, Strong Youth" (1919); "Home"; "Thou Art Mine" (1919); and "Longin."[4] And of course there are others that may emerge or that have resurfaced in various places.

Lucy Hurston has chosen to showcase the poems she included by placing them strategically throughout the book to highlight Hurston's experiences thematically, even using the titles of the poems to name sections and chapters. For example, "Longin" names the section describing the sad and grief-stricken days following her mother's death, and "Love" names the chapter that reveals Hurston's marriage to Herbert Sheen and the blossoming of her friendship with Langston Hughes. In this way, Lucy Hurston underscores the authenticity of expression in the poetry as heartfelt, personal reflections of Hurston's emotional life in contrast to the folklore and fiction that she was producing in her professional life.

Some of Hurston's poems have traditional, formal rhyme schemes, although she puts her pen to a blues lyric in "Longin," and even a bit of comedic Edgar Allan Poe mimicry in "Twas the Night After Lobster—," where Hurston gives the reader a chuckle at either an allergic reaction to lobster, or food-poisoning, perhaps? At the end of this poem, she has written in her elegant penmanship: "return this. I am too indolent to make a second copy." The poem "Home" bemoans the loss of an idyllic, peaceful feeling. A reflective comment follows: "Just a bubbling over of a melancholy heart—momentarily."

Hurston's humor and reflective commentaries do not suggest that Hurston was not "serious" when she wrote these verses nor that she lacked visits from the Muse. Yet it does seem that she was engaging in private, personal musings when she put her pen to paper and created these verses. When Hurston and her cohorts compiled their notorious 1926 "cutting edge" publication *FIRE!!*, Hurston's contributions to the collection were in the genres of short fiction and drama. Work in the poetry genre was submitted by Arna Bontemps, Langston Hughes, Countee Cullen, and Helene Johnson, among others.[5]

Hurston "knew her place" in the pantheon of literary genius, well aware that poetry was not her strong suit, but was very much in admiration of the form and those who were given the gift to produce it. It was a relationship of admiration, knowledge, and respect, yet Hurston did not pose as one of the "anointed" ones in this realm. She had far too much literary training and insight about the genre of poetry to do so, and then, too, she had enough gifts of her own to manage and in more than one area. She knew how to respect the creative divide.

In a 1925 letter to Georgia Douglas Johnson, a gifted poet friend, she praised her colleague for her poetic gifts, calling her a wonderful and soulful poet. At the conclusion of the correspondence in which she had evidently attached a poem of her own, Hurston writes: "Give her this bit of verse, too. She knows I am not trying to be a poet so she wont [sic] think that I think its poetry."[6]

Hurston had an abiding admiration for poetry in general and the poetry of her friends and associates as well. Her admiration of poets and their special call may have been one of the factors that endeared Langston Hughes to her early on. Like those who answered the call to be ministers (a special form of poet), Hurston was well aware of the intense and double-edged sword the poet wielded. After reading his much-lauded poetry collection, *Color*, Hurston wrote a letter to Countee Cullen praising him for the high quality of his work, and then with even deeper admiration, she wrote: "I just sit and wonder as I read poem after poem and wonder how you keep it up so long. I can understand one hitting off a few like that, but I cannot see where it all comes from!"[7]

Here, Hurston graciously admits that this part of literary creation is unfamiliar territory to her on this visceral level. And yet she was involved in a deep professional relationship with the genre throughout her writing life. She read the poetry of her colleagues in public readings, and she sent the poetry of others to influential friends like Carl Van Vechten when she felt that she had discovered a jewel. And she was not afraid to criticize even her closest colleagues who were poets. In the same letter to Countee Cullen referenced above, she continued: "By the way, Hughes ought to stop publishing all those secular folk-songs as his poetry. Now when he got off the 'Weary Blues['] (most of it a song I and most southerners have known all our lives) I said nothing . . . but when he gets off another '*Me and mah honey got two mo' days tuh do de buck*' I don't see how I can refrain from speaking."[8]

In this letter, Hurston makes a strong indictment against Hughes, for what seemed to her inauthentic and inappropriate use of folk idiom in his poetry publications. However, in retrospect, one must consider that she probably considered this complaint to be a private matter between herself and Cullen and though it seemed to be a real concern, it was not necessarily one that she wished to make public. Still, it must be noted that Hurston believed Hughes to be a talented and important poetic voice and personality. Valerie Boyd reports that three years later in 1929 when Hurston returned to New Orleans, Louisiana, to complete her conjure work, she also gave a talk on poetics at the University of New Orleans (later Dillard University). She read six poems by Helene Johnson, "a few from Hughes's *Weary Blues*, and his *Fine Clothes to the Jew* from cover to cover." Hurston later told Hughes "the students et it up."[9]

Hurston's long-standing interest in poetry can be traced throughout her academic career. As a student attending night school in Baltimore, Maryland, Hurston was indelibly impressed with English professor Dwight Holmes. Mesmerized by his reading of *Kubla Khan*, she determined, "This was my world, I said to myself, and I shall be in it, and surrounded by it, if it is the last thing I do on God's green dirt-ball."[10] During her time at Morgan Academy, Hurston worked as a personal assistant in the home of one of the school's trustees. Much of her attention went to devouring their library: "They had a great library, and I waded in. I acted as if the books would run away. I remember committing to memory, overnight—lest I never get a chance to read it again—Gray's Elegy in a Country Church-yard. Next I learned the Ballad of Reading Gaol and started on the Rubaiyat."[11]

At Howard University, "the capstone of Negro education," Hurston was influenced by English Department Head R. Lorenzo Dow Turner:

Listening to him, I decided that I must be an English teacher and lean over my desk and discourse on the eighteenth-century poets, and explain the roots of the modern novel. Children just getting born were going to hear about Addison, Poe, DeQuincey, Steele, Coleridge, Keats and Shelley from me, leaning nonchalantly over my desk. Defoe, Burns, Swift, Milton and Scott were going to be sympathetically, but adequately explained, with just that suspicion of a smile now and then before I returned to my notes.[12]

While at Howard, Hurston was a member of the literary society, The Stylus, and contributed to its journal *The Hill Top*. Hurston transferred to prestigious Barnard College and earned her Bachelor's degree in English in 1928. Her academic background more than qualified her to render lectures on literature, poetry, and poetics. But Hurston's love and connection to poetry actually predates her involvement with higher education, or as Hurston puts it: "I tumbled right into the Missionary Baptist Church when I was born. I saw the preachers and the pulpits, the people and the pews."[13]

She was a minister's daughter. Her father was also at one time the moderator of the South Florida Baptist Association and was considered a true man of the cloth who had genuinely been called to the ministry. Hurston was born with the language of the Bible and the music and parables of African American Christianity and the Baptist liturgy practically in her bloodstream. She became an astute biblical scholar in the source of her writing life and often used the Bible as base for her fiction as well as her anthropological studies. Her book *The Sanctified Church*, published posthumously in 1981 from fieldwork she had begun in the 1930s, illustrates her deep and abiding knowledge of the Black Church and its connection to poetry and poetics.[14] Hurston knew that the African American minister was another manifestation of the poet. She wrote on several occasions that the man who answered the call to be a minister must be heavily endowed with several attributes to fulfill this call, and one of the most important, alongside a good "straining voice" and "fine figure" was the absolute gift of poetry.[15]

In her fictionalized version of her parent's life, *Jonah's Gourd Vine*, she identified poetry as the language of the divine and described the language and structure of late 19th-century African American homily as "primitive poetry." In an examination of Hurston's spiritual life and development, Deborah Plant writes: "His or her [African American clergy's] poetry and artistry is a means by which the minister connects the congregation to its vital Source, just as the Source inspires the minister."[16] Hurston's early and later appreciation of psalmic verse and the lyrical poeticizing of the African American worship service is yet another sustained poetic connection.

As an anthropologist, Hurston found that black poetry was central to any anthropological understanding of African American culture in complex and multidimensional ways. She did not use her own poetry to illustrate these connections in her discourse, but used the poetry of her colleagues, such as Langston Hughes, as well as verses and imagery from the folk idiom and the speech of rural, southern African Americans.

Linguistically, she discovered that the African American's greatest contribution to the English language is the use and development of metaphor and simile and further uses poetry to explain the particular characteristic of Negro expression she identified as asymmetry. In her 1934 essay, "Characteristics of Negro Expression," that first appeared in *Negro: An Anthology*, edited by Nancy Cunard, she chooses lines of verse by Langston Hughes as examples of this quality:

"I ain't gonna mistreat ma good gal any more,
I'm just gonna kill her next time she makes me sore.

I treats her kind but she don't do me right,
She fights and quarrels most ever' night."[17]

Later in this work, she analyzes the literary progress of two folkloric odes: "Uncle Bud," a bawdy tune and "Angeline," verses sung in jooks. Here, Hurston reflects her academic training in formalized poetics describing patterning of stanzas and rhymed couplets as she fleshed out the elements of African American verse in "The Florida Negro," her ethnographic work in progress, begun in the 1930s while she worked for the Works Progress Administration (WPA).

When she sought to express the absolute requirement that artists be free to choose or not choose their own themes and topics for expression, Hurston constructed a poet to illustrate that point. She was commenting on the "race attitude" that mandates that all "Negro" artists must write about race at all times:

Can the black poet sing a song to the morning? Up springs the song to his lips but it is fought back. He says to himself, "Ah, this is a beautiful song inside me. I feel the morning star in my throat. I will sing of the star and the morning." Then his background thrusts itself between his lips and the star and he mutters, "Ought I not be singing of our sorrows? That is what is expected of me and I shall be considered forgetful of our past and present. If I do not someone will even call me a coward. The one subject for a Negro is the Race and its sufferings and so the song of the morning must be choked back. I will write of a lynching instead.[18]

And thus her symbolic artist who represents artistic and political freedom is that special anointed one—the poet.

Can Zora Neale Hurston be titled a poet? In the strict sense of that term, no. That would be an incorrect assignation in terms of who she was and how she used her energies and gift. She did write some poetry. She did understand, study, and love poetry. She was involved with and appreciated the poets she knew and read. Poetry was a vital part of her personal and professional life. Was poetry integral to her use of language? Absolutely, yes. Her novels and other writings are rich and brimming with original imagery, metaphors, and similes as finely honed and poignant as one would find in any poet's lexicon.

As a poet who deeply appreciates Hurston in many ways, I offer the reader two selections of Hurston's prose, converted into verse, for the occasion of looking at Hurston's rhetorical relationship to that form:

This Year Has Been

This year has been
a great trial of endurance
for me.

I don't mind saying
That more than once

I have almost said:
I can't endure.

I shall hold on,
But every time
I see a cat slinking
in an alley
fearing to walk upright
lest again
she is crushed back
into her slink
I shall go to her
and acknowledge
The sisterhood
in spite of
the skin.[19]

And another:

I Know Me

I know
that I'm a reprobate;

I'm cross-eyed,
and my feet ain't mates!

All this I acknowledge
before you say it,
so save your breath
and temper.

Now![20]

NOTES

1. Zora Neale Hurston, "O Night," in *Stylus*, 1 (May 1921): 42.
2. Zora Neale Hurston, "Poem" in *The Howard University Record*, 16 (February, 1922), 236.
3. Zora Neale Hurston, *Zora Neale Hurston: Folklore, Memoirs, and Other Writings*, ed. Cheryl Wall (New York: Library of America, 1995), 963.
4. Lucy Anne Hurston, *Speak, So You Can Speak Again: The Life of Zora Neale Hurston* (New York: Doubleday, 2004).
5. *FIRE!!: Devoted to Younger Negro Artists*, 1 (November 1926).
6. Carla Kaplan, *Zora Neale Hurston: A Life in Letters* (New York: Anchor Books, 2002), 61.
7. Ibid., 84.
8. Ibid.
9. Valerie Boyd, *Wrapped in Rainbows* (New York: Scribner, 2003), 184.

10. Zora Neale Hurston, *Dust Tracks on a Road: An Autobiography*, 2nd edition, ed. Robert Hemenway (1942; repr., Urbana: University of Illinois Press, 1977), 147.

11. Ibid., 149.

12. Ibid., 166.

13. Ibid., 266.

14. Zora Neale Hurston, *The Sanctified Church* (Berkeley, CA: Turtle Island Foundation), 1981.

15. Hurston, *Zora Neale Hurston: Folklore, Memoirs, and Other Writings*, 754.

16. Deborah Plant, *Zora Neale Hurston: A Biography of the Spirit* (Westport, CT: Praeger, 2007), 108.

17. Hurston, *Zora Neale Hurston: Folklore, Memoirs, and Other Writings*, 832, 835.

18. Ibid., 908.

19. Zora Neale Hurston to Fannie Hurst, in *Zora Neale Hurston: A Life in Letters*, 85.

20. Zora Neale Hurston to Countee Cullen, in *Zora Neale Hurston: A Life in Letters*, 83.

A Voice of the South

"Beholding 'A Great Tree in Leaf' ": Eros, Nature, and the Visionary in *Their Eyes Were Watching God*

Gurleen Grewal

A quest narrative about a woman's spiritual journey "tuh de horizon and back," *Their Eyes Were Watching God* is not a love story in any conventional sense.[1] It is, rather, a story of self-discovery and self-revelation, a "biography of the spirit," to borrow the phrase from Deborah Plant's biography of Hurston.[2] We journey alongside a female protagonist who at 16 was called to witness the mystery of a great tree in leaf, an epiphany that impresses on her the blueprint of a quest, for the mystery is one that bespeaks both the blooming pear tree in spring and the self beholding it.[3] This epiphanic tree reveals the "cosmic Zora" that would not be contained by the racialized consciousness prevalent at the time, nor by the deaths and the heartbreak she recounts in her memoir.[4] In *Their Eyes Were Watching God*, Janie will actualize her quest, maturing into a great tree able to contain both "dawn and doom . . . in the branches."[5] This psychic and spiritual synthesis is what the novel achieves.

The novel's exposition and conclusion display a remarkable economy and unity of expression, much like that of a lyric poem. The novel's exposition with its motifs of desire, dream, vision, seeing, horizon and its quest, imbue the novel with a lyric subjectivity. As it opens, the novel registers its own approach to desire different "from the life of men." In contrast to the illusory, phantom dreams of men, the narrator asserts the validity of a different kind of desire that is the pursuit of a vision: Here, "[t]he dream is the truth," here the act of living is propelled by an inner vision.[6]

Janie's perception of the cosmic tree of beauty offers an epistemology and blueprint for all relationships. Janie's is not the torment of a dream deferred, nor is her dream "mocked to death by Time," even though we are first introduced to her as one who has returned "from burying the dead."[7] The novel's concluding pages fulfill the promise of the exposition. Although death is present, the novel ends with the quiet triumph of the spirit, with an affirmation of life that is greater than the deaths it encompasses.

Both *Their Eyes Were Watching God* and Hurston's autobiography *Dust Tracks on a Road* set up a contrast between received wisdom and conventional piety, and one's own understanding based on intuition and direct perception.[8] Nanny's experience of oppression, her lack of autonomy and safety, gives her a pragmatic and transactional view of marriage and a shriveled, gendered script distorted by fear and insecurity from which Janie must free herself. Early on, we get an affirmative vision of life as young Janie herself sees it: The novel introduces us to the dream-like vision of the blossoming pear tree. *More* than an adolescent awakening of sexuality or the representation of orgasmic love as many critics including Robert Hemenway and Carla Kaplan suggest, the tree is a vision of Life that becomes a blueprint for the soul's quest.[9] The lush and blooming buds of the pear tree called Janie to come and see:

It was like a flute song forgotten in another existence and remembered again. . . . This singing she heard that had nothing to do with her ears. The rose of the world was breathing out smell. . . .

She saw a dust-bearing bee sink into the sanctum of a bloom; the thousand sister-calyxes arch to meet the love embrace and the ecstatic shiver of the tree from root to tiniest branch creaming in every blossom and frothing with delight. So this was a marriage! She had been summoned to behold a revelation.[10]

Mystery, revelation, gnosis. This remains one of the most captivating epiphanies in literature, sensuously describing the felt spirituality of the cosmos in a knowing that is intuitive and direct. They form a unitive whole, the flowering tree and the girl budding into womanhood beneath it, her consciousness attuned to its mystery and revelation. While the sinking of the bee into the bloom certainly represents a sexual awakening in the adolescent Janie, the entire section quoted holds the key to understanding the spiritual nature of Janie's, and Hurston's, vision. As Plant observes, this passage bespeaks "the bliss that would yoke [Hurston] to Universal Spirit."[11] Unless the awakening described in this passage is understood in the wider sense as an awakening to the aesthetic and spiritual equivalence of Eros, nature, and life, we risk a narrow understanding of Janie's journey to selfhood. That the awakening is more than sensual/sexual is implied in the declaration that the song Janie hears has nothing to do with anything she hears with her ears, but rather her whole self responding to the world's own nectar.

Hurston's transcendent awareness of her true self, a self beyond the narrow social constructions of identity, is inscribed as early as 1928, in the essay "How it feels to be Colored Me": "Among the thousand white persons, I am a dark rock surged upon and overswept, but through it all, I remain myself. When covered by the waters, I am; and the ebb but reveals me again." And then in the same text: "At certain times I have no race, I am *me*. . . . The cosmic Zora emerges. I belong to no race nor time. I am the eternal feminine with its string of beads."[12]

A blossoming pear tree (*Pyrus calleryana*) with its white blossoms is of such ethereal beauty, a vision of such delicacy, that it has inspired artists before and after Hurston: Vincent Van Gogh's "Blossoming Pear Tree" in Arles, France, March 1888, and James Wright's poem "To a Blossoming Pear Tree" in 1975. However, it is clarifying to juxtapose Wright's vision of the pear tree to Hurston's. The speaker in Wright's poem, while sensitive to the beauty of the tree, is also poignantly distant from it, as if the two occupied different realms, "human" on the one hand, and "natural" or "pure" and "perfect" on the other: "Perfect, beyond my reach, / How I envy you."[13] The tree "beyond [his] reach" inspires envy or separation, not a premonition of identity. Here the tree does not address the speaker nor does the speaker respond with an inner organ of perception to receive *its* message; rather, the speaker wistfully addressing the tree needs the tree's audience for an all too "human" story of alienation and loneliness that follows the quoted stanza.

Hurston's Janie need not envy the tree, for she has a profound and special relationship with it. Every moment she could find, found her beneath the tree. Drawn by its beauty she surrenders herself to the tree, steadily contemplating its numinous presence. Her relationship with the tree is one of reciprocity or call-and-response. Its presence was beckoning and she embraced it. Even if we did not know that Hurston had an affinity for the early modern Dutch philosopher Baruch Spinoza, for whom God was not separate from Nature ("*Deus, sive Natura*," i.e., "God, or Nature"), this epiphany makes it clear that the great flowering tree (Nature) has something to tell Janie about the mystery of existence that is shared by her and the tree.[14] We might say Janie's eyes were watching God: the tree blossoming forth in an emanation of beauty and bliss calls forth her own intuition about the essence of the cosmos, and therefore her very own self.

Hurston had an avid interest in comparative religion. In *Dust Tracks on a Road*, she tells us she has "laid plans" for her old age to "sit around and write . . . and read slowly and carefully the mysticism of the East, and re-read Spinoza with love and care."[15] That she was familiar with Eastern mysticism is apparent in *Their Eyes Were Watching God*. In the novel, Hurston conveys the tree's effect on Janie by describing the experience as a once-forgotten flute song. The flute recalls a popular icon of ancient Indian spirituality and art (literary, musical, and visual), in which human remembrance of the divine is represented in the flute of Krishna; the flute of this dark-hued cowherd awakens all who hear it. When the *gopis* or cowherding maidens hear Krishna's flute they are struck with a restless longing that is described in terms both mystical and erotic. Our relationship to the divine—Krishna is a representation of cosmic consciousness—is something we forget until an upsurge of beauty (a flute song) reconnects us. Beneath the blossoming tree, Janie beholds a revelation, hears the melody of the flute, smells the perfume of the rose, and feels the pulse of life. Like Krishna, Janie is smitten by the beauty of the world. Beneath the tree the senses—seeing, hearing, and smelling—are in a state of arousal, but what the visual beauty "stirs" is in fact the inner ear and the olfactory image refers to a presence that is invisible, accompanying Janie in her waking and sleeping states.[16]

In Indian metaphysical aesthetics, beauty is a dimension of consciousness. The Eros and beauty of nature awaken the subtle, interior awareness of immanent beauty: when inner and outer beauty conjoins in the consciousness of the beholder, the seer experiences the unitive nature of reality as a wave of bliss dissolving the separation of subject and object. In Sanskrit, this unitive state is *yoga*.

The Indian tradition of erotic metaphysics also represents the perfumed consciousness of divinity in terms of the eternal feminine, in figures such as the goddess Lalita, who goes by a thousand names associated with the resplendent beauty of nature—a flowering lotus, a tender vine, radiant dawn, moonlight, the luster of gems, and so on. We can find similar resonances in western art in the figure of Aphrodite, in the Botticelli Venus, and in the Keatsian equation of beauty and truth (as found in his poem "Ode on a Grecian Urn").[17]

Because consciousness is invisible and not an object of thought (as the narrator says of Janie's experience, such matters were "outside observation" and "buried themselves in her flesh"), we are given to epiphanies, to intimate and timeless moments of apperception. And we are given to the work, then, of expressing the ineffable, which can only be represented in the poetic medium of metaphor, so that the numinous is translated back into the concrete language of the sensuous, where it can be shared. This is what Hurston does exquisitely in Janie's epiphany of the flowering pear tree bearing the fragrance of a cosmic consciousness.

Henceforth, the vision of the blossoming tree accompanies her. The awareness of the sacred dimension of existence is a blueprint of sorts that guides her journey to the horizon and back. When Nanny proposes Janie's marriage to her first farmer husband, we are told that the idea of Logan Killicks desecrated Janie's vision of the pear tree. After a few months of marriage and waiting in vain for the kind of marriage she witnessed beneath the tree, she went to Nanny and cried. Standing on the threshold of her world, the adolescent and then the young woman does not know enough about the ways of the world, for such knowing requires experience in time, but she does have direct perception of the world she encounters:

She knew . . . the words of the trees and the wind . . . She knew the world was a stallion rolling in blue pastures of ether. She knew that God tore down the old world every evening and built a new one by sun-up . . .[18]

The repeated emphasis on *she knew* already tells us much of this sojourner who follows her inner compass, her own true north. So much is condensed in this passage: the beauty and power and infinitude of the cosmos; the understanding of the impermanence of the phenomenal world and its eternal renewal. Seeing the stunted worldviews of those around her, young Janie comes to rely on her own vision.

The novel tracks Janie's burgeoning self-awareness from adolescence to maturity over the course of three heterosexual relationships spanning roughly two decades. The novel stages a contrast between hierarchical relationships and egalitarian ones. Each of the men in Janie's life reveals his relational capacities via his relationship to nature and Eros. With his 60 acres and a mule, Logan Killicks's relationship to nature is utilitarian, plodding, and deadly to the imagination as his last name suggests. Leaving him, Janie is remorseless. When she leaves Logan Killicks in search of the horizon, nature prompts her to divest herself of Nanny's apron strings. She unties the apron at her waist, flinging it upon a nearby bush. She walked on, picking flowers and making a bouquet.[19]

Joe Starks waited for Janie up ahead with "a hired rig." But the "high ruling chair" Joe Starks sat on is incompatible with flower dust. Starks didn't represent a blossoming pear tree, "but he spoke for far horizon. He spoke for change and chance."[20] He was her means of escaping the tedium of her present life. As Marilyn Friedman notes, "[w]omen have not been oblivious to the social obstacles that constrained their life choices and that made 'marrying up' a rationally prudent life plan."[21]

But Joe has his own plans. He wants to transform Janie into a housewife. He wants to emulate the protocols of class and make her a lady, a genteel figure, whose feminine propriety would reflect the status of the male as a propertied subject. In keeping with her status as Mrs. Mayor Starks, the relations of ownership (*propre*, Latin, to own) demanded a behavior that was *proper*. Thus, with Joe, Janie is as cut off from engagement with the folk and community as she is from the world of nature. She has lost both intimacy and autonomy and communion with the universe. No less than Killicks, Starks stifles Eros. Spontaneity and sensuality are sacrificed at the altar of false power, and Janie complains to Joe that they are no longer natural with each other.[22]

Through childhood and adolescence, Hurston loved two things: the magical world of myths and fairy tales—Greek, Roman, and Norse— and the enchantments of nature. She writes in *Dust Tracks on a Road*, "I was only happy in the woods, and when the ecstatic Florida springtime came strolling from the sea, trance-glorifying the world with its aura."[23] With her third husband, Janie abandons the alienating security of the big house and declasses herself for the "muck" of the Everglades and all that it offered: intimacy, adventure, existential challenge, and self-discovery. Tea Cake's given name, Vergible Woods, allies him with nature and the necessary greening of Janie's life. If the novel critiques the bourgeois economy of work and relationship based on ownership and possession, it is flouted by Tea Cake, whose legacy to Janie is a packet of seeds he meant to plant.

What unfolds is the dialectic of innocence and experience, for the early beatific vision of nature in springtime is tempered by the fierce destructive element of the hurricane. The Persephone-like image of Janie walking to the horizon, "picking flowers and making a bouquet" as she leaves Logan Killicks and joins Joe Starks in his hired rig, is a presentiment of the "death" Persephone must undergo if the maiden is to become her own queen. The tender and mostly idyllic relationship with Tea Cake, after the "stark" years with Joe, is rent by the destructive element, both within and without: violence surfaces in the relationship even before Tea Cake is bitten by the mad dog. Significantly, Tea Cake succumbs to the mad dog in the course of protecting Janie and, in order to protect herself from Tea Cake, Janie must kill him or end the relationship.

It is tempting to layer the figurative onto the literal scenario, and to draw autobiographical parallels. Hurston knew first hand that unexamined gender roles can be deadly for the questing spirit; that manly "protection" is often a matter of curtailing woman's freedom to travel, to work, to pursue her own dream. In the chapter called "Love" in *Dust Tracks on a Road*, Hurston discloses that the deepest love affair of her life, her relationship with "A.W.P." (Percival Punter), the young student of West Indian background, founders because Hurston is unwilling to end her work-related travel for the sake of the relationship: "He begged me to give up my career, marry him and live outside of New York City. I really wanted to do anything he wanted me to do, but that one thing I could not do."[24] Choosing occupational and existential freedom over the impossible constraints of the relationship, Hurston "sail[s] off to Jamaica" with a Guggenheim fellowship, her feet leaving "tracks of blood . . . [b]lood from the very middle of [her] heart." Shortly thereafter in Haiti outpours the cathartic novel *Their Eyes Were Watching God*, in which she "tried to embalm all the tenderness of [her] passion for [Percival Punter]."[25]

In the novel (as in the autobiography) we learn that Janie and Tea Cake must also contend with jealousy. When Mrs. Turner introduced her brother to Janie, Tea Cake was incensed. To assure himself that Janie was his, Tea Cake beat her.[26] Janie's deep love for Tea Cake withstands this episode, and like the women who "remember everything they don't want to forget," Janie, in her solitude, chooses to remember Tea Cake by his essential "love and light."[27]

Janie's departure from the town of Eatonville and her return to it are both scandalous to the community. First she abandons her husband, and second, she returns *without* the lover she left with. As Friedman comments, "Men's roles in heterosexual love and marriage have long afforded much wider latitude than women's roles for living according to their own distinctive identities and their deep self-defining commitments, whether at home, at work, or in public life."[28] In contrast to the gossiping collective whose voyeuristic gaze tracks Janie, the reliable comfort of her friendship with Phoebe, non-judgmental and receptive, enacts the ideal of a reciprocal, nourishing relationship between an artist and her community. Phoebe feeds Janie's hungry stomach with her platter of food while "Phoebe's hungry listening" compels Janie's story.[29]

Janie ends her life-story to Phoebe with the two things she knows for sure: "[Everybody's] got tuh go tuh God, and they got tuh find out about livin' fuh theyselves."[30] And then we have the lines from the third person narrator: "There was a finished silence after that so that for the first time they could hear the wind picking at the pine trees." Let us register this silence. It is a prelude to the final piece of the narrative. As Michael Cooke has insightfully noted, Janie "ends in what may be called accomplished solitude."[31] To appreciate what such an accomplishment is, we need only consider the distance Janie has traveled between the deaths of her last two husbands.

After Joe Starks's death Janie finds herself in a big house burdened with "the weight of lonesomeness."[32] As Parker Palmer notes, "[s]olitude is a painful condition at first, as are disillusionment and dislocation" but the "fruit of disillusionment and dislocation is the capacity to enter and enjoy our solitude."[33] After Tea Cake's death, we leave Janie to a room of her own, dedicated to the solitary and creative work of contemplation and self-communion: "She pulled in her horizon like a great fish-net. . . . So much of life in its meshes! She called in her soul to come and see."[34] In fact, such solitude is the very ground of great art, what makes it possible. Palmer expresses well what is at stake in this accomplishment: "To be in solitude means to be in possession of my heart, my identity, my integrity. It means to refuse to let my life and my meanings be dictated by other people or by an impersonal culture. To be in solitude is to claim my birthright of aliveness on its own terms, terms that respect the life around me but do not demean my own."[35] Solitude, as Palmer defines it, is synonymous with freedom of the self, a self free to be in intimacy with all of life itself. More than a lover, it is this freedom that Hurston pursued. In *Dust Tracks* she wrote, "But as early as I can remember I was questing and seeking"; "I have achieved a certain peace within myself, but perhaps the seeking after the inner heart of truth will never cease in me."[36]

At the conclusion of *Their Eyes*, as Janie climbs the stairs with a lamp in hand, we see the solitary presence reconciling the polarities of descent and ascent, water and fire, black shadow and radiant sun, in her own ascending light. The death that Janie undergoes is implied in the "shadow" that "fell black and headlong down the stairs," as the resurrection of the spirit is implied through the "sun-stuff washing her face in fire."[37] In lines that evoke Janie's passion, the poet Rainer Maria Rilke addresses the theme of the questing life that wants more: "the darkness of each endless fall, / the shimmering light of each ascent."[38]

The hallmark of a spiritual life is in the serenity achieved from the tumultuous synthesis of polarities. For such synthesis, solitude is essential. Hurston's narrator gives us an image of such creative solitude in the ruminating figure of Janie "[c]ombing road-dust out of her hair.[39] Tested by contraries, met by Nature's beneficence, beauty, and fecundity and by its ferocious, awesome, and destructive force, the mature Janie "saw her life like a great tree in leaf with the things she suffered, things enjoyed, things done and undone. Dawn and doom was in the branches."[40] As Janie Woods, she has integrated the blossoming pear tree with the dark woods, which is the site of both the fatal hurricane at the Everglades and the rape and disappearance of her barely known mother Leafy. The equation of dawn and doom implies equanimity before the vicissitudes of life. Further, the things done and undone were but the leafings, for the whole tree itself is vaster than these.

The novel does not end with the sorrow of Tea Cake's death. The "sobbing sigh" of the room, a spatial symbol of Janie's consciousness, gives way to the image of Tea Cake moving about as in life before. The spirit is not tethered by the body. "He could never be dead until she herself had finished feeling and thinking."[41] Hurston's spiritual under-standing of death informs Janie's point of view. The chapter on "Religion" in *Dust Tracks* ends with this confident acknowledgment of the eternal:

I know that nothing is destructible; things merely change forms. When the con-sciousness we know as life ceases, I know that I shall still be part and parcel of the world. Why fear? . . . I am one with the infinite and need no other assurance.[42]

The ending lines of the novel are a triumph of the spirit, as Janie calls her soul to witness what she discovered at the horizon. Let us recall that this is not the first time her soul has received such an invita-tion. The blossoming pear tree in her backyard had solicited her as well. The parallel invitations to her soul—by the pear tree in the begin-ning and by Janie herself at the end—reiterate the equivalence between the mystery of life that is the great tree and the mystery of life that is Janie wrapped in the fish net of the world's horizon.

Naturally, given the nature of solitude, Phoebe cannot be privy to it, for in these ending lines we have intimation of what poet Wallace Stevens calls the "intensest rendezvous," one with "the interior para-mour."[43] And in the novel's ultimate solicitation *to come and see* is summed up the true function and solace of visionary art: its capacity to extend to the beholder, across time and space and solitude, a numi-nous vision of self.

NOTES

1. Zora Neale Hurston, *Their Eyes Were Watching God* (1937; repr., New York: Harper-Perennial, 1990), 191.

2. Deborah Plant, *Zora Neale Hurston: A Biography of the Spirit* (Westport, CT: Praeger, 2007).

3. Hurston, *Their Eyes*, 11.

4. Zora Neale Hurston, "How it feels to be Colored Me," in *I Love Myself When I Am Laughing . . . and Then Again When I Am Looking Mean and Impressive: A Zora Neale Hurston Reader*, ed. Alice Walker (New York: The Feminist Press, 1979), 155.

5. Hurston, *Their Eyes*, 8.

6. Ibid., 1.

7. Ibid.

8. Zora Neale Hurston, *Dust Tracks on a Road: An Autobiography* (1942; repr., New York: HarperPerennial, 1995).

9. Robert Hemenway, *Zora Neale Hurston: A Literary Biography* (Urbana: University of Illinois Press, 1977); Carla Kaplan, *The Erotics of Talk: Women's Writing and Feminist Paradigms* (New York: Oxford University Press, 1996).

10. Hurston, *Their Eyes*, 10–11.

11. Plant, *Zora Neale Hurston: A Biography of the Spirit*, 117.

12. Hurston, "How it feels to be Colored Me," 154–155.

13. James Wright, "To a Blossoming Pear Tree," *The Nation*, October 18, 1975, 60.

14. Don Garett, "Benedict de Spinoza, Ethics (1677): The Metaphysics of Blessedness," in *The Classics of Western Philosophy*, ed. Jorge E. Gracia et al. (London: Wiley-Blackwell, 2003), 250.

15. Hurston, *Dust Tracks*, 231.

16. Hurston, *Their Eyes*, 10–11.

17. Keats, "Ode on a Grecian Urn," in *John Keats: The Complete Poems* (New York: Penguin, 1977), 344–346.

18. Hurston, *Their Eyes*, 25.

19. Ibid., 32.

20. Ibid., 27, 29.

21. Marilyn Friedman, *Autonomy, Gender, Politics (Studies in Feminist Philosophy)* (New York: Oxford University Press, 2003), 128.

22. Hurston, *Their Eyes*, 43, 46.

23. Hurston, *Dust Tracks*, 41.

24. Ibid., 208.

25. Ibid., 210, 211.

26. Hurston, *Their Eyes*, 147.

27. Ibid., 193.

28. Friedman, *Autonomy, Gender, Politics*, 130.

29. Hurston, *Their Eyes*, 10, 192.

30. Ibid., 192.

31. Michael G. Cooke, *Afro-American Literature in the Twentieth Century: The Achievement of Intimacy* (New Haven: Yale University Press, 1984), 80.

32. Hurston, *Their Eyes Were Watching God*, 89.

33. Palmer, Parker, *The Active Life: A Spirituality of Work, Creativity and Caring.* (San Francisco: Jossey-Bass, 1990), 28.

34. Hurston, *Their Eyes*, 193.

35. Palmer, *The Active Life*, 27–28.

36. Hurston, *Dust Tracks*, 215, 223.

37. Hurston, *Their Eyes*, 192.

38. Rainer Maria Rilke, *The Book of Hours: Love Poems to God*, ed. Anita Barrows and Joanna Macy (New York: Riverhead Trade, 1997), 71.

39. Hurston, *Their Eyes*, 192.

40. Ibid., 8.

41. Ibid., 193.

42. Hurston, *Dust Tracks*, 226.

43. Wallace Stevens, *Collected Poetry and Prose*, ed. Frank Kermode and Joan Richardson (New York: Library of America, 1997), 444.

Zora Neale Hurston: Environmentalist in Southern Literature

Scott Hicks

> There is no single face in nature, because every eye that looks upon it, sees it from its own angle.
>
> —Zora Neale Hurston, *Dust Tracks on a Road*

Despite Cynthia Davis's assertion that Zora Neale Hurston's "focus on the interrelationship of human and natural history, her foregrounding of nonhuman interests and subjects, and her ethical orientation to the environment argue strongly for [her] inclusion in any discussion of the American environmental imagination,"[1] Hurston, by all accounts, remains largely unheralded as an "environmentalist" and writer of environmental literature. Firstly, she is African American, and African Americans, as the story goes, are not environmentalists. "One common assumption is that blacks are rather shallow in their support for environmental protection," sociologist Robert Emmet Jones puts the matter delicately before debunking it firmly.[2] The assumption seems to come from a few ostensibly apocryphal statistics: the low numbers of African American members of the Sierra Club, low rates of visitation by African Americans to national parks, and low numbers of African Americans employed by the National Park Service.[3] Secondly, Hurston is a woman. As ecofeminists have shown, Cartesian dualism "segregates culture from nature, man from woman" and thus affects "the feminization of nature," a process that devalues women and "legitimizes the detrimental exploitation of both women and nature."[4] The conflation of woman and nature, ecofeminists demonstrate, seeks to render the female subject mute and prone to masculinist exploitation and extraction. Finally,

Hurston is southern. In U.S. environmental literature and criticism, the West holds "iconic status . . . as seedbed and Ground Zero of American nature writing, landscape photography, and ecopolitics, relegating other regional landscapes and ecosystems to supporting roles (with the possible exceptions of Thoreau's New England and Aldo Leopold's Wisconsin)."[5] Its swamps no contest for the Grand Canyon, its humidity inferior to the West's aridity, the South compels "a certain stammering as [its literature] attempts to negotiate between the discourses of [John] Muir and [Alexander von] Humboldt, spirit and body, mountains and coast, temperate and tropical, sublime global-northern wilderness and marvelously real global-southern jungle."[6] To be black, female, southern, *and* green? A miracle indeed, according to conventional wisdom.

Because of, and despite, these subjectivities, Zora Neale Hurston grants readers a revolutionary, liberating vision of environmentalism in her autobiography, fiction, and nonfiction—a vision that is anything but "conventional wisdom." Her memories of childhood fixate on sublime transactions between human and wild, while her study of anthropology and folklore gives her access to environmental imaginations across culture and time. On these foundations Hurston sees anew the ecological problems of her era and place, and on these grounds she contests the ideologies of race, gender, class, and nature that would rather render her a cipher. It belongs to us readers, thinkers, and writers across a wide range of fields not only to promulgate the richness of Hurston's vision, but to make much less miraculous, and much more commonplace, the good fortune of being black, feminist, southern, and green—just as we continue to complicate understandings of identity and environment that would otherwise dismiss her.[7]

Hurston's environmental imagination takes root in childhood, the natural richness that surrounded her feeding and freeing her mind. "There were plenty of orange, grapefruit, tangerine, guavas and other fruits in our yard," she writes in *Dust Tracks on a Road* (1942). "We had a five acre garden with things to eat growing in it, and so we were never hungry. . . . There was plenty of fish in the lakes around the town, and so we had all that we wanted."[8] Hurston's catalog of fruits suggests a seemingly untended yet wildly beneficent garden of global Edenic tropicality. Indeed, the vision of their productive home garden rebuts bureaucratic concerns about the capacity of former slaves and their descendents to work their own land, evidenced in U.S. Department of Agriculture pamphlets such as "Negro Families Can Feed Themselves" (1942), just as it signifies a critique of economic and social policies that make migration to the urban North a decision that hundreds of thousands of African Americans made in the 1920s, 1930s, and 1940s, something Richard Wright chronicles in *12 Million Voices* (1941). Like others before them, the Hurstons and their neighbors complement the foods they raise through wild game and fish. That *Dust Tracks* locates this "wildness" in town bespeaks not only a nourishing relationship between humans and nature, but among humans who, in the all-black Eatonville, cultivate a sort of commons and thus share the wealth of nature—a counter-vision to the history of commons and enclosure that Raymond Williams traces in British history in *The City and the Country* (1973). Ensconced in surfeit and protected by community, Hurston is free to enjoy "the mocking birds [that] sang all night in the trees [and a]lligators [that] trumpeted from their stronghold in Lake Belle."[9] The wild and the tame, in other words, coexist in harmony.

The fecundity of Hurston's environmental beginnings enables her to see the porosity between home and away, domestic and wild, and ultimately humankind and nature. She sees herself not as a settler, colonist, or pioneer, someone who sees wilderness as ungodly or dangerous or nature as separate, divisible, and thus conquerable. Instead, she sees herself as but one of many parts in a complex community, as someone who listens to and learns from all living things. Her own maturation, she writes, finds its analogy in nature: she grows like "a gourd vine, and yelling bass like a gator."[10] Just as she celebrates both the domesticity of her family's fruit trees and garden as well as the wildness of the lakes, songbirds, and alligators, she also observes the permeability of wilderness and the impermanence of domestication. The nature she knows is violent and uproarious, "a neighborhood where bears and alligators raided hog-pens, wild cats fought with dogs in people's yards, rattlesnakes as long as a man and as thick as a man's forearm were found around back doors, a fist fight was a small skimption."[11] In Hurston's experience, nature refuses to be segregated from culture, a law that expresses itself throughout her writing: rattlesnakes appear in Della's laundry in "Sweat" (1926) and in the Meserves' orange grove in *Seraph on the Suwanee* (1948), for instance, and wild animals join humans in exodus from the Florida coast in *Their Eyes Were Watching God* (1937). These narratives articulate human and nonhuman nature in balance, as opposed to the notion that the humans take precedence over the wild. As Hurston writes in her autobiography, her realization that the moon does not follow her alone "was my earliest conscious hint that the world didn't tilt under my foot-falls, nor careen over one-sided just to make me happy."[12] This ecocentric appreciation of the interpenetrations of the human and the wild, culture and nature, allows her to imagine herself ecologically and endows her with a synesthetic language to express this subjectivity-altering imagination. She recalls:

I was only happy in the woods, and when the ecstatic Florida springtime came strolling from the sea, trance-glorifying the world with its aura. Then I hid out in the tall wild oats that waved like a glinty veil. I nibbled sweet oat stalks and listened to the wind soughing and sighing through the crowns of the pines. I made particular friendship with one huge tree and always played about its roots. I named it "the loving pine," and my chums came to know it by that name.[13]

Hurston's gift consists not in personifying nature, in which seasons saunter and breezes breathe. More important, she naturalizes the human: disappearing in the wild oats, she becomes another wisp; eating the stalks, she makes the wild landscape part of her bones, marrow, and muscle. Thus she becomes "petal-open" to friendship with the "loving pine," as she has become more willing and able to meet it on its own terms: "The wind would sough through the tops of the tall, long-leaf pines and said things to me. I put in the words that the sounds put into me. Like 'woo woo, you wooo!' The tree was talking to me, even when I did not catch the words. It was talking and telling me things."[14] This shift from anthropocentrism to ecocentrism invites and necessitates a new language, one inspired by and inspiring African American expression. An example of the "double descriptive" that Hurston explicates in "The Characteristics of Negro Expression" (1934), "trance-glorifying" bespeaks the inadequacy of "[t]he stark, trimmed phrases of the Occident" (as well as the austere, truncated environmental imagination of the West) "too bare for the voluptuous child of the sun" (or the lush landscape of the South).[15] Together, Hurston's domestic and wild imaginations collude to plant a revolutionary environmental imagination.

Hurston's study of anthropology, folklore, and Voodoo deepen and extend her revisionary environmental consciousness. Suzanne Clark notes, "Anthropology as Hurston studied it with Franz Boas was a close kin to natural history, with a discursive status similar to the natural history descriptions of the Grand Canyon (for geologist/anthropologists like John Wesley Powell) or the fish of the Amazon River (for biologists like Louis Agassiz)."[16] As an anthropologist and folklorist, Hurston traveled widely, from Harlem and the U.S. South to the Bahamas, Haiti, Jamaica, and other locales—a series of jaunts that, her color and gender notwithstanding, would otherwise put her in the company of, say, John Muir, whose own extensive journeys included California, the Pacific Northwest, Alaska, the Midwest, and the South. The nondenominational, revisionary view of nature that she brings with her from her earliest memories, coupled with her transnational and transcultural mobility, animates her conceptualization of folklore as an explanation of and response to nonhuman phenomena:

Thinking of the beginnings of things in a general way, it could be said that folklore is the first thing that man makes out of the natural laws that he finds

around him—beyond the necessity of making a living. After all, culture and discovery are forced marches on the near and the obvious. The group mind uses
up a great part of its life span t[r]ying to ask infinity some questions about what
is going on around its doorstep.[17]

Unlike many Westerners, Hurston is willing to hear the story of "natural laws" through the mouthpieces of the flora and fauna, not just the
mouths of their human interlocutors.

God, Devil, Brer Rabbit, Brer Fox, Sis Cat, Brer Bear, Lion, Tiger, Buzzard, and
all the wood folk walked and talked like natural men. . . . It did not surprise me
at all to hear that the animals talked. I had suspected it all along. Or, let us say,
that I wanted to suspect it. . . . Animals took on lives and characteristics which
nobody knew anything about except myself.[18]

As Valerie Levy argues, Hurston sees folklore as the cultural result of a
region's natural resources and landscape and thus combines the privileges and responsibilities of the nature writer with those of ethnographer—never distancing herself either from the natural or cultural
environment.[19] Whereas in school she can recite perfectly the myth of
seasons starring Jupiter, Persephone, and Ceres,[20] she gains from folk
stories a counterview of creation and natural phenomena through the
eyes and ears of those who have lived on the land and witnessed the
making of the world.

   Moreover, through Voodoo, its syncretism and creolization of multiple African cultures, and its premise of animism, Hurston articulates a
re-envisioning of environmental consciousness through a global black
lens. As Levy writes of Hurston's Federal Writers Project work, she
"often personifies nature (or shows how black folklore personifies it)
and brings nature from its invisible backdrop status to the forefront of
both plot and structure." She continues: "Indeed, in Hurston's Florida,
the fluid relationship between nature and black folk culture is as
organic as the state's oranges and alligators."[21] Likewise, Rachel Stein
in *Shifting the Ground: American Women Writers' Revisions of Nature, Gender, and Race* (1997) asserts that Voodoo symbolizes "an alternative spiritual model that reframes the binary hierarchies operating within the
denigration of black women as nature incarnate. Through rituals that
locate the sacred within nature and within female sexuality, Voodoo
challenges the degradation of black women as donkeys." Stein analyzes
Their Eyes Were Watching God as an "embalming" of Hurston's "growing knowledge of Voodoo spirituality within the nature imagery of
the novel," noting how "Janie claims kinship and communion with
nature much like that of a Voodoo priestess" and that the novel's
imagery of the Florida muck and hurricane "exemplifies a beneficent

Voodoo disruption of the white culture's false oppositions" that "re-emphasizes and revalues their own blackness."[22] Hurston's turn from anthropology to folklore, and especially Voodoo, reveals her evolving consciousness of the interpenetrations of the human and natural.

Hurston's multifaceted ecological vision allows her to interrogate the ecological problems of Florida in the mid-20th century. Thomas Barbour's *That Vanishing Eden: A Naturalist's Florida* (1944) provides a glimpse into the Florida that Hurston would have known. Indeed, his text centers on Eau Gallie, his grandmother's hometown, and Hurston's place of residence from 1951 to 1956. In *That Vanishing Eden*, the herpetologist and director of Harvard University's Museum of Comparative Zoology details the devastation of a once paradisal place. Rampant ditching, drainage, and deforestation for farming and development deserve the blame, Barbour writes. Quoting John K. Small's *From Eden to Sahara—Florida's Tragedy* (1929), he describes Lake Okeechobee devoid of " '[t]he once deep humus. . . . In its place white sand met the eye. . . . Some of the giant cypress trees (*Taxodium distichum*) were prostrate, some were standing, either dead or alive, but only to emphasize the almost complete destruction!' "[23] What's more, timbering and turpentining have decimated the state's woodlands:

The truth of the matter is that natural scenery, especially in the form of forests, is disappearing from the face of the globe, at an ever-accelerating rate; and the time is not far in the future when man will be living in a treeless world. . . . Between boxing for turpentine and cutting for timber, these vast areas of the [longleaf pine] flatwoods which were so grand and inspiring to see when I was a youngster now are hopeless deserts.[24]

With their habitats ruined, alligator, bear, crocodile, deer, fox, squirrel, and panther stand on the brink of extinction; likewise, thanks to commercial overfishing, it has become next to impossible to land a good-sized sergeant fish or snook in the Indian River. Sobered by these threats to the paradise he once knew, fished, and hunted and pessimistic about the state's future, he can only hope that reforestation efforts and the creation of the Everglades National Park stems the tide of ecological destruction.[25] "[Florida] must cease to be purely a region to be exploited and flung aside, having been sucked dry, or a recreation area visited by people who come only for a good time, who feel no sense of responsibility, and have no desire to aid and improve the land of their temporary enjoyment," he concludes. "It must cease being treated as a colony, and become a vital, integral part of the American Union."[26]

The environmental issues Barbour describes take center stage in Hurston's writing, and her texts decry the degradation of the environment. Her first and last novels, *Jonah's Gourd Vine* (1934) and *Seraph on the Suwanee*, thematize the effects of the timber and turpentine industries in the state. In *Jonah's Gourd Vine*, widespread deforestation worsens flooding and erosion by removing the watershed's groundcover: "The river was full of water and red as judgment with chewed-up clay land. . . . Red water toting logs and talking about trouble, wresting with timber, pig-pens, and chicken coups as the wind hauls feathers, gouging out banks with timber and beating up bridges with logs."[27] *Seraph on the Suwanee* mourns the tendency of logging not only to destroy the region's forests, but to impoverish its agricultural landscapes: "[F]ew of these fields were intensely cultivated," the narrator says of the area surrounding Sawley, Florida. "For the most part they were scratchy plantings, the people being mostly occupied in the production of turpentine and lumber."[28]

Like Barbour's lament, Hurston's novels pay especial reverence to the trees that beckon the lumberman's axe. In *Their Eyes Were Watching God*, Janie Crawford projects onto a blossoming pear tree her budding consciousness of herself and her sexuality, a projection the novel reiterates throughout. The novel likens her marriage to Logan Killicks to "a stump in the middle of the woods" and describes various times of her life in relationship to bloom times, green times, and orange times, as Janie, like Hurston and her "loving pine," contends that she speaks the same language as the trees.[29] In the end, Janie becomes the trees she loves, as her marriage to Vergible "Tea Cake" Woods names her Janie Woods. As Matthew Wynn Silvis asserts, "Hurston merges the two, making Janie a human/tree hybrid,"[30] just as she makes, in *Seraph on the Suwanee*, a similar hybridization for Arvay Henson Meserve and the mulberry tree behind her childhood home. Finally, Hurston's fiction records the profound wealth of nature accumulated in the wetlands featured in her work. In *Their Eyes Were Watching God*, Hurston celebrates the Everglades:

Big Lake Okeechobee, big beans, big cane, big weeds, big everything. Weeds that did well to grow waist high up the state were eight and often ten feet tall down there. Ground so rich that everything went wild. Volunteer cane just taking over the place. Dirt roads so rich and black that a half mile of it would have fertilized a Kansas wheat field.[31]

Such ecologically rich wildernesses liberate Janie and Tea Cake from the oppressions they have endured, though the expeditiousness of the foreclosure of that liberation—the tragic hurricane and its re-inscription of racism and violence—reiterates the precariousness of not only social and psychological, but also environmental, liberation.[32]

Yet Hurston's subjectivity as a complexly classed, black woman homeowner distinguishes her environmental imagination from Barbour's, whose subjectivity as an upper-class white prodigal son leads him to interpret the same territory quite differently. For Barbour, a lamentation of the decline in fish in the Indian River becomes a disparagement of nonwhites' relationships to the environment. Whereas his fondly remembered grandmother respectably appreciates channel bass, for instance, the family cook—a pipe-smoking, crippled resident of "Colored Town" recollected only as "Aunt Harriet"—inelegantly prefers possum. Similarly, he complains of the refusal of "Grandmother's old colored folk," thanks to what he labels superstitiousness, to help in archaeological digs in nearby Indian shell mounds. Finally, he minimizes the presence of Seminole Indians, depicting them as more "Negro blood" than Indian and imagining for them a future role primarily as possible caretakers of a proposed Everglades National Park.[33] Whereas Barbour writes as a "cultured" traveler whose native Florida home he takes for granted from afar, Hurston writes as a committed insider who was, paradoxically, not allowed the opportunity to own the land she loved. Unlike Barbour's masculinist, Eurocentric perspective, Hurston's point of view effects radical, and much-needed, disjunctions in environmental consciousness, disjunctions that privilege the ecoliteracies of a diversity of folk cultures.[34]

For Hurston's characters, Florida represents not ecological conservation through human removal, but cultural preservation through environmental development. John and Lucy Pearson move to Eatonville because it means "[g]ood times, good money, and no mules and cotton." "[S]niff[ing] sweet air laden with night-blooming jasmine and wish[ing] that she had been born in this climate," Lucy perceives "[t]he warmth, the foliage, the fruits" as evidence that here is where "God meant her to be surrounded": "John, dis is uh fine place tuh bring up our chillun. Dey won't be seein' no other kind uh folks actin' top-superior over 'em and dat'll give 'em spunk tuh be bell cows theyselves, and you git somethin' tuh do 'sides takin' orders offa other folks."[35] Such desire for an affirming and secure homeplace haunts Hurston's other characters and expresses itself in a paradoxical pattern of mobility. The once-enslaved Nanny prostrates herself before her white mistress "rak[ing] and scrap[ing] and [buying] dis lil piece uh land so [her granddaughter Janie] wouldn't have to stay in de white folks' yard and tuck yo' head befo' other chillun at school," but her attempt to find freedom for her granddaughter from racist violence and oppression drives Janie into a series of homes that oppress her on the basis of gender. Even as Janie finds affirmation in the pear tree, Nanny recognizes that "us colored folks is branches without roots and that makes things come round in queer ways."[36] In *Jonah's Gourd Vine*, tenant farmers Amy and Ned Crittenden confront and expose sharecropping as a re-inscription of slavery, and African American veterans of World War I refuse rooting themselves to any farm, seeing deep, transnational connections between the interpenetrating violences of war, agriculture, and racism: "God made de world but he never made no hog outa me tuh go 'round rootin' it up. Done done too much bookoo plowing already!"[37] Finally, *Seraph on the Suwanee* provokes, underscores, and rethinks the disjunctive effects of race, class, and gender on the sustenance of a sustainable environmental consciousness. Whereas Janie, Tea Cake, and their black and Bahaman brothers and sisters celebrate the "muck" for the liberation it gives them, "cracker" Arvay Henson Meserve fears the swamp, and her husband and son-in-law drain it, for it is worth more destroyed and turned into a golf course community than it is sustained: "There's a great big fortune hid in that dark old swamp," Jim avers, in part because the labor that transforms the swamp—like all of the Meserves' help—is black and brown, subservient and underpaid.[38] And while *Jonah's Gourd Vine* and *Their Eyes Were Watching God* imagine mobility as intranational or intrastate, *Seraph on the Suwanee* imagines mobility as transubstantiative, turning land into water, as Jim and Arvay trade the liberation of their wealth and real estate for the liberation of the seas. "All water is off on a journey unlessen it's in the sea, and it's homesick, and bound to make its way home some day," the novel's narrator intones as protagonist Arvay Meserve transforms into the ship *Arvay Henson*, unmoored from the gravity of land and culture and freed to sail into the infinite beyond.[39]

Even though Hurston would pen other manuscripts, the end of *Seraph on the Suwanee* reads like a farewell: there exists no place, ultimately, for this black woman to land, to put down roots, in the United States. *Seraph on the Suwanee*'s imagination of the devastation of the muck and the excision of the folk, replaced by golfing suburbanites stratified from the racial and socioeconomic Other by the former swamp as surely as a railroad track,[40] seems to permit no place for a person like Hurston. Such a vision might emanate from Hurston's own quixotic battle—a sort of guerrilla gardening, perhaps—to possess a territory of her own. In the yard that surrounded her rented house in Eau Gallie, Florida, she planted butterfly ginger, pink verbena, and papaya and put an ornamental garden around an artesian spring.[41] She writes in a letter: "Now, you p[e]rhaps question why I am putting so much into this place where I now live. I have a chance to buy it. . . . Somehow, this one spot on earth feels like home to me. I have always intended to come back here. That is why I am doing so much to make a go of it."[42] Yet the property becomes disputed in estate proceedings, and she is evicted. As her fiction and autobiography demonstrate, it is indeed significant that "the only home she ever owned was a houseboat moored on the Indian River."[43]

Put simply, Zora Neale Hurston is an environmentalist *par excellence* because she engages the full complexity of environmental consciousness. Not only does she narrate and critique the ecological depredations of her time; she also explores and exposes the racial, socioeconomic, and gendered interpenetrations of environmental consciousness and inhabitation. Her work as an archivist and sharer of African American folklore and her appreciation and practice of Voodoo introduce her to new realms of community and environmental understanding and advocacy. Finally, her compelling life story—her willingness to hear and speak back to the plants and animals that enlivened her world; her desire for a garden of her own, a garden as rich and fruitful as the gardens she encountered as a child—denies her any recourse as a simplistic, and simplifying, anthropocentrism: her respect for all species, locales, and cultures compels her to engage all life forms seriously, respectfully, and equitably. The result of her environmentalism is the creation, daily, of new worlds, as she suggests in *Their Eyes Were Watching God*, new worlds that increase in richness and beauty, as well as impoverishment and ugliness, before the changed senses of their denizens. Diane Ackerman puts the matter this way in *A Natural History of the Senses* (1990):

[H]ow sense-luscious the world is. . . . We still create works of art to enhance our senses and add even more sensations to the brimming world, so that we can utterly luxuriate in the spectacles of life. We still ache fiercely with love, lust, loyalty, and passion. And we still perceive the world, in all its gushing beauty and terror, right on our pulses. There is no other way.[44]

Put simply, Hurston's environmentalism roots us more firmly in our natural and cultural homegrounds, just as it forces us to engage our homegrounds and homewaters in simultaneously more human, as well as more antihuman, ways. As contemporary readers in a world marked by ecological devastation, environmental injustice, and cultural genocide, we are thankful to "[b]ehold the Jimpson weed putting out roots in the solarium of the orchid!"[45]

NOTES

1. Cynthia Davis, "The Landscape of the Text: Locating Zora Neale Hurston in the Ecocritical Canon," in *Florida Studies: Proceedings of the 2005 Annual Meeting of the Florida College English Association*, ed. Steve Glassman (Newcastle, U.K.: Cambridge Scholars Press, 2006), 155.

2. Robert Emmet Jones, "Blacks Just Don't Care: Unmasking Popular Stereotypes about Concern for the Environment among African-Americans," *International Journal of Public Administration* 25:2–3 (2002): 222.

3. Kirsten Repogle, "The Importance of a Diverse Sierra Club," *EJ Activist: The Sierra Club Environmental Justice Newsletter* 6:3 (Spring 2007): 3; U.S. Department of the Interior, Office of Congressional and Legislative Affairs, *Statement of Marcia Blaszak, Regional Director, Alaska Region, National Park Service, Department of the Interior, Before the Subcommittee on National Parks, House Committee on Resources, Regarding Trends in Visitation to the National Park System,* April 6, 2006, <http://www.doi.gov/ocl/2006/VisitationTrendsInTheNPS.htm>; and James G. Lewis, "A Brief History of African Americans and Forests," U.S. Department of Agriculture, Forest Service, African American Strategy Group, <http://www.fs.fed.us/people/aasg/PDFs/African_Americans_and_forests_March21%202006.pdf>, 4.

4. Jia-Yi Cheng-Levine, "Teaching Literature of Environmental Justice in an Advanced Gender Studies Course," in *The Environmental Justice Reader: Politics, Poetics, and Pedagogy,* eds. Joni Adamson, Mei Mei Evans, and Rachel Stein (Tucson: University of Arizona Press, 2002), 369.

5. Jay Watson, "Economics of a Cracker Landscape: Poverty as an Environmental Issue in Two Southern Writers," *Mississippi Quarterly: The Journal of Southern Cultures* 55, no. 4 (Fall 2002): 497.

6. Jon Smith, "Hot Bodies and 'Barbaric Tropics': The U.S. South and New World Natures," *Southern Literary Journal* 36, no. 1 (Fall 2003): 117–118.

7. We would do well to continue the work of Davis, who critiques mainstream ecocriticism's ignorance of Hurston and offers a foundation for her inclusion in the environmental literary critical canon.

8. Hurston, *Dust Tracks on a Road,* in *Folklore, Memoirs, and Other Writings,* Ed. Cheryl A. Wall (1942; repr., New York: Library of America, 1995), 571.

9. Ibid., 584.

10. Ibid., 579.

11. Ibid., 588.

12. Ibid., 582.

13. Ibid., 595–596.

14. Ibid., 605.

15. Hurston, "Characteristics of Negro Expression," in *The Norton Anthology of African American Literature,* 2nd edition, ed. Henry Louis Gates, Jr., and Nellie Y. McKay (1934; repr., New York: W.W. Norton & Co., 2004), 1043.

16. Clark, "Narrative Fitness: Science, Nature, and Zora Neale Hurston's Folk Culture," in *Restoring the Connection to the Natural World: Essays on the African American Environmental Imagination,* ed. Sylvia Mayer (Munster, Germany: LIT, 2003), 46.

17. Hurston, "Go Gator and Muddy the Water," qtd. Valerie Levy, "'That Florida Flavor': Nature and Culture in Zora Neale Hurston's Work for the Federal Writers' Project," in *Such News of the Land: U.S. Women Nature Writers,* ed. Thomas S. Edwards and Elizabeth A. De Wolfe (Hanover: University Press of New England, 2001), 94.

18. Hurston, *Dust Tracks,* 601, 605, 611.

19. Levy, "'That Florida Flavor,'" 87–88, 94.

20. Hurston, *Dust Tracks,* 591.

21. Levy, "'That Florida Flavor,'" 93, 86.

22. Rachel Stein, *Shifting the Ground: American Women Writers' Revisions of Nature, Gender, and Race* (Charlottesville: University Press of Virginia, 1997), 54, 75, 77–78.

23. John K. Small, qtd. Thomas Barbour, *That Vanishing Eden: A Naturalist's Florida* (Boston: Little, Brown, 1944), 75.

24. Barbour, *That Vanishing Eden*, 77–79.

25. Ibid., 36, 84, 137–144, 178, 224–230.

26. Ibid., 237.

27. Hurston, *Jonah's Gourd Vine* (1934; repr., New York: HarperPerennial, 1990), 86.

28. Hurston, *Seraph on the Suwanee* (1948; repr., New York: HarperPerennial, 1991), 1. For an overview of the turpentine industry in African American environmental history, see Cassandra Y. Johnson and Josh McDaniel's "Turpentine Negro," in *"To Love the Wind and the Rain": African Americans and Environmental History*, ed. Dianne D. Glave and Mark Stoll (Pittsburgh: University of Pittsburgh Press, 2007), 51–62. In this essay, the writers situate African American relationships to wilderness in terms of the exploitive, violent, and racist practices of the turpentine industry in the South during slavery and Jim Crow.

29. Hurston, *Their Eyes Were Watching God* (1937; repr., New York: Perennial Classics, 1990), 25.

30. Matthew Wynn Silvis, "Reading Trees in Southern Literature," *Southern Quarterly* 44, no. 1 (Fall 2006): 96.

31. Hurston, *Their Eyes*, 129.

32. Although too many critics discuss representations of nature in Hurston's work for full discussion here, see especially Martyn Bone, "The (Extended) South of Black Folk: Intraregional and Transnational Migrant Labor in *Jonah's Gourd Vine* and *Their Eyes Were Watching God*," *American Literature* 79, no. 4 (December 2007): 753–779; Keith Cartwright, "'To Walk with the Storm': Oya as the Transformative 'I' of Zora Neale Hurston's Afro-Atlantic Callings," *American Literature* 78, no. 4 (December 2007): 741–767; Glenda B. Weathers, "Biblical Trees, Biblical Deliverance: Literary Landscapes of Zora Neale Hurston and Toni Morrison," *African American Review* 39, nos. 1–2 (Spring and Summer 2005): 210–212; Brian R. Roberts, "Predators in the 'Glades: A Signifying Animal Tale in Zora Neale Hurston's *Their Eyes Were Watching God*," *Southern Quarterly* 41, no. 1 (Fall 2002): 39–50; Sarah Ford, "Necessary Chaos in Hurston's *Their Eyes Were Watching God*," *CLA Journal* 43, no. 4 (June 2000): 407–419; Anna Lillios, "'The Monstropolous Beast': The Hurricane in Zora Neale Hurston's *Their Eyes Were Watching God*," *Southern Quarterly* 36, no. 3 (Spring 1998): 89–93; and Christopher Rieger, "The Working-Class Pastoral of Zora Neale Hurston's *Seraph on the Suwanee*," *Mississippi Quarterly* 56, no. 1 (Winter 2002–2003): 105–124.

33. Barbour, *That Vanishing Eden*, 39–40, 47, 54.

34. Hurston's socially and environmentally engaged consciousness mirrors the revisionary consciousnesses of other southerners writing against traditional southern views, such as Erskine Caldwell, *Tobacco Road* (New York: C. Scribner's Sons, 1932) and *God's Little Acre* (New York: Viking Press, 1933); W.J. Cash, *The Mind of the South* (New York: Alfred A. Knopf Inc., 1941); Marjory Stoneman Douglas, *The Everglades: River of Grass* (New York: Rinehart, 1947); any of William Faulkner's fiction; Charles S. Johnson, *The Shadow of the Plantation* (Chicago: University of Chicago Press, 1934); and Arthur F. Raper,

The Tragedy of Lynching (Chapel Hill: University of North Carolina Press, 1933), and *Preface to Peasantry: A Tale of Two Black Belt Counties* (Chapel Hill: University of North Carolina Press, 1936).

35. Hurston, *Jonah's Gourd Vine*, 103, 109.

36. Hurston, *Their Eyes*, 19, 16.

37. Hurston, *Jonah's Gourd Vine*, 149.

38. Hurston, *Seraph*, 191. For further discussion of labor and environmental consciousness, see Richard White in William Cronon, ed., *Uncommon Ground: Rethinking the Human Place in Nature* (New York: W.W. Norton & Company, 1995), 171–185.

39. Hurston, *Seraph*, 333. The endings of *Their Eyes Were Watching God* and *Seraph on the Suwanee* are uncannily similar: Arvay's transubstantiation into water parallels Janie *Starks*'s transubstantiation into timber as Janie *Woods*, while *Seraph*'s privileging of water reinvokes Nanny's dream of a black man in power: "Maybe it's some place way off in de ocean where de black man is in power, but we don't know nothin' but what we see" (*Their Eyes Were Watching God* 14). Stein argues that like Alice Walker and Leslie Marmon Silko, Hurston "utilize[s] 'monstrous' reconfigurations of nature in order to replace the model of conquest and domination with more interactive and egalitarian social/natural relations" (19). As Hurston asserts in *Dust Tracks on a Road*, "I discovered that all that geography was in me" (634).

40. Hurston, *Seraph on the Suwanee*, 197.

41. Jack Temple Kirby, *Mockingbird Song: Ecological Landscapes of the South* (Chapel Hill: University of North Carolina Press, 2006), 228.

42. *Zora Neale Hurston: A Life in Letters*, ed. Carla Kaplan (New York: Doubleday, 2002), 663.

43. Kirby, *Mockingbird Song*, 228. Many of her letters testify to her deep love of gardening (Kaplan 662, 669), yet even in beautifying the rundown property, Hurston faces racism: "In what was meant to be a compliment, I have been told twice, 'You don't live like the majority of your people. You like things clean and orderly around you'" (Kaplan 663). Dianne D. Glave's "Rural African American Women, Gardening, and Progressive Reform in the South" provides an incisive historical and cultural discussion of gardening and race. She writes: "African American and white gardens possessed distinctive characteristics. . . . By using yards in different ways, African American women took possession of them. They manipulated and interpreted the spaces for sustenance, comfort, joy, and sometimes profit" (in Glave and Stoll 39, 50). For a discussion of the interrelationship of African American landownership and racism in the South, see Raper, *Preface to Peasantry*.

44. Diane Ackerman, *A Natural History of the Senses* (New York: Random House, 1990), xv, xix.

45. Kaplan, *Zora Neale Hurston*, 56.

Narrative Displacement: The Symbolic Burden of Disability in Zora Neale Hurston's *Seraph on the Suwanee*

Michelle Jarman

Zora Neale Hurston's final published novel, *Seraph on the Suwanee*,[1] enjoyed early critical praise, but its release in 1948 was soon overshadowed by an unfounded, highly sensationalized sexual molestation charge against Hurston. Although she was eventually exonerated, the book—and perhaps the author as well—never recovered publicly.[2] Since then, *Seraph on the Suwanee* has been widely dismissed by literary scholars as an insignificant, even regressive text. Many critics have read Hurston's decision to focus on white Florida "crackers" as an unfortunate capitulation to white publishers and readers. Mary Helen Washington suggests that the novel fails because Hurston abandons the wellspring of "her unique esthetic—the black cultural tradition."[3] Alice Walker, who pioneered a revival of public interest in Hurston's work, flatly rejects *Seraph* for lacking the courage or creative vision present in the author's earlier novels and ethnographic writing: "[Hurston's] work, too, became reactionary, static, shockingly misguided and timid. This is especially true of her last novel, *Seraph on the Suwanee*, which is not even about black people, which is no crime, but *is* about white people who are bores, which is."[4] In fairness, Walker's complaint has some validity. Compared to Hurston's celebrated feminist heroine Janie Crawford, *Seraph*'s Arvay Henson Meserve comes across as a whining, indecisive woman, whose great personal triumph entails rejecting moralistic values of her childhood in favor of a more progressive worldview modeled by her charismatic husband, Jim. While the novel does explore social, racial, and gender dynamics of southern Florida, the main focus is the romantic relationship between Jim and Arvay, and the crucial psychological development Arvay must achieve in order to realize happiness with her husband.

In recent years, a few scholars have demonstrated renewed interest in *Seraph* by calling attention to the resistance at play within the text. Claudia Tate, for one, argues that *Seraph on the Suwanee* engages in a persistent joke on white culture's "idealization of passive female desire and its conflation of race and class."[5] Tate refers to Hurston's ruse as a form of "whiteface" used by the author to disguise her critiques of gender roles, marriage, and essentialist ideas about whiteness or blackness. Janet St. Clair also challenges critical dismissals of Arvay as dependent or self-abnegating for failing to acknowledge the "subversive undertow" at work in the "feminist substory . . . [which rejects] both oppression and, more important, the mental submission to oppression."[6] Both Tate and St. Clair argue that Hurston's frustrated (and frustrating) protagonist exposes the idealized passivity of white domesticity, but I would suggest that the material and psychological sacrifices made by Arvay undermine a reading of the novel as a straightforward feminist victory, and instead reveal much more about the social rules— especially among upwardly mobile whites—regulating the parameters of an effective and "successful" marriage.

Specifically, this essay focuses on the melodramatic portrayal and compulsory removal of Arvay's first-born disabled son, Earl. While the novel does expose many levels of oppression and resistance in Jim and Arvay's marriage, the most significant conflicts between husband and wife become symbolically contained in the figure of Earl. Even more troubling and evocative, his death as a young man functions within the narrative to clear the way for Arvay to heal psychologically—and return, physically and emotionally, to her husband and her other, non-disabled, beautiful, and successful children. I examine this depiction of Earl from two directions. First, I argue that Hurston uses disability strategically within the text to negotiate various racial and gender critiques. However, in doing so, she depends on and re-inscribes problematic stereotypes of disability that deserve critical attention. Second, I take issue with critical interpretations of Earl that unquestioningly endorse Hurston's conflation of disability with animalistic, sexual aggression, and champion Earl's death as a feminist breakthrough for his mother.

Broadly, *Seraph on the Suwanee* traces the hasty courtship and nearly 25 years of marriage between Arvay Henson and Jim Meserve, an upwardly mobile, white couple that settles in Citrabelle, a town on the edge of Florida swamplands. When Jim meets Arvay in the small, turpentine and sawmill town of Sawley, he is a brash, self-assured young man determined to win the heart of the shy, nervous, but pretty Arvay. From the beginning, Jim exercises both charm and force in order to win Arvay, and although Hurston exposes Jim's domineering and sometimes oppressive nature, the author seems also to defend his perspective throughout the text. With Jim's reason and understanding as foundation, it falls on Arvay to learn tolerance, and to develop a courageous, rather than a timid, love.

The power struggle that comes to define the marriage begins during their courtship when Jim physically lays claim to his new bride. Troubled by Arvay's emotional and physical reserve, Jim decides to forcefully take her in hand. After instructing Arvay to dress up for a date, Jim arrives at her home with a horse-drawn carriage. Before departing, however, he leads her behind the large mulberry tree in her backyard, pulls her to the ground in all her finery, drags her underclothes "ruthlessly down her legs," and rapes her.[7] Feminist readings of the novel focus not only on Jim's brutality, but critique Hurston for depicting Arvay's response as a terrified enjoyment of a "pain remorseless sweet."[8] After the rape, Jim is tender and doting again, and Arvay, partly out of love, partly out of desperation, clings to Jim. When they finally emerge from behind the mulberry tree, Jim hustles her past her gaping parents straight to the courthouse to get married. Before realizing where Jim is taking her, Arvay confronts him about the rape, an accusation he happily owns: "Sure you was raped, and that ain't all. You're going to keep on getting raped . . . every day for the rest of your life."[9]

At once, Jim sexually lays claim to Arvay, but gives himself to her as well. He is both violent and attentive, devoted and controlling. And in many ways, through the complex figure of Jim, Hurston is at her ethnographic and creative best. Tiffany Ruby Patterson describes Hurston as an "expert witness of her time," who provides a glimpse into the "past present" that was her world.[10] Patterson explains further what the role of witness provides Hurston's readers: "She imagined, as every great artist does, but she also made it her business to see, hear, and write as an ethnographer does—in detail, in depth, and by bringing to bear a deep understanding of human complexity."[11] Thinking of Hurston as a witness becomes an interesting way to provide texture to a reading of Jim, Arvay, and Earl. Of the three, Jim has the most layers: he draws on a depth of character that allows him to see multiple dimensions of other people, which provides him with the social skills and knowledge to connect with anyone—across races, cultures, professions, and economic levels. Arvay, in comparison, seems starkly one-dimensional. She sees everything in relation to herself and judges people outside her small family circle with suspicion and contempt. Earl, by contrast, has no dimension of his own, but instead functions as a template on which the tensions, growth, and resolutions of others can be written. Hurston's characterization of Earl doesn't provide enough texture to depict a complex human, but as a witness of her time, this is notable in its own right because the power of Earl as a symbolic figure depends on his not seeming fully human.

As Patterson suggests, the complexity of character draws readers back to Hurston in an attempt to puzzle out what she really believes about the lives constructed in her writing. In *Seraph*, the attention Hurston pays to developing Jim Meserve as a multi-dimensional character effectively positions him as the authoritative perspective in the novel. Even though readers are allowed access to Arvay's inner thoughts, hopes, and fears, and Hurston at times seems critical of Jim, his perspective overwhelmingly drives the novel. Hurston establishes Jim's authority as well through his close relationships with African Americans, immigrants, and people across class divides. His friendship and respect for Joe Kelsey, his African American overseer and ostensible moonshine partner, and the fluidity with which he crosses racial lines through language and social practice establishes Jim as a savvy, but fair and generous white man. While Hurston makes clear that Jim's racial privilege allows him to reap the lion's share of the economic rewards in such relationships, he also displays an uncommon sense of fair play and reciprocity for the time. Of these human processes, Arvay "had no idea. She had no understanding to what extent she was benefiting from the good will that Jim had been building."[12] Whereas Jim understands that interracial partnership will benefit everyone, Arvay remains aloof and suspicious, wondering why Jim develops loyalties to people outside the *proper* boundaries of the family.

From the beginning of their relationship, initiated by the power struggle under the mulberry tree, Jim and Arvay are caught in a clash of wills. In many ways, their differences are reflected in Hurston's depiction of Earl. He becomes the stage on which the psychological gulf between them is enacted: their interpretations of him reflect the correctness or distortions of their worldviews—of Jim's progressive rationale and Arvay's timid rigidity. Disability studies scholars David Mitchell and Sharon Snyder have argued that although disabled figures are in many ways pervasive in Western literary traditions, the representational role of these figures has been widely under-theorized. In *Narrative Prosthesis*, they point out that while literature has depended on the presence of disability as metaphorical and transgressive—as a means of conveying cultural critiques—the social stigma of disability remains unchallenged: "Literature borrows the potency of the lure of difference that a socially stigmatized condition provides. Yet the reliance upon disability in narrative rarely develops into a means of identifying people with disabilities as a disenfranchised cultural constituency."[13] In other words, even as disability becomes saturated with symbolic and metaphorical meaning, people with disabilities continue to be read in static terms. This is certainly true of the figure of Earl: he embodies all of the marital and psychological tensions between his parents, but reveals very little about the social realities of disability oppression or stigma. Instead he is rendered an aberration, a problem, and a threat.

This is evident even at his birth. Noting Earl's small hands and misshapen head, Jim accepts his responsibilities to provide for Earl, but does "not enthuse at all" over the child.[14] Arvay becomes particularly upset when Jim avoids choosing a name. Sensing his ambivalence, she preemptively names the baby Earl and devotes herself to the child with a missionary zeal. At the same time, she begins to react instinctively to Earl as a manifestation of the tainted biology she had hoped to escape by marrying Jim. Her anguish around Earl follows two commonplace interpretations of disability during this period: moral punishment or hereditarian determinism. From one side, she thinks Earl could be God's judgment for her "sinful" teenage infatuation with Reverend Carl Middleton, who eventually married her sister Larraine: "This is the punishment for the way I used to be . . . I never thought it would come like this, but it must be the chastisement I been looking for."[15] She also considers her own "hysterical seizures" and Earl's resemblance to her Uncle Chester, "the one who was sort of queer in his head" as biological explanations for her son's impairments.[16] These thoughts reveal deeply naturalized and internalized narratives of disability: either her "unfit" bloodline or impure nature has caused "deformity" in her child.

Arvay's devotion to Earl intensifies after the birth of their second child. "A damn fine baby you had for me, honey," Jim exclaims.[17] Comparing the baby's auburn hair and beautiful eyes to those of his own mother, he immediately bestows her name of Angeline on his new daughter. At that moment, "Arvay found out what Jim was like as a father. He was hanging over the baby's crib practically all the time." This adoration, however, only underscores his rejection of Earl, and redoubles Arvay's commitment to him: "The lines were drawn, and she had become a partisan."[18]

Although Arvay's partisanship seems laudable, Hurston resists this reading by foreshadowing Earl's violent and uncontrollable nature. When he is five and Angeline three, Arvay hears "inhuman screams" and immediately thinks some "wild beast had crept in from the swamp" to attack her children in the yard. In actuality, Earl is "emitting those animal howls" as he fights with his sister over a piece of fruit.[19] So distressed is she by Earl's unnatural cries that she fears the child in her womb might "be marked" by it,[20] thereby evoking another common fear evoked by the presence of disability. Yet even as she begins to fear Earl, she continues her unwavering protection of him through silence and self-denial.

As the novel unfolds, however, Arvay's continued insistence on Earl's harmlessness is increasingly undermined by Hurston's representation, which reifies cultural narratives linking cognitive impairment to immorality, animalistic violence and criminality. Following this trajectory, readers are not surprised when Earl's sexual awakening takes the form of an animalistic frenzy. When Earl is near 16, one of Jim's friends, Alfredo Corregio, moves his family into the cabin behind the Meserve home. The Corregios have two lovely daughters, the eldest of whom—the teenage Lucy Ann—immediately becomes the object of Earl's obsessive and violent desire. The day the Corregios arrive, he is driven to distraction by something new in the air. Like a "hound dog hunting for a scent," Earl begins to throw himself at his screened window to propel himself out of his room.[21] When Arvay opens the door to investigate, Earl runs her down and races toward the cottage, and is thwarted only because Jim intercepts him on the path.

After subduing Earl, Jim suggests a *practical* solution, one Hurston seems to endorse. "Earl has got to be put away," Jim pleads with Arvay, "He'll do harm to other folks. We ought not to risk it." Arvay's adamant refusal to send her son to "a crazy house" seems irresponsible in the face of such evidence.[22] Her reasoning is rendered even more questionable in her relentless prejudicial accusations that Jim is choosing the Corregio "furriners" over his own son. Jim also points out to Arvay that over the years, he has noticed in Earl "some great craving after guns."[23] Earl had aimed an unloaded rifle at his younger brother Kenny, and since then, Jim had been locking his guns and ammunition away. Jim urges Arvay to be sensible and assures her that he doesn't blame her for Earl's "condition," because it "come through your father's folks."[24] This comment, intended to comfort her, only works to confirm Arvay's long-held suspicion that Jim blames her for Earl's disability, further fueling the feeling that "she and Earl were shut off in loneliness by themselves."[25]

Hurston seems to suggest, however, that this loneliness results less from Jim's indifference than from Arvay's own misplaced devotion. Predictably, within days of this argument, Earl escapes the watchful eye of his mother and attacks Lucy Ann. Sitting at her sewing after dinner one night, Arvay is startled by shrieks mixed in with "howl[s]" and "yelps" coming from the grove.[26] Immediately recognizing Earl's animal-like cries, she runs toward the cottage to find a group now crowded around Lucy Ann, who lies unconscious on the ground. The girl's skirt was torn and pulled up to reveal "a bleeding wound on one thigh." Arvay notices blood running from a "mangly spot" on her neck, and even her fingers are "chewed and bloody."[27] Judging from her wounds, Lucy Ann looks as if she has been attacked by a wild creature, not a human being.

Hurston's depiction of Earl's attack echoes deterministic rhetoric of the time that equated cognitive impairment with sexual "deviancy." The frenzied nature of Earl's violence fits the picture of "mental defectives" developed by eugenicists in the early 20th century. Martin Barr, a physician and strong supporter of surgical sterilization, explained the threat of this population: "[M]ental defectives suffer not only from exaggerated sexual impulses, but from mental and moral debility, causing always a minimum of judgment and of will-power, leaving them greater slaves to the impulse of the moment."[28] Rendered both hypersexual and morally impaired, people perceived as fitting into this category were understood to be aggressive time bombs just waiting to go off. Re-inscribing this stereotype, Hurston portrays Earl as incapable of reining in his impulses, and his mother becomes complicit in his crime by refusing to accept the inevitability of violence.

Once Earl attacks Lucy Ann, Arvay can no longer protect or hide him. Within minutes a posse forms outside their home, and in an effort to keep them from killing Earl, Jim joins the manhunt for his own son. Ultimately, however, after a standoff in the swamp where Earl has his rifle locked on his father, the men are forced to shoot Earl to save Jim. As I argue elsewhere,[29] Earl's sexual attack and subsequent death at the hands of this posse posits a re-scripting of the all-too-common lynching stories: Instead of a falsely accused black man falling victim to a racist mob, Earl is positioned as an authentic sexual menace within the community. In order to represent Earl's death as inescapable, and ultimately beneficial, Hurston constructs him as static and atavistic: as a sexual predator, a killer incapable of higher human emotions. Through Earl, Hurston attempts to displace the black male rapist as the villain of the lynch narrative, suggesting instead that specific white men should be rightly understood as a very real threat to women of all races. In making this argument, Hurston draws on the cultural similarity of lynching and eugenic narratives that position black men and cognitively impaired men as sexual predators. However, in her effort to free black men from the trap of false accusations, she positions cognitively impaired men in a similar rhetorical prison.

Not only does Earl's death evoke images of the lynch mob, but as a bona fide "sexual deviant" loose in the community, the threat of his presence displaces the sexual transgressions of everyone else in the novel. Jim's rape of Arvay, specifically, becomes more an act of passion and love when contrasted to Earl's violence and "animalistic" impulses. In other words, while it does seem that Hurston endeavors to expose Jim's rape for what it is, she dampens this critique by continually authorizing his perspective, and by representing Earl as *the real* social menace. Further, Jim's recognition of Earl as a threat positions him as the rational protector, unbiased by his own familial connections, and committed to protecting the community—even from his own son.

Following Jim's understanding of Earl's death as inevitable and ultimately beneficial, Hurston sets up Arvay's final struggle as an inner battle of accepting the *truth* of this perspective. Hurston constructs Arvay's choice in binary terms: either sever herself emotionally from Earl or lose her marriage. After a month of grieving for Earl, Jim challenges her to admit that she must be somewhat relieved. Although she "would have died rather than admit that Jim was telling the truth . . . [s]he acknowledged to herself that she had put on the greatest show of grief when she caught herself feeling relieved."[30]

This internal confession represents a turning point in the novel—the beginning of Arvay's transformation. As she comes to accept Earl's death, she also admits to herself that her love for Earl had been "something that stood between her and Jim" and had distracted her from Angie and Kenny.[31] This familial narrative of disability was very common in the first half of the 20th century. Professionals routinely argued for institutionalization on the grounds that mothers were not able to balance the care demanded by the disabled child with the needs of other family members. As historians Tyor and Bell explain, "a mentally defective child could exhaust the mother, forcing her to slight her responsibilities to other family members resulting in the disruption of the entire household."[32] Hurston's depiction of Arvay follows this model. Throughout Earl's life, Arvay uses her love for and protection of him to separate herself from Jim, Angeline, and Kenny. Within this context, Earl's death represents the psychological breakthrough that allows Arvay to *come back* to her family. The tacit understanding, of course, is that Earl is not an appropriate member of the family, and this unstated truth allows his death to represent a psychological healing rather than a trauma—as the death of any non-disabled child would naturally evoke.

Through Arvay and Earl, Hurston bears witness to the enduring cultural salience of eugenic ideas that disability cannot be contained in the family or the community—and that disabled figures should be removed, either through confinement or, in the case of Earl, through death. This is a stark and troubling conclusion, and if critics are to examine the "static" or "reactionary" nature of Hurston's final novel, her endorsement of such deterministic understandings of disability represents an important area to explore. Most critical readings of Earl, however, are not interested in the meanings associated with disability, and unquestioningly accept his death as crucial to his mother's emancipation. Returning to the feminist interpretations offered by Claudia Tate and Janet St. Clair, both critics read Earl, not as a representation of disability, but as a metaphorical reflection of Arvay's internal life. Tate reads Earl as a psychological projection of Arvay's insecurity, so his death is interpreted as finally free-ing Arvay from "her guilty burden."[33] St. Clair also interprets Earl reduc-tively as a metaphorical construct of Arvay's mental state: "Earl, Arvay's idiot firstborn, serves as an image of the deformed and illogical con-sciousness that restricts her growth and potential . . . But Earl himself is full of destructive potential; and like Arvay's deformed mentality, which invites and expects oppression, he is destroyed so that productive life can resume."[34] This critical endorsement of Earl's characterization perpetu-ates an exceedingly dehumanizing, tragic conception of a cognitively impaired child within the family—especially as a care-giving burden to the mother. While Hurston does position Earl's death as a central event that continues to shape Arvay's internal identity, the necessity of his death enacts a distinctly eugenic rationale, and does much to challenge such liberating feminist readings of the text.

Arvay's psychological maturation and her ability to reunite with Jim do indeed depend on her reconciling Earl's death as an unfortunate but necessary event. At this point, Arvay begins to understand his death as central to her ultimate fulfillment:

Yes, Earl had been bred in her before she was even born, but his birth had purged her flesh. He was born first. It was meant to be that way. Somebody had to pay off the debt so that the rest of the pages could be clean. God must have thought that she was one who could shoulder the load and bear it . . . Earl had served his purpose and was happily removed from his sufferings . . . She had been purged out, and the way was cleared for better things.[35]

Earl functions, in effect, as a canvas on which Arvay paints her own psychological growth, not as a complex character in his own right. By never challenging the sacrifice at the heart of Arvay's return to her family, and further, by effectively demanding Earl's death, Hurston develops a eugenic script that precludes the existence of a positive, lov-ing, supportive, or productive role for children with disabilities within the domestic site of the (white) middle-class family. In some ways, we might credit Hurston with witnessing this static perception of disabil-ity, but knowing her incredible ability to depict the complexity of human experience, it seems that she also accepted these cultural stereo-types as accurate, and even depended on them to provide cohesion to the excessive symbolism contained in her figuration of Earl.

In *Seraph on the Suwanee*, Hurston broke with traditional rules and expectations of the period that African American writers should write about African American people, and constructed her story around an insecure white woman, and her journey toward psychological fulfill-ment. Arvay's arrival at contentment, however, ultimately depends, not only on the fatal sacrifice of her disabled son, but on her acceptance of his death as a *happy removal*—clearing the way within *her* for "better things." This unapologetically able-ist and eugenic solution to the novel's central conflicts—which revolve around Earl—should be the subject of greater critical concern. Instead, however, Hurston's use of Earl as the metaphorical container for Arvay's personal growth has been widely accepted as an effective—even liberating—narrative strategy.

In many ways, Hurston's method for negotiating the racial dimensions of the novel reveals a great deal about the enduring saliency of static, limiting, and dehumanizing thinking about disability. Specifically, Hurston's strategic use of Earl to embody the discord between Jim and Arvay presents cognitive disability as a social threat around which whites, blacks, and immigrants can unite. While Hurston routinely challenged and complicated racial or gendered stereotypes, her conceptualization of disability in *Seraph* depends heavily on deterministic assumptions. Arguably, in fact, she trades on the stigmatization and rejection of disability in her negotiation of race—both in writing about white people, and in realizing her vision of a more racially integrated and egalitarian social space. This remains a troubling paradox: racial openness and marital happiness come to rest on the social exclusion of disability. Hurston's capitulation to this eugenic solution suggests a compelling need for critical analyses that foreground and analyze race, gender, and disability *in relationship*—whether complementing, intersecting, or opposing each other.

NOTES

1. Zora Neale Hurston, *Seraph on the Suwanee* (1948; repr., New York: Harper, 1991). Citations refer to the 1991 publication (hereafter cited as *Seraph*).

2. Valerie Boyd, *Wrapped in Rainbows: The Life of Zora Neale Hurston* (New York: Scribner, 2003), 387–401.

Before the original 1948 publication of Zora Neale Hurston's *Seraph on the Suwanee* (New York: Harper, 1991), the author was arrested and booked on charges of sodomizing three young boys. She denied the charges vehemently and demanded a full investigation. She even provided evidence that she had been in Honduras during the time the alleged molestations were to have taken place. Even though the accusations were completely fabricated by the boys involved, Hurston's name was not formally cleared for over a year. During that time, her final novel was published. At the time Hurston felt particularly betrayed by African American critics who used the scandal to exploit the sexual content in the book.

3. Mary Helen Washington, "A Woman Half in Shadow," in *I Love Myself When I Am Laughing: A Zora Neale Hurston Reader*, ed. Alice Walker (New York: Feminist Press, 1979), 12.

4. Alice Walker, foreword to *Zora Neale Hurston: A Literary Biography*, by Robert Hemenway (Urbana: University of Illinois Press, 1977), xvi.

5. Claudia Tate, "Hitting 'A Straight Lick with a Crooked Stick': *Seraph on the Suwanee*, Zora Neale Hurston's Whiteface Novel," in *The Psychoanalysis of Race*, ed. Christopher Lane (New York: Columbia University Press, 1998), 381.

6. Janet St. Clair, "The Courageous Undertow of Zora Neale Hurston's *Seraph on the Suwanee*," *Modern Language Quarterly* 50.1 (1989): 38.

7. Hurston, *Seraph*, 51.

8. Ibid.

9. Ibid., 57.

10. Tiffany Ruby Patterson, *Zora Neale Hurston and a History of Southern Life* (Philadelphia: Temple University Press, 2005), 7.

11. Ibid.

12. Hurston, *Seraph*, 83.

13. David T. Mitchell and Sharon L. Snyder, *Narrative Prosthesis: Disability and the Dependencies of Discourse* (Ann Arbor: University of Michigan Press, 2000), 55.

14. Hurston, *Seraph*, 68.

15. Ibid., 69.

16. Ibid., 6, 68.

17. Ibid., 85.

18. Ibid., 85–86.

19. Ibid., 100.

20. Ibid., 101.

21. Ibid., 123.

22. Ibid., 125, 126.

23. Ibid., 127.

24. Ibid., 125.

25. Ibid., 131.

26. Ibid., 143.

27. Ibid.

28. Martin W. Barr, "Some Notes on Asexualization; With a Report of Eighteen Cases," *Journal of Nervous and Mental Disease* 51.3 (1920): 232.

29. Michelle Jarman, "Disability and the Lynch Mob: Violence and Sexuality in Eugenic and Lynching Narratives," in *Sex and Disability*, ed. Robert McRuer and Anna Mollow (Durham: Duke University Press, forthcoming).

30. Hurston, *Seraph*, 158.

31. Ibid.

32. Cited in Janice Brockley, "Rearing the Child Who Never Grew: Ideologies of Parenting and Intellectual Disability in American History," in *Mental Retardation in America*, ed. Steven Noll and James W. Trent Jr. (New York: New York University Press, 2004), 136. Brockley further suggests that in 19th-century fiction, disabled sons were often represented as punishment for an incompetent or weak father. Because masculinity was supposed to be passed down from father to son, a child with a disability tended to reflect on the father's virility.

33. Tate, "Hitting 'A Straight Lick,'" 390.

34. St. Clair, "Courageous Undertow," 51.

35. Hurston, *Seraph*, 350.

Zora Neale Hurston and the Challenge of Black Atlantic Identity

Shirley Toland-Dix

Zora Neale Hurston was a novelist, folklorist, anthropologist, and some say, a conjure woman. In all of her work, she was committed to portraying the full, complex humanity of black people. In *Zora Neale Hurston: A Biography of the Spirit*, Deborah Plant describes Hurston as "the first social scientist to not only recognize the *undiminished* humanity of Africana peoples, but also to extensively document the cultural expressions that were indicative of their particular and original genius."[1] Hurston's research was fueled by her deeply held conviction that "the greatest cultural wealth on the continent" could be found in the "sayings and doings of the Negro farthest down."[2] With the publication of her first ethnography, *Mules and Men* (1935), Hurston became the first black anthropologist to record southern black folk culture. In her second ethnography, *Tell My Horse* (1938), she broadened the scope of her research and focused on the African Caribbean cultures of Jamaica and Haiti. With these studies, she granted black Atlantic folk cultures a scholarly legitimacy that white supremacist ideology had denied them. In both collections, she explored the complex connections between West African and black Atlantic cultures.

Defined simply, the black Atlantic refers to descendants of the Africans who experienced the trauma of the Middle Passage, those who are part of the diaspora created by the Atlantic slave trade. A recurring theme within black Atlantic discourse is the desire for reconnection. For most of the history of the United States, people of African descent have not been acknowledged or treated as full citizens of the nation; in various ways, they have been marginalized and constructed as the deviant

Others against whom those who "belonged" were measured. The African American community's response to enslavement, oppression, and exclusion has included both the struggle for freedom, equal rights, and belonging within the community of the nation as well as the desire to reconnect with others of African descent across the boundaries of nation. Therefore, African Americans constitute part of the larger community of the black Atlantic world—blacks of the West"[3]—a community imagined on the basis of shared historical experiences, shared cultural foundations, shared origin, and shared struggle.

In *The Black Atlantic: Modernity and Double Consciousness*, Paul Gilroy provides a more political definition of black Atlantic identity as an intercultural positionality beyond nationality: "a global, coalitional politics in which anti-imperialism and anti-racism might be seen to interact if not to fuse." Gilroy argues that nationalist identity is "antithetical" to the multifaceted, "fractal structure of the transcultural, international formation I call the black Atlantic."[4] Black Atlantic identity can be an alternative or an addition to an exclusively nationalist focus, as black Atlantic sensibility involves the desire to "transcend structures of the nation state and the constraints of ethnicity and national particularity."[5] It is experienced as an empowering, self-defined identity that focuses on reconstruction of historical, cultural, and potentially political links. The black Atlantic is conceived as a space of legitimacy and affirmation, beyond the constraints of societies where those of African descent were deemed void of history or culture and required to prove their humanity.

As an anthropologist, Hurston did groundbreaking research in establishing the cultural connections between West Africa, the Caribbean, and the American South. She was a pioneer in developing awareness of the African diaspora as "a transnational and intercultural multiplicity."[6] A focus of her studies was the interconnectedness of diasporic religions and spiritualities. The deeply personal impetus of spiritual quest became as much a reason for her study as the intellectual curiosity of the social scientist. Hurston developed a strong diasporic consciousness through research trips to the Bahamas, Jamaica, and Haiti, and she was able to place Southern black folk within the context of a shared black Atlantic experience.

Scholars who study the black Atlantic identity of diasporic blacks often discuss the extent to which political solidarity beyond national identity can come out of an awareness of intercultural and historical connectedness. Gilroy asserts that the challenge of "weighing the claims of national identity against other contrasting varieties of subjectivity and identification has a special place in the intellectual history of blacks in the west."[7] In reality, most black people who are aware of diasporic connectedness hold it in tension with national identity. This was certainly true of Zora Neale Hurston. Like many African Americans, she experienced contesting loyalties between her identity as an American citizen and her identity as a member of the transnational African diaspora. Susan Stanford Friedman emphasizes the multiple identities that diasporic blacks balance "partially based on multiple and continuously negotiated affiliations linked to class, sexuality, religion, gender, ethnicity, nation, age, and so forth."[8] To state the obvious, black Atlantic cultural identity does not erase distinct differences among diasporic black people. This is particularly evident in the complex interactions between Hurston and the communities she studied in Jamaica and Haiti. June Roberts observes that despite her black American folk roots, as an educated American woman, Hurston was *petit blanc* in Haiti.[9]

In the Introduction to *Mules and Men*, Hurston comments on the challenge of returning to Eatonville as a Columbia University-trained anthropologist to study her own folk culture from an academic perspective: "I couldn't see it for wearing it. It was only when I was off in college, away from my native surroundings, that I could see myself like somebody else and stand off and look at my garment. Then I had to have the spy-glass of Anthropology to look through at that."[10] Karen Jacobs observes that the spy-glass not only implies the "penetrating male gaze of science," it also invokes the "imperial white gaze of colonialism, both of which inform the ambiguous history of anthropology."[11] The "spy-glass" could thus be seen as particularly problematic when turned on African Caribbean communities in Jamaica and Haiti by an American anthropologist. Part of this dynamic is that despite her race and gender, Hurston was privileged because of her status as a highly educated American. In *Tell My Horse*, she reports that in Haiti and Jamaica, this allowed her access to some spaces routinely denied to women. The challenge of balancing her dual identity as citizen of the United States and member of the transnational black Atlantic diaspora is particularly evident in Hurston's second ethnography.

Published in 1938, *Tell My Horse* is significant among ethnographic studies because Hurston offers narratives that are not only critical of colonialism and color and class hierarchies in the Caribbean, but also of oppressive gender politics, especially the brutal treatment of black women. In a chapter entitled "Women in the Caribbean," Hurston observes satirically that in the Caribbean, "sex superiority is further complicated by class and color ratings": "Of course all women are inferior to all men by God and law down there. But if a woman is wealthy, of good family and mulatto, she can overcome some of her drawbacks. But if she is of no particular family, poor and black, she is in a bad way indeed in that man's world. She had better pray to the Lord to turn her into a donkey and be done with the thing. It is assumed that

God made poor black females for beasts of burden, and nobody is going to interfere with providence."[12]

Hurston arrived in Haiti to study Vodou in 1936. As a conjure woman trained in New Orleans by renowned hoodoo doctors, Hurston was knowledgeable of the similarities between hoodoo and Vodou, and confidently became the apprentice of a houngan or Vodou priest in Haiti. She soon realized that even though African diasporic religions share a common spirituality rooted in Africa, they were not homogeneous. According to Joseph Murphy, because these religions evolved in a variety of enslaved and emancipated communities throughout the Americas, each one "possesses a unique heritage" and has faced "unique challenges" in its survival and development.[13] In *Tell My Horse*, Hurston voices her astonishment at how highly developed and prolific Vodou practices in Haiti were. After providing some initial explanations of the intricacies of Vodou belief systems and rituals, Hurston allows that "it would require several volumes to attempt to cover completely the gods and Voodoo practices of one vicinity alone. Voodoo in Haiti has gathered about itself more detail of gods and rites than the Catholic church has in Rome."[14] In her research into Vodou, Hurston encountered the specific challenge of assuming the insider position of the native anthropologist and discovering that she was more of an outsider than she had imagined.

Hurston arrived in Haiti during the aftermath of the United States' 19-year (1915–1934) occupation of the country. *Tell My Horse* is a balanced ethnographic study of Vodou that includes an examination of this political history that both explicitly and implicitly dismantles racist interpretations and representations of Vodou. Her ethnographic work directly refutes reasons advanced by American politicians to justify their invasion and occupation of Haiti. Interestingly, however, as evidenced by her overwhelmingly positive depiction of an occupation whose racist, anti-democratic, and brutal policies and practices had been documented extensively, Hurston's black Atlantic cultural identification does not seem to have displaced her political loyalty to the United States.[15] Arguably, the most controversial section of *Tell My Horse* is Part II, "Politics and Personalities of Haiti," because of, among other things, Hurston's apparent endorsement of the American occupation, of the stories she tells about Haitian leaders, and because she actively omits the details of an occupation described by one historian as "unprecedented in both its duration and the extreme racism that characterized American behavior in the black republic."[16] Her stances are read as paradoxical if not contradictory. The challenge of black Atlantic identity is made clear by the way Hurston's positionality is critiqued. Some critics begin by assuming that as an African American, Hurston should have demonstrated "racial solidarity" with the Haitians, not based on some inherent racial essence, but on shared ancestral experiences of racial oppression.

Scholars offer a fascinating range of critiques, challenges, and explanations for some of the clearly provocative statements Hurston makes. Hazel Carby describes *Tell My Horse* as "blindly patriotic" and "reactionary."[17] Perhaps the most outraged critic is J. Michael Dash, as suggested by the title given the section of his book that discusses African American writers' responses to the occupation: "From Hughes' Dream to Hurston's Nightmare." Dash scathingly dismisses *Tell My Horse*, charging that for Hurston, Haiti was "a nightmare world fit only to be probed anthropologically and to be rehabilitated militarily. Hurston's comments on Haitian folk culture are consistent with her reactionary politics. Other black writers could be forgiven because their sensationalist fictions were often motivated by the urgent need to establish a common folk heritage. Hurston's only motivation seems to have been unmitigated contempt."[18] Significantly, these dismissive judgments avoid acknowledging the complex politics of identity of African Americans as citizens of the United States. Annette Trefzer observes that while in Haiti, Hurston frequently encountered anti-United States sentiment. She notes the difficulties Hurston faced as "a minority anthropologist who occupied marginal positions in both American and Haitian society and who was a woman in a predominately male discipline."[19] However, Trefzer also concludes that Hurston was "trapped" in the "imperialistic and nationalistic American discourses" used to justify the occupation.[20] Leigh Anne Duck and Mary Renda offer thoughtful, complex analyses of Hurston's nuanced rhetorical strategies and her possible political reasons for avoiding a direct critique of the American occupation, even though it had been a *cause célèbre* among African American civil rights activists.[21]

In fact, Haiti has historically held a uniquely conflicted place in the African American imagination. At the height of the slave trade, in a New World built on enslaved labor, Haiti was the only place where the enslaved staged a successful Revolution, violently seizing freedom from their masters and defeating three colonial powers before becoming in 1804 the second independent nation in the Western Hemisphere. The Haitian Revolution also upended the philosophical discourse that supported and justified the enslavement of Africans. Consequently, throughout the black Atlantic world, Haiti has been symbolic of a people's willingness to die rather than be enslaved, of courage and skill in the face of seemingly insurmountable odds, of black manhood, black womanhood, heroism, and the claiming of self-determination. Dash observes that from the 19th century, black writers consistently depicted Haiti as "exemplary in its assertion of black nationalism and racial defiance."[22] Writing in 1893, Frederick Douglass declared that "the negro" had been seen as "a sheep-like creature, having no rights which white men were bound to respect; a docile animal, a kind of ass, capable of bearing burdens and receiving stripes from a white master without resentment or resistance. The mission of Haiti was to dispel this degrading and dangerous delusion and to give to the world a new and true revelation of the black man's character. This mission she has performed and has performed it well."[23] More than anything, the Haitian Revolution was a symbol of possibility for the enslaved throughout the rest of the Americas and for abolitionists, black and white. African Americans viewed the island with pride, investing hope in the possibilities of a self-governed black nation. However, many were also afraid that if Haiti failed to govern itself effectively, if it seemed that Haitians were "reverting" to anarchy and savagery, as white supremacist social science predicted, that would be used as evidence that people of African descent were not sufficiently evolved to govern themselves. Thus, in 1915, in the early days of the occupation, an editorialist for the *New York Age,* a black newspaper, declared: "We long to see Haiti demonstrate to the world the capacity of the Negro for self-government and self-improvement . . . and each time that she suffers from revolution and lawlessness we experience a feeling of almost personal disappointment."[24]

In a comprehensive historical essay, Brenda Gayle Plummer documents African American response over the course of the American occupation, establishing that at first response was muted, in part because the invasion of Haiti happened during World War I. However, one who responded from the outset was Booker T. Washington, whose self-help philosophy Hurston deeply admired.[25] In an essay published in November 1915, Washington expressed his belief that the Haitians were "a backward people in need of discipline and enlightenment." In his opinion, the Caribbean nation's "economic stagnation and political violence owed much to its neglect of sound industrial education." At the same time, Washington disagreed with America's occupation of Haiti. Washington warned of "the limitations of military rule and the adverse effects of racism. Haiti should be civilized, but not at gunpoint. . . . Care should be taken to send them no negrophobes."[26] Plummer notes that after World War I, with a resurgence of black nationalism and an increased sense of international black Atlantic identity, along with growing awareness of American authoritarian control of Haiti's government and finances, and spurred by reports of the brutal suppression of the Haitian people by American soldiers, African American organizations, writers, leaders, and publications began protesting the American occupation in earnest. Plummer shows that the racist beliefs and actions of the occupying officers combined with the abuses being suffered by African Americans at home created an impetus:[27]

The Bloody Summers of 1918 and 1919, the agitation for a federal anti-lynching bill, and the rise of militant nationalism put racial matters at the forefront. Black Americans perceived the Haitians as related to themselves.[28]

The National Association for the Advancement of Colored People (NAACP) was the first major black organization to mobilize against the American occupation of Haiti. In 1920, the NAACP sent James Weldon Johnson to Haiti on a two-week investigative mission. As a lawyer, journalist, novelist, poet, former diplomat, and the field secretary for the NAACP, Johnson had impeccable credentials. Although the invasion had been explained officially as essential for America's strategic defense needs and as an effort to provide paternal guidance to an anarchic republic, Johnson discovered and emphasized the role of the National City Bank of New York in determining U.S. policy in Haiti. In 1918, the Americans had forced the Haitian Congress to adopt a new constitution that allowed foreign ownership of Haitian banks.[29] While in Haiti, Johnson met with Haitian President Dartiguenave and other members of the occupation government as well as with opposition leaders, peasants in the rural areas, and U.S. Marines "who spoke casually of rape, killing, and torture." When he returned to New York, Johnson became one of the most effective crusaders working to end the American occupation of Haiti.[30] Notably, his arguments in support of the Haitian people also reflect African American investment in a particular vision of what Haiti's "mission" should be. Speaking in 1920, Johnson declared that the United States should get out of Haiti "as quickly as it can and restore to the Haitian people their independence and sovereignty. The colored people of the U.S. should be interested in seeing that this is done, for Haiti is the one best chance that the Negro has in the world to prove that he is capable of the highest self-government."[31]

Hurston's analysis is structured by a similar investment in a particular vision of Haiti's possibilities and promise. Hurston arrived in Haiti two years after the last American Marines were withdrawn. By that time, African American political discourse on Haiti had begun to change. There had always been tensions between the Haitian nationalists and African American progressives who worked together for the liberation of Haiti. Part of the tension arose from different valuations of color and class. In addition, while the NAACP was essential in the negotiations between the U.S. government and the Haitian leaders, the two groups had different visions of what a liberated Haiti should look like.[32] African American activists were elated when Haitian political independence was restored in August 1934. The NAACP had played a decisive role in securing Haiti's freedom from U.S. occupation; in a 1934 letter to the NAACP's *Crisis* magazine, President Stenio Vincent publicly expressed the gratitude of the Haitian people. However, by the end of the year, African Americans who had been among Haiti's staunchest supporters were criticizing President Vincent for imprisoning the writer Jacques Roumain, expressing their fear that the "authoritarian and intolerant nature" of former Haitian governments was reemerging. By May 1935, *Opportunity*, journal of the National Urban League, had published an editorial expressing "disapproval of Vincent's despotic regime" and "surprise that Haitians who protested against the infringement of their rights by the American government should now deny freedom to their own citizens."[33] At their Twenty-Sixth Annual Conference, the NAACP adopted a resolution condemning the Vincent administration for suppressing free speech and imprisoning critics of his government.[34]

Many of those reading *Tell My Horse* when it was published in 1938 would have been aware of this context. In "Politics and Personalities of Haiti," Hurston enters a conversation that African Americans were already having about Haiti. She also expresses apprehension that old patterns of class exploitation and despotic government are reemerging. Throughout *Tell My Horse,* Hurston differentiates sharply between her deep sense of connection with the Haitian people and a scathing indictment of the greed and opportunism she identifies as the legacy of Haitian politicians. She also draws a sharp distinction between Haiti's proud revolutionary past and the intense socioeconomic crisis, exacerbated by the Great Depression that the country faced. So while Hurston respectfully acknowledges the grandeur and heroism of Haiti's founding and the sacrifice and dedication of its revolutionary leaders, she counterbalances that with her conviction that "oppression did not cease" when the "white oppressors" were driven out; she argues that by the time of the American invasion, "Haiti's internal foes" had become "more dangerous to Haiti than anyone else."[35] With her terse summary of the current situation in Haiti, Hurston establishes the parameters and focus of her analysis and she strategically omits inconvenient facts that do not fit this version of events:

The occupation is ended and Haiti is left with a stable currency, the beginnings of a system of transportation, a modern capitol, the nucleus of a modern army.
So Haiti, the black republic, and where does she go from here?[36]

Thus Hurston chooses to present the aftermath of the occupation as an opportunity for Haitian rebirth. She also chooses to omit discussion of or give representations of the abusive behavior of the American occupiers or to account for the adverse effects of their exploitative policies on the country. She focuses instead on Haitian responsibility for the invasion and on what she thinks their best course of action going forward should be.

In discussing Hurston's autobiography, *Dust Tracks on a Road*, Deborah Plant argues that Hurston "constructed a history of her life based on empowering metaphors of self."[37] While Hurston acknowledged that virulent white racism existed, she maintained that black people could not allow it to diminish them. They had to find a way to achieve despite those facts. Plant observes that in the autobiography, the narrator "creates the image of the ideal, industrious individual who, in accordance with Booker T. Washington's philosophy, lifts herself up by her own bootstraps." However, Plant continues, this representation of the narrator's struggle to achieve was "oversimplified"; Hurston's strategy was to emphasize her persona's "courage and tenacity" and to deemphasize the impact of "oppressive forces in the lives of African Americans."[38] This is the approach Hurston takes when, in *Tell My Horse*, she addresses the "oppressive forces" that the Haitians face. Plant describes Hurston as a "staunch individualist" who, like Washington, believed fervently in "personal industry, individual merit, and self-empowerment"; she was determined "to achieve self-reliance, self-definition, and self-direction, an autonomy conceived as nothing short of a mastery of self."[39] However, Plant also emphasizes the cost of this strategy, concluding that this orientation required "rationalization and reconciliation . . . with a history of oppression and dehumanization." Realizing that "the weight of an oppressive history" was "potentially self-defeating," Washington and Hurston created "an emotional distance from the past that would allow them an emotional and intellectual space in their present. Both believed that too much contemplation of the past was just so much time taken from present endeavors, thus their ahistorical stance and their willingness to 'settle for from now on.'"[40] This philosophy informs what Hurston criticizes and what she advocates in *Tell My Horse* and illuminates why she forecloses further discussion of abuses perpetrated by the American occupiers. Adopting a role that African Americans have claimed for themselves in the black Atlantic world, she admonishes the Haitians to focus on the major internal problems Haiti must confront and overcome.

"Politics and Personalities of Haiti" is a methodically organized, deliberately slanted argumentation. With the controlling thesis of "Whither Haiti?" Hurston presents the period after American occupation as an opportunity for Haitian rebirth—just as she presents the post-Reconstruction era in America as an opportunity for African American rebirth. Her approach, after the fact of the occupation, is to argue that there were some benefits for Haiti and then, to move the discussion forward to "where do we go from here." Hurston opens this section with the riveting chapter "Rebirth of a Nation," an affecting rationale for the American invasion. In fact, what Hurston dramatizes actually happened: the massacre, allegedly ordered by President

Guillaume Sam, of 167 political prisoners, many from elite families; the horrific murder, "in retribution," of Sam by an enraged mob. Silencing the less flattering (to the Americans) aspects of the story, Hurston represents the Marines as a force divinely guided to rescue the Haitian people from a succession of destructive leaders, thus providing Haitians with the peace for which they had "yearned" for 400 years: "The people were weary of the 'generals,' and their endless revolutions and counter-revolutions. Their greed and ambition were destroying the nation. They breathed a great prayer for Peace!"[41] The fact that the Americans had ulterior motives and already planned to invade Haiti for reasons of their own is not mentioned and, in the face of the horror she describes, seems almost beside the point. The depiction of the Americans as saviors, however, was a distortion of history, something Hurston must have known, given her interests in politics and her acquaintance with NAACP leaders. This chapter is also a vivid example of Hurston's efforts to negotiate between her identity as an American citizen and her very real concern for the Haitian people.

Speaking as an American, Hurston offers advice on what Haitians must do to develop a viable democracy. Observing that Haiti "is not now and never has been a democracy according to the American concept," she first focuses on the crippling patterns of class stratification as a major impediment to the country's development: "Haiti has always been two places. First it was the Haiti of the masters and slaves. Now it is Haiti of the wealthy and educated mulattoes and the Haiti of the blacks." She concludes that "Haitian class consciousness and the universal acceptance of the divine right of the crust of the upper crust is a direct denial of the concept of democracy" and repeatedly asserts that the extreme poverty and illiteracy of the poor had to be addressed before Haiti could become a true democracy, as it is much more "difficult to discover the will of the people in a nation where less than ten percent of the population can read and write."[42]

In comments that echo her critiques of African Americans, Hurston takes the Haitians to task for what she considers defeatist habits of mind, especially fatalism, living in the past, and "self-deception."[43] Significantly, in her discussion of Haiti's history, she strives for balance. On the one hand, she empathetically describes the particular challenges Haiti has faced since its founding and praises the commitment and pragmatism of leaders like "L'Ouverture, Christophe, Petion and Dessalines," who faced the challenge of "trying to make a government of the wreck of a colony" and a "nation out of slaves to whom the very word government sounded like something vague and distant." At the same time she insists that although "what happened in 1804 was all to Haiti's glory . . . this is another century and another age."[44] In her analysis, she consistently draws a sharp distinction between politicians and leaders, arguing passionately that throughout its history, Haiti's curse has been the politicians she describes colorfully as "demagogues," "rattlers-of-bones," "self-seekers," and "treasury-raiders" who prostitute Haiti's historical legacy for personal gain while failing to provide roads, schools, and services that would improve the lives of the Haitian people. She castigates them as "blood brothers to the empty bags who have done so much to nullify opportunity among the American Negroes." At the same time, she applauds the practical, honest, and earnest "class of new and thinking young Haitians who are on the side lines . . . becoming more and more world- and progress-conscious all the time." Hurston praises them as "realists" willing to confront and solve problems, willing to focus on what is best for Haiti rather than on personal gain, men (and they are all men) who minister to and care about the poorest of Haitian peasants: "They see that . . . public education, transportation and economics need more attention, much more than do the bones of Dessalines."[45]

In the last two chapters of "Politics and Personalities of Haiti," Hurston tells the stories of two past Haitian presidents—General François Antoine Simon, president of Haiti from 1908 to 1911, and Cincinnatus Leconte, president from 1911 to 1912. The stories are parables or cautionary tales: she presents Simon as a disastrous example of someone unqualified to be president who was put in office by those who saw him as a useful tool. On the other hand, Leconte who was widely praised for being progressive and committed to the welfare of the Haitian people—but who died tragically in an explosion—was proof that good governance is possible in Haiti. Hurston uses the stories to call on the Haitian people to take the responsibility that is required of citizens of a democracy, to demand more of their leaders and to hold them accountable. Her critiques, like those of other African Americans, are inflected by the sense that Haitians owe it not only to their own people but also to their African American supporters to govern wisely. African Americans did not see their support of Haitian independence as purely racial solidarity. From Du Bois and Johnson and the NAACP to Langston Hughes to Hurston, they expected the Haitians to share their vision of a progressive, democratic black republic. As a subjugated minority, many African Americans have long imagined a nation state where black people could be full citizens in a society free of the racism that haunted and hindered them in the United States. Their imagining of Haiti was often intertwined with what they needed Haiti to be. To some extent, African Americans had made Haiti the receptacle of their yearnings and aspirations. Haiti had succeeded in freeing itself. Surely it could also build a viable black democratic nation-state.

As an anthropologist who had lived among the Haitians for over a year, Hurston had an intimate knowledge of conditions on the ground in Haiti. She had examined the challenges Haitians faced and she was concerned about the future of the Haitian peasants with whom she had lived and worked. "Whither Haiti?" was thus more than academic for Hurston. Apprehensive about the dangers Haiti faced and the direction in which Haiti seemed to be going, she presents it as a country at the crossroads. She concludes her examination of the challenges Haiti faced by specifically addressing the threat posed to Haiti by Dominican President Trujillo. Hurston is troubled by the vulnerability of the Haitian people and conveys a sense of urgency and sorrow despite the understatement she uses when she describes the massacre of 20,000 Haitians in the Dominican Republic as "the recent border trouble."[46] Would a "few thousand Haitians" have been murdered if the Marines had still been in Haiti? Were the Marines the worst thing that could happen to the Haitians—or the lesser of evils? Was President Vincent more concerned with protecting his power than with protecting his people? Hurston ultimately addressed Haitian issues with the same pragmatism with which she addressed African American issues. At the same time, the contradictions in her ethnography are indicative of her negotiation of dual identities. There is no seamless ideology put forward. Ultimately, "Politics and Personalities of Haiti" reflects a yearning for Haiti to be a successful democratic black Atlantic nation-state.

NOTES

1. Deborah Plant, *Zora Neale Hurston: A Biography of the Spirit* (Westport: Praeger, 2007), 60.

2. Quoted in Valerie Boyd, *Wrapped in Rainbows: The Life of Zora Neale Hurston* (New York: Scribner, 2003), 174.

3. Paul Gilroy, *The Black Atlantic: Modernity and Double Consciousness* (Cambridge: Harvard University Press, 1993), 2.

4. Ibid., 4–6.

5. Ibid., 19.

6. Ibid., 195.

7. Ibid., 30.

8. Susan Stanford-Friedman, *Mappings: Feminism and the Cultural Geography of Encounter* (Princeton: Princeton University Press, 1998), n. 17, 269.

9. June Roberts, *Reading Erna Brodber: Uniting the Black Diaspora Through Folk Culture and Religion* (Westport: Praeger, 2006), 43.

10. Zora Neale Hurston, *Mules and Men* (1935; repr., New York: Harper and Row, 1990), 1.

11. Karen Jacobs, "From 'Spy-Glass' to 'Horizon': Tracking the Anthropological Gaze in Zora Neale Hurston," *Novel: A Forum on Fiction* 30, no. 3 (Spring 1997): 330.

12. Zora Neale Hurston, *Tell My Horse: Voodoo and Life in Haiti and Jamaica* (1938; repr., New York: Harper and Row, 1990), 58.

13. Joseph Murphy, *Working the Spirit: Ceremonies of the African Diaspora* (Boston: Beacon Press, 1994), 1.

14. Hurston, *Tell My Horse*, 131.

15. See especially Hans Schmidt, *The United States Occupation of Haiti, 1915–1934* (New Brunswick, Rutgers University Press, 1971), and Mary A. Renda, *Taking Haiti: Military Occupation and the Culture of U.S. Imperialism, 1915–1940* (Chapel Hill: University of North Carolina Press, 2001).

16. Brenda Gayle Plummer, "The Afro-American Response to the Occupation of Haiti, 1915–1934," in *Freedom's Odyssey: African American History Essays from Phylon*, ed. Alexa Benson Henderson and Janice Sumler-Edmond (Atlanta: Clark Atlanta University Press, 1999), 313.

17. Hazel Carby, "The Politics of Fiction, Anthropology, and the Folk: Zora Neale Hurston," in *Zora Neale Hurston's Their Eyes Were Watching God: A Casebook*, ed. Cheryl Wall (New York: Oxford University Press, 1990), 131.

18. J. Michael Dash, *Haiti and the United States: National Stereotypes and the Literary Imagination* (New York: St. Martin's Press, 1988), 59–60.

19. Annette Trefzer, "Possessing the Self: Caribbean Identities in Zora Neale Hurston's *Tell My Horse*," *African American Review* 34, no. 2 (2000), 308.

20. Ibid., 302.

21. See Leigh Anne Duck, "'Rebirth of a Nation': Hurston in Haiti," *Journal of American Folklore* 117.464 (2004), 127–146; Mary A. Renda, *Taking Haiti: Military Occupation and the Culture of U.S. Imperialism* (Chapel Hill: University of North Carolina Press, 2001).

22. Dash, *Haiti and the United States*, 48.

23. Quoted in Leon D. Pamphile, *Haitians and African Americans: A Heritage of Tragedy and Hope* (Gainesville: University Press of Florida, 2001), 8.

24. Quoted in Plummer, 315.

25. See Deborah Plant, *Every Tub Must Sit on Its Own Bottom: The Philosophy and Politics of Zora Neale Hurston* (Urbana: University of Illinois Press, 1995), 37–41.

26. Plummer, "The Afro-American Response," 314–316.

27. For example, General John B. Russell, for many years the most powerful administrator in the "treaty government" the United States had forced on Haiti, stated publicly that the mental age of the average Haitian was seven. Secretary of State Robert Lansing believed that, like Liberians and African Americans, Haitians had an "'inherent tendency to revert to savagery'" and lacked the capacity to govern themselves (Plummer 318). These racist beliefs led to abusive and exploitative policies and practices.

28. Plummer, "The Afro-American Response," 319.

29. See Schmidt, *The United States Occupation of Haiti*, 108–134.

30. Renda, 190. See Renda, 188–196, and Plummer, 319–322, for more detailed discussion of Johnson's activism. See also Pamphile, 102–128, for discussion of the critical role the NAACP played in African American agitation against the occupation of Haiti.

31. Quoted in Dash, *Haiti and the United States*, 50.

32. See Pamphile, *Haitians and African Americans*, 122–128. Pamphile comments that in negotiations with President Hoover, "the NAACP chose an uncompromising approach . . . focusing on Haiti's interests instead of [Haitian President] Vincent's

personal quest for power." Ultimately, the Vincent administration and the Roosevelt administration signed an executive agreement in 1933, thus bypassing both the U.S. Congress and almost certain rejection by the Haitian legislature. NAACP Secretary Walter White refused to accept the agreement, seeing it as a betrayal of the Haitian people's fifteen-year struggle for "full freedom" (127).

33. Dash, *Haiti and the United States*, 54.

34. Pamphile, *Haitians and African Americans*, 128.

35. Hurston, *Tell My Horse*, 65, 72.

36. Ibid., 74.

37. Plant, *Every Tub Must Sit on Its Own Bottom*, 9.

38. Ibid., 17.

39. Ibid., 33.

40. Ibid., 41.

41. Hurston, *Tell My Horse*, 68.

42. Ibid., 73–75.

43. Hurston explains that the Haitians have developed the habit of deceiving "themselves about actualities" and throwing "a gloss over facts" as a way "to save [their] own and the national pride" (82–83). Ironically, this also applies to her strategy of glossing over the facts of the American occupation, to save her national pride.

44. Hurston, *Tell My Horse*, 81, 80.

45. Ibid., 92, 80.

46. Ibid., 90.

Premonition: Peering through Time and into Hurricane Katrina

Dawood H. Sultan and Deanna J. Wathington

Sometime that night the winds came back. Everything in the world had a strong rattle, sharp and short . . . Louder and higher and lower and wider the sound and motion spread, mounting, sinking, darking [sic]. It woke up old Okechobee [sic] and the monster began to roll in his bed. Began to roll and complain like a peevish world on a grumble . . . The monstropolous beast had left his bed. The two hundred miles an hour wind had loosed his chains. He seized hold of his dikes and ran forward until he met the quarters; uprooted them like grass and rushed on after his supposed-to-be conquerors, rolling the dikes, rolling the houses, rolling the people in the houses along with other timbers. The sea was walking the earth with a heavy heel.[1]

INTRODUCTION

Author and anthropologist Zora Neale Hurston experienced what powerful tropical hurricanes could do to property, landscape, and people's lives while living in Florida, during the time she spent in the Caribbean, and well before she wrote her seminal work *Their Eyes Were Watching God*.[2] However, her vivid account of black society around Lake Okeechobee and a hurricane's devastating impact on people and landscape was grounded in information and facts she collected firsthand during a catastrophic hurricane that swept through Florida. As such, her documentation of both black social life, the marginalization of black people, and how such marginalization intensified the damage the hurricane caused among them could be generalized to contemporary black society with similar socioeconomic and sociospatial characteristics.

The argument we are making in this essay is that the collision of poverty and racial segregation which banished the black people in the narrative to a hazardous work and living place which they defined pejoratively as "the *muck*," has been an ever-present reality for poor black people in the United States. That is, contemporary landscapes occupied by poor black people are likely to be hazardous and are likely to pose significant mortality risks.[3] For instance, the ground occupied by the majority of poor black people in New Orleans when Hurricane Katrina battered and drowned the city and scores of its black inhabitants in August 2005 was a landscape marred by socioeconomic dynamics which made it structurally violent and life threatening.[4] It was symbolically and substantively identical to the *muck* which hemmed Lake Okeechobee in Hurston's narrative. Therefore, in a sense, a casual reading of *Their Eyes Were Watching God* should be enough to frighten black people who lived too close to a massive body of water on ground that would be heavily flooded if the dikes which protected it were ever breached during a hurricane.

THE *MUCK*: A 20TH-CENTURY BLACK *LIFEWORLD* AND DISASTER LANDSCAPE

The segregation of black "*folks*" in "quarters that squatted so close that only the dyke separated them from great, sprawling Okechobee [sic]"[5] from white "*people*" in "the big houses further around the shore"[6] meant that the communicative relationships which existed between the two groups were primarily over work in the *muck*. Yet, through these formal relationships or other more complex forms of social interaction, the subjective feelings and thoughts of collective ontological security expressed by whites before the arrival of the hurricane reached blacks and were accepted by the majority of them as valid.

It is reasonable to assume that in this highly segregated and economically stratified world, this apparent deference to whites' "thinking" or feelings[7] about an impending natural disaster is a signal of white group monopoly over the subjective meanings of some of the technical elements of the social structure in the *muck* (specifically, the strength of the seawalls) and their capacity to communicate these meanings to black people. Indeed, a considerable volume of sociological research has often indicated that in societies marked by extreme socioeconomic inequality, the social relations ideologies and symbolic meanings created by dominant social groups were often effectively communicated to minority communities for the general purpose of maintaining the social order. Therefore, it stands to reason that forewarnings about a strong potential for dike failure and imminent danger were not socioeconomically instrumental or productive for a group that collectively depended on the services rendered by the poor blacks who inhabited the hazardous landscape. A presentation of seawalls as indestructible and an outward expression of feelings of safety by whites were essential to avert a black public panic that had the potential for destabilizing economic production and the social order. However, deference to white "thinking" about the hurricane threat and apparent acceptance of ideas about the effectiveness of the seawalls "to chain the senseless monster in his bed"[8] does not necessarily serve as an indication of an interracial exhaustive commonality of subjective definitions of situations or that of a potential for consensual coordination between blacks and whites in the event of hurricane-caused disaster. Certain elements of the narrative point to the evolution of a separate black world in the *muck* and an oppressive exclusion of blacks from white society even at moments when such exclusion threatened their lives.

The black folks in Hurston's narrative constructed the equivalent of what Jurgen Habermas called *"lifeworld"* and *"public sphere"* and what sociologists now refer to as identity construction sites:[9] transcendental social sites at Tea Cake's and Janie's house and in the quarters. There, they reduced their productive and living space to a poignant symbolic sobriquet, the *muck*, reflecting a keen collective sense of a harsh existence. Also there, black ethnic identity and interpersonal relationships were negotiated and defined, the symbolic meanings of a range of life events were collectively generated and any subjective claims that were made were assiduously contested. It is also there where peaceful and frequently rowdy and not-so-peaceful dialogues and "big arguments"[10] were normative. And, though not directly addressed throughout the narrative, those who gathered around at these sites were very poor, economically exploited, and without immediately accessible health care. It is likely that they discussed some of the social injustices and oppression that marked their social life in the *muck* and elsewhere. Hence, their deference to whites' "thinking" appears partial and restricted only to the technical aspects of an outer-reality which blacks did not directly manage. Furthermore, the fact that blacks in the narrative could not find space to occupy on the bridge at Six Mile Bend during the hurricane because "White people had preempted that point of elevation and there was no more room"[11] ruled out any notion of consensual cooperation, a condition which becomes highly instrumental during a catastrophe. In sum, when the hurricane arrived at Lake Okeechobee, the blacks and whites in the vicinity inhabited substantively separate and mutually exclusive *lifeworlds* that were marked by economic inequality and differential political power. Current public health research shows that the relative poverty of black people, their lack of access to health care, their social distance from white society and a general reticence against and mistrust of medicine which they have historically displayed are some of the major causes of their lower health status profile. These factors are also some of the major determinants of an observed contemporary tendency among black people to present themselves at clinical or other health care settings with illnesses at advanced stages of diagnosis, illnesses that should have been diagnosed and treated had the patients presented themselves to health caretakers much earlier. Delaying or altogether foregoing medical treatment are sick role behaviors which are typically conditioned by social distance from and mistrust of institutional medicine, relative poverty, and the fatalism which is typically associated with poverty and lack of education.[12] Hence, Tea Cake's attitudes and behaviors toward injuries he sustained during fights with gamblers or when he was attacked by a dog and, later, toward the symptoms of rabies were not uncommon in the *muck* and bear a remarkable resemblance to the contemporary attitudes and sick role behaviors of the majority of poor black people in the United States.

Finally, the hurricane in Hurston's narrative claimed the lives of both whites and blacks.[13] Yet, mass death did not seem to undermine the power of existing social structures and race-based power relations which dictated a fierce structural separation of blacks and whites and enforced the servitude of blacks to white society. The black folks in Hurston's narrative were made against their will to recover dead and decomposing bodies from land and flood waters polluted by washedaway debris, organic matter, and the chemical fertilizer and pesticides which were in heavy use then. And, against their thinking about death and the afterlife, they were forced to racially separate the burial rites of those who were killed by the hurricane. Even in death, local authorities saw to it that dead blacks were not allowed final symbolic entitlements: burial alongside the whites they knew or burial in a wooden coffin. Hence, as it stands in Hurston's narrative, the *muck* was a landscape of hard existence, oppressive structural separation from white society, powerlessness, relative poverty, and exposure to environmental hazard. It is eerily similar to the landscape inhabited by black people in New Orleans when the city was battered and catastrophically drowned by Hurricane Katrina on August 29, 2005.

BLACK NEW ORLEANS: A 21ST-CENTURY *MUCK*

In the last week of August 2005, the entirety of Hurston's vivid account of how artificial barriers that protected the habitat of poor black people were breached by a massive lake that was aroused by strong hurricane wind recurred in New Orleans. The city was severely battered by Hurricane Katrina and catastrophically drowned when the waters of Lake Pontchartrain breached seawalls and dikes.[14] The majority of the hurricane's damage was concentrated in black neighborhoods where houses and other structures were totally destroyed. The majority of those who perished were poor black people. To understand the reasons for the disproportionate destruction of the New Orleanian black *lifeworld*, one has to examine the socioeconomic and sociospatial status of the city's black population.

In New Orleans, decades of economic inequality relegated the majority of the city's black population to low socioeconomic status, low-paying jobs, widespread extreme poverty, and little access to health care and other entitlements which come with citizenship in a postindustrial and developed society (such as personal and community security, workplace safety, literacy, clean living environment). By some calculations, on any given year between 2000 and 2005, close to half of the city's working-age black adults were unemployed and more than two-thirds of the city's black population lived in households with annual incomes below the poverty threshold.[15] The overwhelming majority of the city's black population resided in almost entirely black neighborhoods, all of which were located on flood-prone terrain protected by artificial earthen levees and concrete seawalls. Blacks and whites in the city were structurally separated and ran significantly different levels of risk of exposure to flood-related disaster. When Hurricane Katrina battered and drowned the city, it exposed this separation and the fundamental weakness of the socioeconomic and sociospatial attributes of the city's black *lifeworld*. Furthermore, not only did Hurricane Katrina expose the city's soft socioeconomic underbelly, but also a civil society in which poor black people were routinely stigmatized and in which public institutions were quick to brutally enforce the spatial separation of whites from poor blacks even at a time when this separation threatened the lives of black people. Three days after the city was flooded, St. Bernard Parish police officers prevented a group composed largely of poor black people from crossing the bridge over the Mississippi River to safety. Crossing the bridge would have brought them to a dry and a predominantly white neighborhood.[16] So, it stands to reason that in 2005, the socioeconomic conditions of black people in New Orleans, their collective image in the minds of civic authorities, and their distance from the main structures of white society differed very little from the conditions which characterized the *muck* in Hurston's narrative.

In communities where ethnic minorities wield a disproportionately heavy demographic weight, poverty and low socioeconomic status often produce powerful negative public health outcomes which can be seen in a variety of measures. Collectively, the black folks in Hurston's *muck* were "tired looking" and "broken" by poverty and lack of education.[17] The New Orleanian blacks who suffered the ravages of

Hurricane Katrina exhibited similar physical and educational attributes. Their educational profile was very low and reflected the devastating impact of concentrated poverty.[18] Their access to health care was very limited and whatever care they received was largely inadequate. They appeared as perpetually tired and broken as those in Hurston's *muck*. It is no surprise to note that before the arrival of the hurricane in the city, almost one-third of the black residents who were segregated in the poorest neighborhoods reported some form of disability. The disability index for this population was twice as high as the national average and significantly higher than the average for the whole city, and by some accounts was a major cause for the inability of many people to evacuate flood-affected neighborhoods during the hurricane. Collective and individual ontological security is often undermined by particular behavioral predispositions directly linked to poverty and lack of education. In New Orleans, fatalism, a behavioral predisposition typically associated with lack of education and poverty, led many poor black residents to ignore official calls to leave the city before the arrival of Hurricane Katrina. The effect of the fatalistic tendencies of the poor New Orleanian blacks (also seen among some of the black folks in Hurston's *muck* during the hurricane) was further exacerbated by a long history of unnecessary hurricane evacuations and a widespread lack of any means of rapid mobility. In 2005, an estimated one-third of the residents of New Orleans failed to evacuate because they had no means of transport.[19] Undoubtedly, the majority of them were poor black people. So, just as it was in the *muck* when Lake Okeechobee breached the dikes, the black people of New Orleans who were drowned by Lake Pontchartrain were either too poor to have the necessary transport to evacuate or were of a behavioral temperament made recalcitrant by fatalism. And just as it was in the *muck* during the hurricane, many of those who survived Hurricane Katrina came in contact with flood waters polluted by organic matter and synthetic chemicals. The fact that the official reports published in the days following the drowning of New Orleans have suggested that the levels of pollutants in the flood waters were not an immediate health hazard did not bring comfort to observers of the city's post-hurricane environmental state.[20] The landscape inhabited by black people in New Orleans and the waters of southern Louisiana have long been considered polluted.[21] Only time will reveal the health damage sustained by those who were exposed to the waters that inundated the New Orleanian black *lifeworld*.

Finally, though homicide was not a part of the behavioral complex in the *muck*, there were sufficient indications of spousal physical abuse and rampant interpersonal fighting to suggest that the *muck* was a volatile place. In comparative terms, the segregated black *lifeworld* of New Orleans was no different from Hurston's *muck*. By all local and national official accounts, violence, which is now considered a public health problem,[22] was a common characteristic of New Orleans' poor neighborhoods. From 2002 and up to the arrival of Hurricane Katrina, the annual murder rate in the city was nearly eight times the national average and the per capita homicide rate, at 59 per 100,000 residents, was the highest in the United States.[23]

CONCLUDING REMARKS

The concentration of black people in New Orleans in landscape long known to be susceptible to massive flooding, their inability to move their communities to higher and safer ground, and the catastrophic drowning of these communities by Hurricane Katrina in 2005 were not accidental. These were direct outcomes of a long history of apartheid-like racial segregation, mass poverty and relative socioeconomic deprivation.[24] The same socioeconomic, political, and historical factors which determined individual and collective health status, safety, and general well-being of New Orleans' poor blacks before the arrival of Hurricane Katrina in the city were the ones which afflicted the black folks in Hurston's *muck*. Poverty, powerlessness, and Jim Crow laws segregated Hurston's black community into dilapidated quarters located too close to a massive lake that was reined in only by artificial barriers. Ultimately, an untold number of them perished when a powerful hurricane caused the lake waters to breach the barriers and flood the surrounding terrain. The *lifeworld* of black folks in Hurston's hurricane narrative is separated from the *lifeworld* of black people in New Orleans during Hurricane Katrina by about 70 years. But, the eerie similarity of the impact of both hurricanes on black people and the similarity of their socioeconomic and sociospatial conditions place Hurston's work at a prominent place in contemporary dialogues over the future of very poor black people in the United States. Hurston's 20th-century *muck* and the *lifeworld* of poor black New Orleanians in the 21st century shared structural and behavioral commonalities which readily allow any cursory reading of *Their Eyes Were Watching God* to reach the conclusion that she wrote a narrative which successfully identified a host of structural, socioeconomic, and behavioral variables with strong predictive qualities as they relate to contemporary poor black communities in the United States.

NOTES

1. Zora Neale Hurston, *Their Eyes Were Watching God* (1937; repr., Urbana: University of Illinois Press, 1991), 189, 193.

2. John Lowe, *Jump at the Sun: Zora Neale Hurston's Cosmic Comedy* (Urbana: University of Illinois Press, 1994), 202–203.

3. Alan Berube and Bruce Katz, *Katrina's Window: Confronting Concentrated Poverty Across America*, The Brookings Institution Metropolitan Policy Program (Washington, D.C.: Brookings Institution, 2005); Robert D. Bullard, "Ecological Inequalities and the New South: Black Communities Under Siege," *Journal of Ethnic Studies*, 17 (Winter 1990): 101–115; Institute of Medicine, *Towards Environmental Justice* (Washington, D.C.: National Academy Press, 1999).

4. The concept of "structural violence" which refers to structural socioeconomic and sociopolitical conditions responsible for causing negative impacts on poor people and communities was developed by Paul Farmer in *Pathologies of Power: Health, Human Rights, and the New War on the Poor* (Berkeley and Los Angeles: University of California Press, 2005).

5. Hurston, *Their Eyes*, 157.

6. Ibid., 189.

7. Ibid.

8. Ibid.

9. Jurgen Habermas, *The Theory of Communicative Action. Vol. 2: Lifeworld and System: A Critique of Functionalist Reason*. Thomas McCarthy (trans.) (Boston, MA: Beacon Press, 1987); Jurgen Habermas, *The Structural Transformation of the Public Sphere: An Inquiry Into a Category of Bourgeois Society*. Thomas Burger with the assistance of Frederick Lawrence (trans.) (Cambridge: MIT Press, 1991); Stephen Cornell and Douglas Hartmann, *Ethnicity and Race: Making Identities in a Changing World*, 2nd ed. (Thousand Oaks, CA: Sage Publications, 2006).

10. Hurston, *Their Eyes*, 162.

11. Ibid., 196.

12. Institute of Medicine, *Unequal Treatment: Confronting Racial and Ethnic Disparities in Healthcare* (Washington, D.C.: National Academy Press, 2003); Thomas A. LaVeist, "Beyond Dummy Variables and Sample Selection: What Health Services Researchers Ought to Know about Race as a Variable," *Health Services Research*, Vol. 29, No. 1 (1994): 1–16.

13. Hurston, *Their Eyes*, 204–205.

14. Douglas Brinkley, *The Great Deluge: Hurricane Katrina, New Orleans, and the Mississippi Gulf Coast* (New York: HarperCollins Publishers, 2006).

15. Berube and Katz, *Katrina's Window*, 2005; Thomas J. Durant and Dawood Sultan, "The Impact of Hurricane Katrina on the Race and Class Divide in America," in *Seeking Higher Ground: The Hurricane Katrina Crisis, Race and Public Policy Reader*, ed. Manning Marable and Kristen Clarke (New York: Palgrave Macmillan Ltd., 2008), 191–201.

16. Gardiner Harris, "Police in Suburbs Blocked Evacuees, Witnesses Report," The *New York Times*, September 10, 2005, 13.

17. Hurston, *Their Eyes*, 159.

18. Durant and Sultan, "The Impact of Hurricane Katrina," 2008.

19. Ivor Van Heerden and Mike Bryan, *The Storm: What Went Wrong and Why During Hurricane Katrina—The Inside Story from One Louisiana Scientist* (New York: Viking, 2006), 49.

20. John Manuel, "In Katrina's Wake," *Environmental Health Perspectives*. Vol. 114, No. 1 (2006): A32–A39.

21. Bullard, "Ecological Inequalities and the New South," 1990.

22. Thomas J. Durant, "Violence as a Public Health Problem: Toward an Integrated Paradigm," *Sociological Spectrum*, Vol. 19, No. 3 (1999): 267–280.

23. Nicole Gelinas, "Who's Killing New Orleans?: It's Hard to Worry about Racism and Poverty after You've Been Murdered," *City Journal*, Vol. 15, No. 4 (2005), available at http://www.city-journal.org/html/issue_15_4.html.

24. Berube and Katz, *Katrina's Window*, 2005; Durant and Sultan, "The Impact of Hurricane Katrina," 2008; Douglas S. Massey and Nancy A. Denton, *American Apartheid: Segregation and the Making of the Underclass* (Cambridge: Harvard University Press, 1993).

The Legacy of Zora Neale Hurston in the 21st Century

"That Man in the Gutter Is the God-Maker": Zora Neale Hurston's Philosophy of Culture

Catherine A. John

> That man in the gutter is the god-maker, the creator of everything that lasts.[1]
>
> —Zora Neale Hurston

As Spike Lee's 1986 film *She's Gotta Have It* opens, the first two paragraphs of Zora Neale Hurston's novel *Their Eyes Were Watching God* roll across the screen.[2] The text is offset by a quiet piano solo composed by Spike's father, Bill Lee. The feature was an instant success, one that launched Lee's career with a bang. Being both proverbial and poetic, the opening of Hurston's novel functioned, for viewers of the film who were familiar with Hurston's work, as an ideal backdrop for the heroine—sexually liberated Nola Darling. This novel, Hurston's second and most celebrated, fused the proverbial folk language and the mores of her people into a story about black love. While much has been written about Hurston as both a writer of fiction and a collector of folklore, and while her current influence spreads far and wide as evidenced both by Lee's use of text from the novel *Their Eyes Were Watching God* and Oprah Winfrey's production of the film—little has been said about Hurston's philosophy of culture as it is expressed and espoused in her short essays and articles in particular.

Consistently rooting her research and analyses within the context of "low down folk" practices, Hurston spent February of 1928 collecting work songs in lumber camps in the Florida Everglades.[3] From there, she moved on to rural Alabama where she studied local speech patterns and collected stories, and then she traveled to New Orleans where she conducted research on hoodoo that was partially published in her collection *Mules and Men*.[4] By the time she traveled to Haiti in 1936, she was 45 years old. Having freshly arrived from her research among the Maroons in Jamaica, Hurston wrote *Their Eyes Were Watching God* over a seven-week period from an apartment in Port-au-Prince and then immediately began her passionate and near-fatal love affair with the ancient Haitian religion, Vodou, which she described as "the old, old mysticism of the world in African terms . . . a religion of creation and life."[5]

Her research throughout the black South as well as in Jamaica, Haiti, and, later, Honduras profoundly informed her deep comprehension of African diaspora culture. Written primarily between 1928 and 1955, Hurston's essays and short articles espouse a cultural philosophy that is a product of both the syncretic worldview and the lived experience of the descendants of formerly enslaved Africans in the Americas. This is a worldview in which the political, the spiritual, and the cultural are all intertwined portions of a philosophical whole. This abstract description of Hurston's theory is expressed more succinctly in folk parlance when Hurston states, "[T]hat man in the gutter is the god-maker, the creator of everything that lasts."[6] Hurston makes this statement sometime after having collected lore in rural towns and investigating hoodoo in New Orleans. Her subsequent trips to Jamaica and Haiti further solidified these beliefs. The gutter metaphor is at once political in the sense that it privileges the class of people lowest down, economically, in the capitalist economy. The "god-maker" reference suggests that there is a spiritual root to the creative power that influences cultural production. Additionally, Hurston's use of folk parlance is significant because it situates the system of making sense or meaning out of these ideas within, rather than outside, the philosophical worldview of the people being referenced.

The privileging of the folk in an era when the black bourgeoisie was struggling to differentiate itself should also be interpreted as an inherently progressive move politically. Additionally, Hurston's analyses of the culture of "the man in the gutter" reveal it to be implicitly spiritual, which in this context means—rejuvenating and enabling. This is a central rather than peripheral characteristic of the culture. The work songs, spirituals, and folklore that Hurston collects *are not*, in and of themselves, the culture, but rather products of the culture. The culture itself appears to be *the ability* to create and recreate something that is life sustaining and that moves the spirit. Within this context, an analysis of several of Hurston's essays seems apropos. While her essays, "Spirituals and Neo-Spirituals," and "The Sanctified Church" emphasize the "god-maker" quality implicit in the culture, her essay "Art and Such" as well as her well-publicized literary disagreement with

Richard Wright demonstrate that her views about the black artist's role and his or her relationship to the cultural matrix on one hand and the larger society on the other, was deeply insightful although understudied. On the other hand, essays such as "The Pet Negro System," "My Most Humiliating Jim Crow Experience," and "High John de Conquer" fuse scathing and ironic political critique with the spiritual ethos that characterizes the culture as a whole.

In her 1934 essay, "Spirituals and Neo-Spirituals," Hurston begins with this statement: "The real spirituals are not really just songs. They are unceasing variations around a theme . . . These songs, even the printed ones, do not remain long in their original form. Every congregation that takes it up alters it considerably."[7] Hurston's initial emphasis on the variation within the form of the classic spiritual places the focus on the *process* of creating the spiritual rather than on the finished product. The ability to create is what is really being emphasized and this is further demonstrated by her definition of what characterized the early spirituals. In defining them, she states, "The nearest thing to a description one can reach is that they are Negro religious songs, sung by a group and a group bent on expression of feelings and not on sound effects." Her definition, at its core, states that the tradition of the spirituals is most characterized by a group focused on expressing certain feelings rather than on things like pitch, melody, and unison. "The real Negro singer cares nothing about pitch." To emphasize this, she observes that "the jagged harmony is what makes it, and it ceases to be what it was when this is absent . . . The congregation is bound by no rules. No two times singing is alike, so that we must consider the rendition of a song not as a final thing, but as a mood."[8]

She goes on to make a distinction between the spiritual and the neo-spiritual which she describes as fixed versions of the original songs arranged by trained musicians and sung by glee clubs and concert singers. Seeing formal training as ruining rather than enhancing the real spiritual, Hurston states, "Its truth dies under training like flowers under hot water." This rather humorous analogy directs the student of her theories back to the spirit at play in the creation of the music as the primary defining characteristic. Training kills the raw impulse which for Hurston is the source of the creativity. She states, "European singing is considered good when each syllable floats out on a column of air, seeming not to have any mechanics at all."[9] By contrast, the de-emphasizing of the characteristics that usually characterize "good singing" in the Western sense, in favor of something that privileges "mood" and the expression of feeling situates the spirituals within the "god-maker" context, becoming something whose primary goal is to affect or touch the spirits of both the performer and the listener. So, functional—rather than primarily aesthetic—art forms characterize Africana culture. In this context, the emphasis is not placed on the finished "product" or "object" but rather the ability to both communicate an emotion and affect the feelings of the participant/observer. This issue, while being subtle, may have certain larger implications. In Western aesthetics, the overwhelming focus on cultural objects has by and large guided much of the study of indigenous cultures. The language and linguistic patterns, as well as stories, dances, and rituals retained by a group, are usually viewed as the primary evidence of that group's cultural authenticity. Hurston's analysis here suggests that the mode of creation and the ability to create certain things is more important than the artifact, because it is the mode that makes the artifact possible.

In "The Sanctified Church," Hurston further develops and extends the conceptual terrain established in "Spirituals and Neo-Spirituals." She makes a distinction between the Sanctified church and what are typically called Holy Rollers, whether of the black or white variety. She identifies the Church of God in Christ and the Saints of God in Christ as the two branches of the Sanctified church and argues ostensibly that the style of the service as well as the approach to worship suggest significant retention of indigenous African spirituality, re-shaped and revised into a New World format. She informs us that "the Negro has not been Christianized as extensively as is generally believed. The great masses are still standing before their pagan altars and calling old gods by a new name. As evidence of this, note the drum-like rhythm of *all* Negro spirituals."[10] Celebrating rather than critiquing what she sees as the "pagan" aspects of black religion, the hallmark of Christianity for Hurston is not so much the privileging of Christ as it is the culture surrounding how the worship is enacted. Hurston's observations here crystallize something that has been understudied generally although long suggested by scholars of the religious practices of New World Africans—and that is the significant extent to which there has been an Africanization of Christianity rather than a wholesale Christianizing of Africans.[11]

A careful study of this dynamic would help to account for the significant historical difference between the religion of the slave master and that of the slave, even when both were theoretically Christians. It has been a long-established fact among scholars of Haitian Vodou, Cuban Santeria, and Brazilian Candomblé that Catholicism has functioned as a vessel for the practice of West African religions in Christian-face.[12] As Valerie Boyd notes in her biography of Hurston, "She [had] attended numerous ceremonies in which *hougans* (voodoo priests) invoked Jesus, Mary, Joseph, and a long list of Christian saints right alongside the *loa* (divinities) of the voodoo pantheon."[13] In addition to the rhythm of the spirituals in Sanctified churches, Hurston refers to the practice of "bearing up" which is a call-and-response exchange between the minister and the congregation. While the bearing up is apparently spontaneous and random to an outsider, Hurston argues that the congregation is well aware of prescribed forms and formats. She also refers to the practice of "shouting"—spontaneous expressions of emotion that erupt during the service—which she describes as "nothing more than a continuation of the African 'Possession' by the gods."[14] Describing the whole Sanctified church movement as primarily a "rebirth in song-making" and a "new era of spiritual-making" Hurston ostensibly links the essence of the Sanctified church back to the spirituals and the fluid process by which they are made. The ability to evoke strong emotion in the participant/observer, even to the point where he or she becomes "possessed" is not only the main point of the experience but it also functions as a cathartic. The "song-making" and "spiritual-making," the tools used in the process, are ultimately the products of the culture that are consumed by the society at large.

At the end of the essay, Hurston states, "There is great respect for the white man as a law-giver, banker, builder and the like, but the folk Negro does not crave his religion at all. They are not angry about it, they merely pity him because it is generally held that he just can't do any better that way . . . they go on making their songs and music and dance motions to go along with it, and shooting new life into American music." Hurston's observations here are two-fold. She essentially notes that despite segregation and gross inequality, the dominant society's spiritual *ethos* was never a source of envy or jealousy for the black masses. Furthermore, the implicitly African spirituality informing black American religion infused itself into the music, dance, and cultural expression of the Sanctified church.[15] The suggestion here is also that while the Sanctified churches may have retained the largest amount of continental African cultural practices, other black churches in varying degrees were also repositories for some of these practices and modes of expression.

The sacred sensibility that Hurston describes in the Sanctified church is manifest in contemporary and secular modes of expression. David LaChappelle's 2005 documentary *RIZE* is one example.[16] The film examines the dance phenomenon known as "Krumping" that was created by youth in abandoned sections of South Central Los Angeles in the decades following the Rodney King riots. "Clowning," from which "Krumping" develops, was invented by Tommy the Clown, a resident of South Central who originated the idea of a hip-hop-style dancing clown who entertains young kids at birthday parties and celebrations in the 'hood. Surveying the absence of social outlets for local youth beyond sports and gangs, Tommy created a movement of sorts with Clowning. Over 50 clown groups developed, and as the documentary shows, not only did they function as a source of enjoyment and activity, but they became an alternative to joining gangs as well as a positive outlet for the frustration and tension experienced by these youth in everyday life. As one participant states, "It's like getting out your anger but on the dance floor." In the Sanctified church, song-making and dancing are the rituals that lead to possession, which functions as collective release, for both the individual and the congregation, from the stresses of everyday life. Hurston states, "The gods possess the body of the worshipper and he or she is supposed to know nothing of their actions until the god decamps. This is still prevalent in most Negro protestant churches and is universal in the Sanctified churches."[17] In the documentary *RIZE*, the dancing is so frenetic that the director LaChappelle puts a disclaimer at the opening of the film stating that the footage has not been speeded up in any way, shape, or form.[18] While Clowning functions as both entertainment and release, Krumping seems to be more of a ritualized activity solely used for the cathartic release from the stresses of everyday life. As one of the participants says of the activity, "there is a spirit in the midst of krumpness," and as one of the young women states, "you can't just do it; you have to have love for it."[19] The pace and intensity of Krumping is so frantic that it suggests a kind of spiritual possession; and while both groups compete against each other in what is called "The Battle Zone," the Krumpers describe their activity as spiritual. In one particularly striking instance in the documentary, a young Krumper named Daisy goes into a trance in the middle of a Krumping session. As the documentary crew perplexedly inquires what has happened, Baby Tight Eyez, one of the younger Krumpers, says, "She's been struck. That's what we've all been waiting on." Daisy, whose eyes were the eyes of one in a trance, is lifted up and taken away by some of the male Krumpers. The scene that immediately follows is one with Baby Tight Eyez in church sitting at the piano surrounded by his adopted church parents. He is telling the director that while he is dancing to the beat of the music being played as he Krumps, he thinks of the words to a song his grandfather taught him, "Lord Lift Me Up and Let Me Stand," and uses it as inspiration while he dances.[20] What we see in "Krumping" is arguably a secular manifestation of the Sanctified church as described by Hurston. Music and dance are the tools used to reach the place of cathartic release, sometimes bordering on actual trance-like possession. The film reveals that a good portion of the Krumpers and Clowns have parents who were incarcerated for drug addiction. One Krumper's father committed suicide and another was shot by his own grandfather. In the midst of all this tragedy, these youths recreate their own extended family structures, finding a way to "work the good out of evil" and make "a way out of no way." The products of the culture in this instance are new dance styles now known as "Krumping" and "Clowning" which are being consumed and adopted within American popular culture.

In her 1938 essay, "Art and Such," Hurston makes plain her position on the role of the artist in relation to the culture. Twelve years earlier, the role of the black artist was contended in a series of well-publicized essays, all written by black men. George Schuyler in his essay, "The Negro Art Hokum," argues that there is really no such thing as African American art. He states, "the literature, painting, and sculpture of Aframericans—such as there is—is identical in kind with the literature, painting and sculpture of white Americans: that is they show more or less evidence of European influence."[21] The folk culture that Hurston sees as the source, Schuyler argues, is real but is specific to a marginalized peasant caste that can hardly be seen as representative of the black population as a whole.

In his response to Schuyler in the essay, "The Negro Artist and the Racial Mountain," Langston Hughes raises questions about the psychological freedom shaping the choices of the black artist. Describing a theoretical "Negro poet," Langston tells us that he—this theoretical poet—comes from a "Negro middle class environment" in which "the mother often says, 'Don't be like niggers' when the children are bad . . . [and] a frequent phrase from the father is 'Look how well a white man does things.' And so the word white comes to be unconsciously a symbol of all the virtues. It holds for the children beauty, morality, and money. The whisper of 'I want to be white' runs silently through their minds." Arguing that under these conditions, the choice to be a European artist culturally, as Schuyler suggests, is frequently a function of racial shame rather than true artistic freedom; Hughes states, "this [is] the mountain standing in the way of any true Negro art in America—this urge within the race towards whiteness, the desire to pour racial individuality into the mold of American standardization, and to be as little Negro and as much American as possible."[22]

W.E.B. Du Bois's "Criteria of Negro Art," published six months after Hughes's and Schuyler's essays, sees the role of black art as promoting a form of propaganda that will humanize the race in the eyes of whites. Yet unlike Schuyler, Du Bois believes that there is a difference between the kind of art that comes out of black culture and the kind of art produced in mainstream America. He resonates with a Hughes-ian politic when he states, "We can afford Truth. White folk today cannot. As it is now we are handing everything over to a white jury. If a colored man wants to publish a book he has to get a white publisher and a white newspaper to say it is great; and then you and I say so. We must come to a place where the work of art when it appears is reviewed and acclaimed by our own free and unfettered judgment."[23]

Challenging both the black audience and artist to liberate their collective psyche when judging black art, Du Bois unwittingly exposes the terms on which much of Hurston's writing was misjudged by many of her contemporaries. Chief among them was Richard Wright, whose

"Blueprint for Negro Writing" was published a year before Hurston's "Art and Such," and privileged a Marxist approach to the production of black art, suggesting that the primary goal of the black writer should be to expose and fight against social injustice.[24] In "Art and Such," Hurston categorically refuses Wright's and Du Bois's notions that the primary purpose of black art should be social justice propaganda. Yet, while she feels that the black artist should be free to write about things other than race and oppression, she at the same time holds a staunch conviction about the integrity and self-sufficiency of "the-man-in-the-gutter-godmaker-culture." Hurston writes of the black artist who limits him- or herself to representing race and oppression, not because of issues of inferiority, as Hughes suggests, but rather because of the imposition of cultural expectations and societal limitations. So while Hughes's "Negro poet" has no desire (due to shame) to use the forms and contents of his culture as a source of inspiration, Hurston's "Negro poet" believes that no white publisher will print poems that fall outside "the AMERICAN MUSEUM OF UNNATURAL HISTORY . . . [where] it is assumed that all non-Anglo-Saxons are uncomplicated stereotypes."[25] Describing this poet, Hurston states:

Can the black poet sing a song to the morning? Up springs the song to his lips but it is fought back. He says to himself, "Ah this is a beautiful song inside me. I feel the morning star in my throat. I will sing of the star and the morning." Then his background thrusts itself between his lips and the star and he mutters, 'Ought I not to be singing of our sorrows? That is what is expected of me and I shall be considered forgetful of our past and present. If I do not some will even call me a coward. The one subject for a Negro is the race and its sufferings and so the song of morning must be choked back. I will write of a lynching instead.[26]

For Hurston in the quotation above, the black poet's sole focus on oppression highlights the group's victimization at the expense of more nuanced and varied forms of expression. But her alternative to this is not to see "black" or "Negro" as negative and limiting and thus something to be escaped, but rather to see it as positive and limit-less. Such an artist would be proud of the uniqueness of the culture and should be capable of responding to filmmaker Julie Dash's questions, "Where is our *Lord of the Rings* trilogy? Where is our [*Chronicles of*] *Narnia*?"[27] In some sense, it is hard in the contemporary moment to understand how radical Hurston's refusal to write primarily about racial oppression was then. Ultimately she believed that much of black art in that era had been reactive instead of original and had been pigeon-holed into focusing on the sorrows of "the Negro problem" rather than the vitality of the culture. Her legacy has been confusing to some because she both refused to be reduced to focusing on race *and* because she passionately loved her people and their uniqueness.

There is no name or category in academic parlance for the position that Hurston represents. She actively criticized stereotypical portraits of blacks and resisted these depictions in her work. But those who presumed that any representation of the folk laughing or doing wrong was a stereotype, apparently did not understand the culture of the "man in the gutter" enough to tell the difference. Nowhere are these contradictions more apparent than in her well-publicized critical disagreements with Richard Wright. While Wright's disagreement with Hurston was the most notorious, his views were a crystallization of the sentiments expressed by several prominent black male writers who had also, at various points, accused Hurston's work of trafficking in stereotypes. As Carla Kaplan notes in her introduction to *Hurston: A Life in Letters*, Wright's critique of *Their Eyes Were Watching God* accused it of "pandering 'to a white audience' by exploiting 'the phase of Negro life which is "quaint," the phase which evokes a piteous smile on the lips of the "superior" race.' Her writing, he declared, has 'no theme, no message, no thought.'"[28] Commenting on other sections from Wright's review of *Their Eyes*, Hurston biographer Valerie Boyd notes that although Wright admitted that Hurston was skilled as a writer, he saw her as perpetuating a minstrel image of black folk for the benefit of white readers. He states, "Her characters eat and laugh and cry and work and kill; they swing like a pendulum eternally in that safe and narrow orbit in which America likes to see the Negro live: between laughter and tears." When *Moses, Man of the Mountain* was published in 1939, it received rave reviews from the *New York Times*, the *Saturday Review of Literature,* and the *New York Herald Tribune,* but Harlem Renaissance scholar Alain Locke described it as "caricature instead of portraiture," and Ralph Ellison stated that "For Negro fiction . . . it did nothing."[29]

Hurston's 1938 review of Richard Wright's *Uncle Tom's Children* incisively cuts back, carving and exposing the issues at stake in her own way. She states:

This is a book about hatreds. Mr. Wright serves notice by his title that he speaks of people in revolt, and his stories are so grim that the Dismal Swamp of race hatred must be where they live. Not one act of understanding and sympathy comes to pass in the entire work . . . Since the author himself is a Negro, his dialect is a puzzling thing. One wonders how he arrived at it. Certainly he does not write by ear unless he is tone-deaf. But aside from the broken speech of his characters, the book contains some beautiful writing.[30]

While Locke, Wright, and Ellison awaited the moment when Hurston would write what Locke called "social document fiction," Hurston's critique of Wright's text sees it as trafficking in types rather than emerging organically from the reality of the lived experience. While some saw her position as politically conservative her views as expressed in her essay, "Negroes Without Self-Pity" suggest that she judged her people's pride and self-respect by their cultural and political independence and self-determination. Ironically, Wright saw Hurston as pandering to white stereotypes, while she saw him as trapped in a Hegelian struggle with white power, one that left no space for the humanity of either. He saw her as politically bankrupt and she saw him as culturally illiterate. In her essay, "On Richard Wright and Zora Neale Hurston: Notes Towards a Balancing of Love and Hatred," June Jordan suggests that we need the realities that both Wright and Hurston present to be whole. She states, "Richard Wright was a Black man born on a white, Mississippi plantation . . . In short, he was born into the antagonistic context of hostile whites wielding power against him . . . Zora Neale Hurston was born and raised in an all-Black Florida town . . . And without exception, her work—as novelist, as anthropologist/diligent collector and preserver of Black folktale and myth—reflects this early and late, all Black universe that was her actual as well as her creative world."[31]

At the end of the day, "High John de Conquer" is in many ways Hurston's ultimate essay. In her introduction to the collection *The Sanctified Church*, Toni Cade Bambara tells us that "High John had been on [Zora's] mind and in her mouth since childhood, as were other folk figures and heroes."[32] Fusing the political, cultural, and spiritual into one piece, High John is a folkloric embodiment of the energy of the culture. He is described as "a whisper, a will to hope, [and] a wish to find something worthy of laughter and song . . . The sign of this man was a laugh, and his singing-symbol was a drum-beat." Hurston tells us further, "It did not call to the feet of those who were fixed to hear it. It was an inside thing to live by. It was sure to be heard when and where the work was the hardest, and the lot the most cruel."[33] If, as seems evident in "Spirituals and Neo-Spirituals" and "The Sanctified Church," Hurston moves the definition of diasporic culture away from the *object* and toward the *ability* to express emotion and move the spirit, then describing High John de Conquer as the culture's hope-bringer synthesizes the energy at the heart of the culture into one folkloric symbol. Telling us that High John came from Africa "walking on . . . waves of sound," Hurston describes him as having the ability to outwit sorrow, using laughter, song, and rhythm as his tools. He is also a trickster who outsmarts "Old Massa" and "Old Miss" while appearing to be submissive and subservient.

In several of these anecdotes, High John is described outsmarting Old Massa without upstaging him. In one instance, he is a slave on the plantation who takes to stealing and cooking some of Massa's pigs when he has a hankering for pig meat. Suspecting him, Massa shows up at John's cabin one night when he knows he is cooking a pig he has stolen. John is shocked to hear Massa's voice outside, insisting he let him in and he says, "[Massa] Youse too fine a man for that. It would hurt my feelings to see you in a place like this here one."[34] But Massa persists and John lets him in with great reluctance. When Massa, in an authoritarian tone, insists on a plate of whatever delicious smelling meat is cooking, ignoring John's protestations about the meal being too humble for someone of Massa's status, John tells Massa that although he thought he was cooking a possum, if it turns out to be a pig, he can't be held accountable. Massa laughs before he can catch himself and the tale ends with the listener being told that from then on Massa "gave John and all the other house servants roast pig at the big house."[35]

The tale seems innocuous enough, and for those who catch the humor, that may appear to be the only point. For others, the tale may be an example of the kind of subservience that made the racist power structure comfortable because it does not threaten the imperialist hierarchy in any concrete fashion. Yet Hurston seems to give us another way to interpret the dynamics at play. John outwits Massa while appearing to submit and in the end, no one is dead and everybody gets more food. But the deeper message is that High John symbolizes surviving trauma while neither losing one's spirit nor destroying that of someone else. The lesson is to preserve one's humanity at all costs, and laughter and song, rather than being the symbols of complacency and subservience are in fact the most underestimated and powerful weapons in the toolkit. Hurston's own statements within the body of the essay situate what some may misread as simple humor as a scathing political critique of oppression also coded as a complex strategy of resistance. She states:

And all the time, there was High John de Conquer playing his tricks of making a way out of no-way. Hitting a straight lick with a crooked stick. Winning the jack pot with no other stake but a laugh. Fighting a mighty battle without outside-showing force, and winning his war from within. Really winning in a permanent way for he was winning with the soul of the black man whole and free. So he could use it afterwards. For what shall it profit a man if he gain the whole world, and lose his own soul? You would have nothing but a cruel, vengeful, grasping monster come to power . . . Way over there, where the sun rises a day ahead of time, they say that Heaven arms with love and laughter those it does not wish to see destroyed. He who carries his heart in his sword must perish. So says the ultimate law. High John de Conquer knew a lot of things like that. He who wins from within is in the "Be" class. *Be* here when the ruthless man comes, and *be* here when he is gone . . . Moreover, John knew that it is written where it cannot be erased, that nothing shall live on human flesh and prosper.[36]

Taking on an almost prophetic tone, Hurston situates real power as the internal power to master negative emotion and "work the good out of evil." We hear echoes of the Hurston who had moved beyond Christianity calling forth the force of ancient African gods while reminding us that all religious principles worth their salt privilege good over evil and humanity over vengeance. It also can't help but to be interpreted as a critique of imperialist aggression and violence in whatever form. And at the same time, she vindicates her people by letting the audience know that this powerful strategy of survival comes from her culture— and no matter their weaknesses, any culture or group that can produce such a strategy is not a destroyed people. They are instead, in the "Be" class; those who will ultimately "be here when the ruthless man comes and be here when he is gone."[37]

Hurston drops one last bomb in her essay. She says, "It is no accident that High John de Conquer has evaded the ears of white people. They were not supposed to know. You can't know what folks won't tell you. If they, the white people, heard some scraps, they could not understand because they had nothing to hear things like that with."[38] With this comment Hurston suggests that at the end of the day, the cultures that have emerged from Africans in the diaspora are still heavily coded and symbolic. Strategies of survival and resistance are handed out in plain sight of the oppressor and taken for pleasantries. The implication is that wherever the lore is being made and remade in the contemporary context, strategies of resistance unique to the culture are encoded there—waiting for the descendants of the old folks who invented them to unearth them and renew their power. This piece is one of the most effective examples of the syncretic nature of black art. Hurston's philosophical worldview, as put forth implicitly and explicitly in her essays, moves beyond a monolithic notion of the political or even a dualistic view of the political and cultural, towards a helix-like model in which spiritual, political, and cultural energies interact simultaneously.

Scholar and critic Hazel Carby's essay, "The Politics of Fiction, Anthropology, and the Folk: Zora Neale Hurston," highlights some of the contemporary tensions surrounding Hurston's work in the academy despite her rebirth.[39] In this essay, Carby sees Hurston's resistance to the commercialization of traditional forms as a refusal to accept the changes that urbanization was making on both black people and their music. Carby simultaneously suggests that urbanization categorically shifts rural black culture away from the *ethos* that Hurston identifies and toward something else. The something else is signified primarily by modern 20th-century gadgets such as the record, the phonograph, and the theatre.[40] Yet history appears to have vindicated Hurston, because some 20 years shy of a century after she wrote "Characteristics of Negro Expression," her identification of the cultural characteristic she calls "asymmetry" is an uncannily accurate description of the lyrical flow of rappers like the Notorious B.I.G. and Goodie Mob. Hurston states, "The presence of rhythm and lack of symmetry are paradoxical, but there they are. Both are present to a marked degree. There is always rhythm, but it is the rhythm of segments. Each unit has a rhythm of its own, but when the whole is assembled it is lacking in symmetry."[41] Any close study of rap music reveals both the fragmenting of the iambic pentameter as well as many of the "verbal nouns" and "double descriptives" that Hurston identified as characteristics of the culture, 80 years prior.

Carby's view is a view of black culture from the outside, and Hurston's biggest contribution to the conversation seems to have been creating a space for the culture to be viewed from the inside, on its own terms. Hurston saw her goal and job as identifying modes of expression that were endemic to the culture. This necessarily happened in context where there was the least outside influence. As she studied black Southern rural culture, she began to realize that it was comparable to African diaspora cultural forms in places like Jamaica, Haiti, and the Bahamas, where cultural forms such as Jonkunnu, Nine Night, and Vodou were New World survivals of ancient Old World West African practices. The cultural modes that Hurston identified in rural contexts, rather than vanishing as Carby suggests, re-appear in urban contemporary space in various forms.

The cultural separation between the rural and the urban is not as categorical in Hurston's work or in lived reality, as Hazel Carby suggests. Bessie Smith was born in Chattanooga, Tennessee, an urban space in the middle of the Deep South, yet her parents came from a small rural town. Bob Marley was born in Nine Mile, a rural town in the parish of St. Ann in Jamaica, but his music is a fusion of a nature-oriented Rastafari worldview inflected through the prism of the violence in urban Trench Town. The rural agrarian space deeply influenced these artists by their own admission. If one is looking for the old-time spirituals to be performed in exactly the same way (a point that even Carby acknowledges Hurston refutes), then there will be a failure to recognize their rebirth in the "changing same" mode. Krumping, clowning, and break dancing suddenly seem like continuations of the expression endemic to the spirituals and the Sanctified church in a new form. The external form has changed but the internal function has not. If the focus is on the object produced (be it a song with a particular tune or a dance with certain steps) rather than on what the object is used to express, then what is identified as culture will seem static; but this is a Western projection, not a diasporic reality.

Thirteen years before her death, on March 24, 1924, Bessie Smith, when interviewed by the *Pittsburgh Courier*, stated, "Of course the modern songs are greatly modified, but the original blues songs are deep, emotional melodies, bespeaking a troubled heart."[42] If the focus instead is on the creation process itself—then the modes of cultural expression that Hurston identifies are all around us, and like the old spirituals, they are "being made and forgotten everyday."

NOTES

1. Zora Neale Hurston to Langston Hughes, November 22, 1928, in *Zora Neale Hurston: A Life in Letters*, ed. Carla Kaplan (New York: Doubleday, 2000), 131–132.

2. Spike Lee, *She's Gotta Have It* (New York: Forty Acres and a Mule Filmworks, 1986). This film was made on a budget of $175,000 but grossed over $7,000,000. This brought Lee to the attention of the commercial film industry as well as into relative prominence.

3. I borrow this term from Langston Hughes's essay, "The Negro Artist and the Racial Mountain," in *The Norton Anthology of African American Literature*, edited by Henry Louis Gates, Jr. (New York: Norton, 1997), 1266–1269.

4. Zora Neale Hurston, *Mules and Men* (1935; repr., New York: Harper & Row, 1990).

5. Valerie Boyd, *Wrapped in Rainbows: The Life of Zora Neale Hurston* (Los Angeles: Scribner Book Company, 2003), 295–296.

6. Hurston, *Life in Letters*, 131–132.

7. Zora Neale Hurston, "Spirituals and Neo-Spirituals," in *Zora Neale Hurston: Folklore, Memoirs, and Other Writings*, ed. Cheryl Wall (New York: Library of America, 1995), 869. All essays cited are collected in this volume.

8. Ibid., 870, 871.

9. Ibid.

10. "The Sanctified Church," in *Zora Neale Hurston: Folklore, Memoirs, and Other Writings*, 901.

11. This case is made persuasively by Mervyn C. Alleyne in his text *Roots of Jamaican Culture*. Sterling Stuckey also makes this case in his text Slave Culture when he focuses on the creation of a singular African American culture from the disparate African ethnicities that were brought to North America. Historically, in the Caribbean setting religious sects referred to as Myal, Pocomania, Zion Revival, Shango Baptists, and Shakerism have been seen as transitional practices caught somewhere between formal Christianity and traditional African religions, many of which originated from West African Yoruba and Akan societies.

12. See *The Faces of the Gods* by Leslie G. Desmangles which is a study of Vodou and Roman Catholicism in Haiti.

13. Valerie Boyd, *Wrapped in Rainbows*, 298.

14. Zora Neale Hurston, "The Sanctified Church," in *Zora Neale Hurston: Folklore, Memoirs, and Other Writings*, 902.

15. Ibid., 903.

16. David LaChappelle, *RIZE* (Los Angeles: David LaChappelle Studios, 2005).

17. Zora Neale Hurston, "The Sanctified Church," in *Zora Neale Hurston: Folklore, Memoirs, and Other Writings*, 902.

18. David LaChappelle, *RIZE*.

19. Ibid.

20. Ibid.

21. George Schuyler, "The Negro-Art Hokum." *The Nation* 122 (June 16, 1926): 662–663.

22. Langston Hughes, "The Negro Artist and the Racial Mountain," *The Nation* 23 (June 26, 1926).

23. W.E.B. Du Bois, "Criteria of Negro Art," *The Crisis*, Vol. 32 (October 1926): 290–297.

24. Richard Wright, "Blueprint for Negro Writing," *The New Challenger*, 1937.

25. Zora Neale Hurston, "Art and Such," in *Zora Neale Hurston: Folklore, Memoirs, and Other Writings*, 951.

26. Ibid., 908.

27. Julie Dash, "'From Black Insurgent' to Negotiating the Hollywood Divide—A Conversation with Julie Dash," Michael T. Martin, *Cinema Journal*, 49.2 (Winter 2010), http://muse.jhu.edu/journals/cinema_journal/v049/49.2.martin.html

28. Carla Kaplan, "Introduction," *Zora Neale Hurston: A Life in Letters*, 26.

29. Valerie Boyd, *Wrapped in Rainbows*, 306, 336.

30. Zora Neale Hurston, "*Review of Uncle Tom's Children*," in *Zora Neale Hurston: Folklore, Memoirs, and Other Writings*, 912–913.

31. June Jordan, "On Richard Wright and Zora Neale Hurston: Notes Towards a Balancing of Love and Hatred," in *Civil Wars* (Boston: Beacon, 1981), 84–89.

32. Toni C. Barbara, "Foreword," in *Sanctified Church*, by Zora Neale Hurston (Olympia: Turtle Island, 1983), 9–13, 12.

33. Zora Neale Hurston, "High John de Conquer," in *Zora Neale Hurston: Folklore, Memoirs, and Other Writings*, 922.

34. Ibid., 926.

35. Ibid., 927.

36. Ibid., 923–924.

37. Ibid., 924.

38. Ibid., 923.

39. Hazel Carby, "The Politics of Fiction, Anthropology and the Folk: Zora Neale Hurston," in *The Politics of History and Memory in African American Culture* by Geneviève Fabre & Robert O'Meally (New York: Oxford University Press, 1994), 28–44.

40. Carby's critique privileges Wright's view of culture, when she states that Hurston wanted to "preserve an aesthetically purified version of blackness [while] the antagonism between them reveals Wright to be the modernist and leaves Hurston embedded in the politics of Negro identity."

41. Zora Neale Hurston, "Characteristics of Negro Expression," in *Zora Neale Hurston: Folklore, Memoirs, and Other Writings*, 55.

42. Quoted in "Black Music Critics and the Classic Blues Singers," by Phillip McGuire, in *The Black Perspective in Music*, 14:2 (Spring 1986), 103–125, 105.

Dear Zora: Letters from the New Literati

Kendra Nicole Bryant

Dear Zora Neale Hurston,

I know a professor who acts like you're the manna from heaven. I asked her why she reveres you so much. She told me: Zora points the way to God.

Dear Zora Neale Hurston:

In a 20th-Century African American Literature class I took, my professor required the class to read an article by Barbara Christian titled "A Race for Theory" (1987), wherein she argues that the academic lens through which theory is viewed is "inappropriate to the energetic emerging literatures in the world today," particularly in regard to "people of color, feminists, radical critics, and creative writers."[1] Reading her article was a relief, because, as a black and female student in a predominantly white university—where the English department is entrenched in theories written for and by white people (usually white men)—I have often found myself confused in my efforts to understand what theory is because the manner in which the academy talks about and defines theory, more often than not, disregards black people and their historical and cultural experiences.

According to the *Oxford English Dictionary*, a theory is "a scheme or system of ideas or statements held as an explanation or account of a group of facts or phenomena; a hypothesis that has been confirmed or established by observation or experiment, and is propounded or accepted as accounting for the known facts; a statement of what are held to be the general laws, principles, or causes of something known or observed." However, because theoretical discourse traditionally happens among white men, when the majority of these men theorize, they talk in a mechanistic language unfamiliar to mainstream black people; they over-generalize about black culture when they do write about it; and they disregard black people's way of being in the world *as* pure theory itself. In so doing, they reinforce white patriarchal superstructures—media, law, education, religion—that function to silence or repress people of color—within the imagination of the critic, within the classroom, and within the broader public discourse beyond the academy. Christian says, "People of color have always theorized—but in forms quite different from the Western form of abstract logic."[2] She says that black people's theorizing "is often in narrative forms, in the stories we create, in riddles and proverbs, in the play with language."[3] Then she asks, "How else have we managed to survive with such spiritedness the assault on our bodies, social institutions, countries, our very humanity?"[4] In other words, black people from Africa to the Middle Passage, from the plantation to Jim Crow, from store front porches to kitchen tables, from "yo mama" jokes to hip-hop slang, have survived in an oppressive world because their knowing how to *be* in the world is their knowing how to theorize about themselves and the world(s) in which they live.

After reading Christian, I thought of you, and, laughing to myself, I whispered, "My People! My People!"[5]

Dear Zora Neale Hurston:

I read *Their Eyes Were Watching God* for the third time. The first time I read it, I was in tenth grade and only remembered Tea Cake because his name reminded me of the nicknames black people give each other, like Cookie and Pumpkin, Peanut and Rooster. The second time I read it, I was a graduate student and the love between Janie and Tea Cake became relevant as I was also looking at the relationship between Tish and Fonny in James Baldwin's *If Beale Street Could Talk*. But this third go-around, as a post-graduate student, I read *Their Eyes Were Watching God* as social biography: as your retelling of black people's humanity.

In an article you wrote called "What White Publishers Won't Print," you said, "To grasp the penetration of western civilization in a minority, it is necessary to know how the average minority behaves and lives."[6] Therefore, *Their Eyes Were Watching God* is your theoretical offering, not so much to evoke critical discussion among literary critics—particularly those of the 1930s like Alain Locke, who claimed your work was "simply out of step with the more serious trends of the time,"[7] or Richard Wright, who argued your novel "carries no theme, no message, no thought"[8]—but to record the *African* American ethos, the moral nature or guiding principle of a person, as you experienced it growing up in Eatonville.

Dona Marimba Ani in *Let the Circle Be Unbroken*, says the African ethos expressed itself in America by means of our black expressions: language, music, dance, thought patterns, laughter, walks, spirituality. She claims, "The system and circumstances of slavery in New Europe sought to destroy African value, African self-image and self-concept."[9] In other words, slavery was an attempt to dehumanize Africans. But Africans survived because their spirits survived, which were manifested in their ability to recreate the world, in their ability to express themselves.

Ms. Hurston, you were obviously ahead of your time. Your preoccupation with Negro expressions as a means of understanding Negro life in America only seemed like one more minstrel show for critics like Locke and Wright, who didn't seem to understand the significance of your reclaiming black traditions. Instead, they thought a novel about the downtrodden black was more situated in the Renaissance's idea of social protest, and was thus more appropriate for the times.

I wonder if they are rolling around in their graves, and if you are rolling around too, but rolling around like the sun rolls around heaven.

Dear Zora Neale Hurston:

I think your writing about black people's expressions was a political act.

Dear Zora Neale Hurston:

I keep thinking about black expressions, especially after reading your "Characteristics of Negro Expression," and came across Henry Louis Gates's *The Signifying Monkey*. Because of the dialect you use in *Their Eyes*, he calls your story a "speakerly text," a spin-off from Roland Barthes' opposition between the "readerly" text—a text that is reader-friendly, and the "writerly" text—a text that requires the reader to work for comprehension.[10] Gates claims *Their Eyes* "is the first example in (black) tradition . . . to represent an oral literary tradition, designed 'to emulate the phonetic, grammatical, and lexical patterns of actual speech and produce the illusion of oral narration,'" thus the term "speakerly text."[11] Before Gates examines *Their Eyes* for rhetorical strategies, however, he summarizes "Negro Expressions" as your claim that dialect is Negro speech. This summation becomes the foundation for Gates's arguments. Nevertheless, what intrigued me most about his essay is his historical account of black poetic diction, as well as critics' responses to its use.

Did you know that Paul Laurence Dunbar is considered the most accomplished black dialect poet, and that his presence engendered "the turn of critical attention to matters of language and voice"?[12] And did you know in 1866 a white woman claimed that "'The Coming American Novelist' would be 'of African origin'"? She wrote in *Lippincott's Monthly Magazine*, "This great author would be one 'With us' but 'not of us,' one who 'has suffered everything a poet, a dramatist, a novelist need suffer before he comes to have his lips anointed.'"[13] She goes on to say, "The African 'has given us the only national music we have ever had,' a corpus of art 'distinctive in musical history. 'She says this great author will be "'a natural story-teller,' uniquely able to fabricate . . . 'acts of imagination,' discourses in which no 'morality is involved.'"[14] And although this white woman referred to "The Coming American Novelist" as a man, because using the male pronoun was more "convenient," she declares that it will be a woman who will claim the title.[15]

Zora, do you think she conjured you up?

Dear Zora Neale Hurston,

The way I see it, hip-hop culture encompasses—and I am inclined to argue, hyper-encompasses—all of the expressions that you evaluated in your "Characteristics of Negro Expression." You would have had such a writing good time with hip-hop.

DRAMA

Everything that is hip-hop is dramatic. With lyrics from excess money to pimps and hos, *Self Destruction* and *Cop Killer*; from dances that require lines and breaks, krumps and shoulder leans; from styles that range from Phat Farm to Sean Jean, penny loafers and hot pink high top PUMA sneakers; and language from *bootylicious* to *fo shizlle my nizzle*, *bling-bling*, and *sippin' on some sizzurp*, hip-hop resonates with "Every phase of Negro life [being] highly dramatized."[16]

WILL TO ADORN

Indeed, black is beautiful, and there is nothing more beautiful than to see how black people adorn themselves, especially in hip-hop culture (and church). In your essay you said, "Whatever the Negro does of his own volition, he embellishes."[17] Clearly, that is an understatement in regard to hip-hop.

In hip-hop, artists are always dressed to impress whether they are wearing tailored three-piece suits, baggy fatigues, ballroom gowns, or skinny jeans. However, their attire is never complete without their bling-bling or their iced jewelry (worn either in their mouths or on their extremities); their designer shades, shoes, and handbags; and their groomed hair, which, if cut for a male, may have art work shaved on the head, and if styled for a female, may be brightly colored. In addition to adorning their bodies, hip-hop artists also adorn (or pimp) their automobiles with hydraulics, tinted windows, booming sound systems, and spree wheels, to name a few adornments. Hip-hop artists pride themselves in their ability to adorn, as this expression expresses whether or not they are deemed a "rubberband" man (or woman).[18]

ANGULARITY AND ASYMMETRY

Graffiti, one of the four elements (the others being rapping, break dancing, and DJing) of hip-hop culture, encompasses both angularity and asymmetry. "Wild-style," a form of graffiti involving interlocking letters, arrows, and connecting points, is an example of hip-hop art that welcomes deep angles and the rhythm of segments.[19] Although your spiel on angularity and asymmetry is in reference to Negro dancing, poetry, and furniture placement, graffiti can be posited in this exploration of your Negro expressions, for the images that graffiti artists produce are fluid, and therefore, letters dance with each other, and their placements on the abandoned wall, the subway door, or the Harlem tunnel is poetic, each piece creating a rhythm of its own.

DANCING

Hip-hop can't be hip-hop without break dancing. But in addition to cardboard boxes laid on dance floors, upside-down head spins, and holding one's body up with one arm, with legs (angular) poised to the sky while striking a pose, dance includes almost any movement that a black person involves him- or herself in while listening to music. From simple head nodding and hand clapping, to an all-out line dance like the Electric Slide, "the Negro must be considered the great(est) artist, his dancing is realistic suggestion."[20]

NEGRO FOLKLORE

Hip-hop music is a form of folklore, as rappers' lyrics are usually autobiographical stories about their own black experiences. According to Deborah Plant, you saw your own culture "as the source of renewed Black national dignity and pride."[21] Plant claims you "saw in it the foundations of African American self-affirmation and independence and the foundation of resistance to European cultural domination."[22]

Rapper Christopher Wallace, aka Biggie Smalls, who was noted for his storytelling abilities, seemed to share the same sentiments, for in his lyrics he remembers and celebrates his growing up black in Brooklyn, New York.

Biggie Smalls, who reminds me much of Richard Wright's Bigger Thomas (because he was a poor black subjugated male who hung out with his friends on street corners committing crimes), created music about his life; he created music, which eventually liberated him. In short, Biggie Smalls used hip-hop music as a vehicle in which he embraced his essential self.

Throughout his song titled "Juicy," Biggie tells his listeners about living in public housing, dropping out of high school, and fulfilling all of the "stereotypes of a black male misunderstood."[23] In his chorus, however, he tells his listeners "don't let 'em hold you down, reach for the stars," and provides his life as an example of a black person who went from birthdays being the worst days to sippin' champagne when he is "thirst-ay."[24] Like you, Zora, Biggie's "creative expression . . . [was] as much protest against establishment dictates, both white and Black, as they were affirmations of Black folk culture."[25]

In addition to hip-hop music being a form of folklore, call-and-response, which was popular in traditional African cultures during public gatherings, civil affairs, and religious ceremonies, is a dynamic of folklore. Similarly, the rapper and audience interact with one another spontaneously. Perhaps one of the most popular call-and-response interactions employed in hip-hop music include this now formulaic structure:

DJ/Rapper: *Now throw yo hands in the air*
                    An' wave 'em like you jus' don't care.
Then the DJ/Rapper makes up the third line. For example: *an' if you like bein' black ya know it's all that*
DJ/Rapper: *Let me hear ya say "oh yea!"*
Audience: *Oh yea!*
DJ/Rapper: *Oh yea!*
Audience: *Oh yea!*
DJ/Rapper: *Ya don't stop.*

Finally, free-style battling, an aspect of hip-hop perFORMances, is similar to playing the dirty dozens, which is another form of folklore. Like the dirty dozens, wherein two people go back and forth insulting one another, two rappers are pitted against each other, rapping it out for the title of lyrical genius. Usually each rapper's verse includes insults toward the other, and the more insulting and clever the rhyme, the more "props" the rapper receives.

In short, hip-hop music is the word on the street. Says Plant, "through words, the individual could assume autonomy, naming and unnaming self and world."[26] Biggie Smalls never thought hip-hop would be the answer to his challenges in life. However, with words, Biggie narrated his own story and "create[d] a world wherein [he could] survive and become a self-determined individual."[27]

CULTURE HEROES

Although Rudy Ray Moore can be considered a culture hero in regard to hip-hop culture because his 1970s "Dolemite" character influenced rap lyrics, Rudy Ray Moore was a comedic folklorist who used Africa's culture hero tales in his stand-up comedy performances. According to critics, Moore's "Dolemite" routine was filled with rhyme, arrogance, and profanity, and was, therefore, an example of blaxploitation, a hyperbolic exploitation of blacks in film.[28] However, for rap artists like Snoop Dog, Dr. Dre, and 2 Live Crew, who worked with Moore, imitated him, and/or included snippets of his "Dolemite" routine in their own music, Moore portrayed black expressions with truth, humor, and appreciation for black culture. Perhaps one of his most popular culture hero stories is his signifying monkey routine, wherein a monkey uses his wiles and an accommodating elephant to fool a lion. Says Douglas Martin of the *Chicago Tribune*, the tale, which originated in West Africa, became a basis for Gates's *The Signifying Monkey*.[29] But Zora, it was through you, as well as through Ishmael Reed, Ralph Ellison, Richard Wright, Jean Toomer, Sterling Brown, Wole Soyinka and others, that Rudy Ray Moore was able to narrate his story in the first place.[30] Zora, because of you and your comrades, Gates is able to talk 'bout signifyin'.

ORIGINALITY

Zora, you asserted "to get back to original sources is much too difficult for any group to claim very much as certainty. What we really mean by originality is the modification of ideas."[31] There is no doubt that hip-hop artists have modified ideas. Perhaps one of the biggest illustrations of modification is the hip-hop artist's ability to modify language. However, since you are fully aware of black people's ability to transform language and noted how black people have modified "whites' musical instruments, so that his interpretation has been adopted by the white man himself and then re-interpreted,"[32] I want to tell you how hip-hop artists have used and modified instruments used to create hip-hop music.

Hip-hop technology (instruments) includes turntables, amplifiers, and synthesizers, as well as voices (for beat boxing, rapping, and call-and-response), and hands (for scratching, clapping, and spinning vinyl) to create sounds reflective of the African diaspora.[33] One of the most modified technologies, however, is the turntable, whose intended use was limited to spinning records. However, the expressive dynamics of hip-hop culture—which is a mixture of *African* American cultures—merged with the ever-present DJ who spins the records, transformed the turntable into a multipurpose piece of machinery. The traditional record spinning of DJs, in combination with other technologies, resulted in the use of turntables to scratch, as well as mix songs and beats, originating a hybridity of sounds unique to black music. Eventually the sampler, which is closely related to the synthesizer, was invented. The user records multiple sounds on the sampler, which then plays each recording back based on how the instrument is configured. With the sampler, sounds didn't have to be generated by scratch, which not only led to the elimination of turntables, but also the elimination of the use of the voice to beat box, imitating a drumming sound. Now that blacks have reinterpreted instruments to fit the demands of hip-hop sound, hip-hop technologies have been further modified, allowing anyone to *do* hip-hop music.

IMITATION

Because hip-hop music is a mixture of be-bop, blues, R&B, gospel, rag time, jazz, [and more], hip-hop artists heavily imitate (sample) other artists. However, what made me smile really big was your reference to dances that imitate animals. When it comes to hip-hop, the dances are endless. Not only do dances imitate animals, but they imitate personal traits and machinery. A few of my favorite dances include the California worm, which requires the dancer, standing erect, to squiggle her arms, neck, and torso as a worm would; the Young Joc (named after rapper Young Joc), which requires the dancer to pretend she is sitting on a motorcycle, back leaning, and arms extended as if gassing a motorcycle; the Superman, which requires the dancer to extend his arms in front of him like the Superman hero, and hop to the side as if flying; the pony, which requires the dancer to trot in place like a pony; the toilet bowl, which requires the dancer to move her lower torso (legs closed) imitating a flushing down of water; the sissy, where the dancer prances around snapping his fingers, winding his arm in large circles, and walking rapidly (but with short steps) on his toes; and the robot, which requires the dancer to stiffly move her arms, feet, and head like a robot with limited movement.

ABSENCE OF THE CONCEPT OF PRIVACY

One of the characteristics of hip-hop is braggadocio. Therefore, very little of a rapper's life is kept private. Your claim, "The community is given the benefit of a good fight as well as a good wedding. An audience is a necessary part of any drama,"[34] is right on in regard to the hip-hop community. (I might argue, however, that the media's interest in black people's defamation plays a role in the lack of privacy associated with hip-hop artists.) Nevertheless, perhaps the most talked about, most publicized, and most criticized debate—after the openly East Coast, West Coast rivalries that left rappers Tu Pac and Biggie Smalls dead—is R&B singer Rihanna and hip-hop artist Chris Brown's public domestic dispute. Every detail about their quarrel, from the cause of the argument, to the location, to the car Chris Brown was driving, to Brown's public apology and images of Rihanna's bruised face, was made available to the public. Obviously, with the advancement of communications technology, people have more access to information than ever before. However, hip-hop culture is notorious for airing out its dirty laundry, for negative publicity is better than no publicity at all.

JOOK

After watching Steven Spielberg's rendition of Alice Walker's *The Color Purple*, I wanted Harpo to build me a Jook joint. Watching those black folks jook to Jook music was my pleasure, and listening to Shug Avery singing "Miss Celie's Blues" was my dream. Nevertheless, hip-hop artists Andre 3000 and Big Boi of OutKast played in the 2006 film "Idlewild," which reminds me of Harpo's Jook Joint.

"Idlewild" is a juke (jook) box (guitars) musical set in the Prohibition-era American South, where Rooster (Big Boi), a speakeasy performer and club manager, must contend with gangsters who have their eyes on the club, while his piano player and partner Percival (Andre 3000) must choose between his love, Angel, or his obligations to his father.

> I thought you might appreciate knowing that Rooster's wife's name is Zora.

Nevertheless, "Idlewild" is filled with the characteristics of the Jook joint you describe in "Negro Expressions." The club is a bawdy house where the men and women dance (mainly the jitterbug), drink, and gamble. In addition, the guitarist and pianist play blues and jazz, as the movie is set in the 1930s. Many of the musical numbers were written and performed by OutKast and were previously featured on their albums *Big Boi and Dre Present . . . OutKast and Speakerboxxx/The Love Below.*

DIALECT

There is not a hip-hop artist whom I am aware of who does not use dialect as you have described in your "Negro Expressions." Even if lyrics are written in standard American English, the performance of the English is undoubtedly dialectical, as rappers tend to (purposely) fail to enunciate every letter sound in particular words, similar to your explanation of "I" versus "Ah." Although you claim "the lip form" is responsible for blacks failing to pronounce a sharp "I," because "By experiment the reader will find that a sharp 'I' is very much easier with a thin taut lip than with a full soft lip," I believe black people purposely alter the pronunciation of standard English as a means of claiming their own language, a rejection, if you will, of standard English. Rapper Mos Def, begins his song, "Hip Hop," stating that he speaks in a tongue native to his community, culture, and political history. He used to speak in standard American English, "But caught a rash on my lips / So now my chat just like dis."[35] In other words, it seems Mos Def is claiming that before colonization, *African* Americans spoke a language particular to their divinity. However, because standard English was forced on them as an oppressive tool to further dehumanize them, *African* Americans abandoned the standards of American English as a way of reclaiming their humanity; therefore, *this* is *dis*. Moreover, and Zora, I am sure you can appreciate this, instead of positioning himself as a downtrodden black who wallows in race matters, Mos Def celebrates black people's resilience and creative spirits, claiming that black people went from working in chain gangs to working in hip-hop, a culture that has rendered them visibility. Like Tea Cake, in your *Their Eyes Were Watching God*, Mos Def is another black man who, while making a living, is creating and jooking to good music. Mos Def is making the "mos" out of his Negro Expressions, even marketing them, I might argue, in order to expose *African* Americans' ability to theorize.

Dear Zora Neale Hurston,

If my professor believes you lead the way to God, do you think she believes hip-hop artists can lead her there too?

Dear Zora Neale Hurston,

I'm up to my eyeballs in criticisms about you and about your work. I asked my professor about how she still comes up with so much to write about in regard to you. Her response: "How many poems are there about roses?" But *everyone* still has *so much* to say about you: Alice Walker, Robert Hemenway, Henry Louis Gates, Jr., Maya Angelou, Hortense J. Spillers, Marjorie Pryse, Barbara Christian, Valerie Boyd, Carla Kaplan, Cary D. Wintz, Cheryl A. Wall, Sterling Brown, Ruby Dee, Rita Dove, bell hooks, Nathan Huggins, June Jordan, Ishmael Reed, Mary Helen Washington, Addison Gayle, Deborah Plant. They call you a fore-mother, say you gave them voice, like you were their *nommo*—the *force* within the universe that they used in order to effect other beings.[36] You were their vehicle, they merely the vessel. I guess you were the "Genius of the South."[37]

Dear Zora Neale Hurston,

I hadn't thought about black people being geniuses until I heard you were named one. In my academic training, "genius," looked like Albert Einstein, or Mozart, or William Shakespeare. And black people— although I knew they were politicians, artists, inventors, warriors, and scholars—I thought them brilliant, never *genius*. But Alice Walker claimed you "Genius of the South."[38]

Says Harold Bloom, in order to discover one's genius, a person must look inside her or himself, because ". . . there is a god within us, and the god speaks."[39] I think you knew black people were geniuses all along—and by speaking for them, you introduced the world to God.

Dear Zora Neale Hurston,

I get it.

Black expressions derive from the black ethos, which is the divine self. In order for *African* Americans to survive in an oppressive state, they create. They create language, music and dance, art, stories, drama, church. They create hip-hop. And because creation is divine, as God— the ultimate Creator—dwells in people acting as their spirits, the Creator manifests itself in people's ability to create. Creating, then, is not only an expression of the divine, but it is an expression of humanity. It is theorizing.

Through your storytelling, you, too, are theorizing, as well as giving black people voice and exposing their divinity, which is also their humanity, to a world that did not view them as human beings. You see, to be able to speak in your mother tongue (black dialect, dramatics, folklore, adornments) is to be able to maintain your identity and sense of belonging in a world that attempts to exclude you by imposing values on you that are foreign—that are not your own. So, Zora, your story about a black woman who washes white people's clothes in order to support herself and her cheating husband,[40] and your story about a black couple whose love survives despite adultery because the wife thinks that sleeping with another man will earn her a gold piece for her husband,[41] and your story about a black man believed to be killed by a bobcat, which is actually the spirit of the man he murdered[42]— along with the secondary stories told on Joe Stark's storefront—stories told in jest in order to keep from crying—was your way of re-narrating black ethos. Matter of fact, you, as storyteller, are the embodiment of Negro expression. You are divine Truth, as are the black characters in your stories.

Zora, do you see yourself as the storyteller of God? Or as God's journalist, trying to explain everything that happens around us?

Dear Zora Neale Hurston,

I'm on a roll now. I've read your *Dust Tracks on a Road* and all of your short stories—"John Redding Goes to Sea," "Drenched in Light," and "Story in Harlem Slang," being among my favorites—and I think I'm on my way to seeing God. I realize, although spirit cannot be seen, one's language gives it voice so that it can be heard, and then deemed visible. However, to strip somebody of her ability to speak, that which makes a person heard, is to strip her of her identity, which is deeply rooted in spirituality. So, it's like as a storyteller, telling stories from the time you were a little girl, to re-narrating stories you heard orated (and often fabricated) on Eatonville's storefront, I've come to the conclusion that language is home, and Gloria Anzaldúa says it is essential that people be given permission to be at home in their language,[43] for home is where the heart is. Albeit, a trite phrase, it is one that is very appropriate, for the spirit dwells in the heart, and "where the spirit is, there is liberty."[44]

Dear Zora Neale Hurston,

According to Paul DeMan in Lea Ramsdell's article, "Language and Identity Politics: The Linguistic Autobiographies of Latinos in the United States," "the self is constituted by language."[45] Says DeMan, "language precedes identity [and] language is what grants humans 'the self-reflexive dimension of their consciousness' and their ability to interact with others, thereby developing their own subjectivity."[46] In other words, without language, human beings cannot develop their own individuality. So, if a person is stripped of her language, she is unable to interact with other human beings, and unless she creates a new language, the language becomes dead, as does the spirit of that culture and its people. Therefore, since language is an art, as an artist, you wrote about Negro expressions in your re-narrations of *African* American folklore, in order to sustain *African* American culture, as well as to showcase how Africans used their ethos (theories) to survive in America.

Dear Zora Neale Hurston,

Don Miguel Ruiz, who wrote *The Voice of Knowledge*, says, "If other people try to write your story, it means they don't respect you. They don't respect you because they consider that you are not a good artist, that you cannot write your own story, even though you were born to write your own story. Respect comes directly from love; it is one of the greatest expressions of love."[47] Although Ruiz's "you" refers to the individual self, I think "you" can also mean a cultural group, as Toni Morrison, Paule Marshall, and Alice Walker—who stand on your genius—are in the business of re-narrating *African* American history in an attempt to debunk myths that suggest *African* Americans inhuman. But Zora, you celebrated *African* Americans and all of their Negro expressions. You *were* born to write your story, as well as the stories of those blacks who were silenced. And your respect for *African* Americans as human beings *is* a great expression of love; it is an expression of God.

Dear Zora Neale Hurston,

Your mother told you to jump at the sun, and in the spirit of her genius, you encouraged others to do the same. I'm jumping Zora. I'm jumping at the sun, and I can see God in the horizon.

Fondly Yours,

Kendra Nicole
Daughter and Negro Artist

NOTES

1. Barbara Christian, "The Race for Theory," *Cultural Critique*, 6 (1987), 53.

2. Ibid., 52.

3. Ibid.

4. Ibid.

5. Zora Neale Hurston, *Dust Tracks on a Road* (New York: Arno Press, 1942), 223.

6. Hurston, "What White Publishers Won't Print," in *Within the Circle: An Anthology of African American Literary Criticism from the Harlem Renaissance to Present*, ed. Angelyn Mitchell (Durham: Duke University Press, 1994), 121.

7. Quoted in Zora Neale Hurston, *Their Eyes Were Watching God* (New York: Harper and Row, 1990), viii.

8. Ibid.

9. Dona Marimba Ani, *Let the Circle Be Unbroken: The Implications of African Sprituality in the Diaspora* (Lawrenceville: The Red Sea Press, 1980), 14.

10. Henry Louis Gates, Jr., *The Signifying Monkey: A Theory of African American Literary Criticism* (New York: Oxford University Press, 1988), 198.

11. Ibid., 181.

12. Ibid., 174.

13. Ibid., 174.

14. Ibid.

15. Ibid.

16. Zora Neale Hurston, "Characteristics of Negro Expression," in *Voices from the Harlem Renaissance*, ed. Nathan Higgins (New York: Oxford University Press, 1995), 225.

17. Ibid., 227.

18. A "rubberband" man is a person who is carrying so much money that he has to use a rubberband to secure all of it.

19. Sacha Jenkins, "Graffiti: Graphic Scenes, Spray Fiends, and Millionaires," in *The Vibe of Hip Hop*, ed. Alan Light (New York: Three Rivers Press, 1999), 39.

20. Hurston, *Negro Expression*, 228.

21. Deborah G. Plant, *Every Tub Must Sit on Its Own Bottom: The Philosophy and Politics of Zora Neale Hurston* (Urbana: University of Illinois Press), 64.

22. Ibid.

23. Biggie Smalls, "Juicy," *Ready to Die*, Executive Producer, Sean "Puffy" Combs (New York: Arista Records, 1994).

24. Ibid., verse 3.

25. Plant, *Every Tub*, 70.

26. Ibid., 78.

27. Ibid.

28. Douglas Martin, "Rudy Ray Moore, 81, 'Dolemite' star, precursor of rap, dies," *Chicago Tribune.com* Oct. 2008. *Chicago Tribune*, 8 May 2009.

29. Ibid.

30. Gates, *Signifying Monkey*, preface.

31. Hurston, *Negro Expression*, 230.

32. Ibid.

33. Houston Baker, "Hybridity, the Rap Race, and Pedagogy," in *Black Music Research Journal* 11.2 (1991): 217–221.

34. Hurston, *Negro Expression*, 231.

35. Mos Def, "Hip-Hop," Verse 1, *Black on Both Sides* (Los Angeles: Rawkus Records, 1999).

36. Ani, *Let the Circle*, 40–41.

37. Alice Walker, "Looking for Zora," in *In Search of Our Mother's Garden: Womanist Prose* (San Diego: Harcourt Brace Jovanovich Publishers, 1983), 107.

38. Ibid.

39. Harold Bloom, *Genius: A Mosaic of One Hundred Exemplary Creative Minds* (New York: Warner Books, 2002), 12.

40. Zora Neale Hurston, "Sweat," in *The Complete Stories*, ed. Henry Louis Gates, Jr. and Sieglinde Lemke (New York: HarperCollins Publishers, 1995), 73–85.

41. Zora Neale Hurston, "The Gilded Six-Bits" in *The Complete Stories*, 86–98.

42. Zora Neale Hurston, "Spunk" in *The Complete Stories*, 26–32.

43. Gloria Anzaldúa, "How to Tame a Wild Tongue," in *Bordering Fires: The Vintage Book of Contemporary Mexican and Chicano/a Literature*, ed. Christina Garcia (New York: Vintage Books, 2006), 45.

44. 2 Corinthians, *Holy Bible*, King James Version, A Regency Bible (Nashville: Thomas Nelson, Inc., 1978), 508.

45. Lea Ramsdell, "Language and Identity Politics: The Linguistic Autobiographies of Latinos in the United States," *Journal of Modern Literature* 28.1 (2004), 167.

46. Ibid.

47. Don Miguel Ruiz, *The Voice of Knowledge: A Practical Guide to Inner Peace* (San Rafael: Amber-Allen Publishing, 2004), 66.

Their Eyes Were Watching God: The Novel, the Film—An Interview with Valerie Boyd

Deborah G. Plant

Valerie Boyd is the author of *Wrapped in Rainbows: The Life of Zora Neale Hurston* and the forthcoming *Spirits in the Dark: The Untold Story of Black Women in Hollywood*.

DP: *In order to create a context for our readers, would you please first give us the historical background of the novel* Their Eyes Were Watching God?

VB: Zora Neale Hurston wrote *Their Eyes Were Watching God* under emotional duress. She'd kept the novel "dammed up" inside for months, as she recalled, and she wrote it under what she called "internal pressure."

Basically, Hurston wrote the novel as a tribute to a younger man she was dating—a man who we could describe as her very own Tea Cake. About 20 years younger than Hurston, his name was Percival McGuire Punter. When the two of them began dating, he was only 23 years old; Hurston, on the other hand, was 44. But it wasn't the age difference that gave them problems, at least not on the surface.

The fundamental conflict in their relationship was that he wanted Hurston to give up her career, marry him, and leave New York. The marrying and leaving New York parts were fine, she said, but giving up her career was out of the question. As she put it: "I had things clawing inside of me that must be said."

Hurston and Punter continued to see each other, but this fundamental conflict in their relationship drove a wedge between them. They began to argue more and more, and their mutual jealousies escalated. One night, as Hurston remembered it, an argument turned particularly ugly and she found herself in physical combat with Punter. "No broken bones," she recalled, "and no black eyes," but combat nonetheless.

Realizing that the relationship was unhealthy for her, Hurston jumped at the chance to put some distance between herself and Punter when she received a Guggenheim fellowship to study Haitian Vodou and Caribbean culture. With only a hasty goodbye, she took off for Jamaica, where she threw herself into her research in an attempt to "smother" her feelings for Punter. Once her research took her to Haiti, however, all the feelings that she'd dammed up inside came flooding out. Commanded by a "force somewhere in Space," as she dramatically put it, Hurston started writing a novel, working urgently for days on end. All the while, her love for Punter stayed on her mind. "The plot was far from the circumstances," she noted, "but I tried to embalm all the tenderness of my passion for him in *Their Eyes Were Watching God.*" In just seven weeks, right before Christmas 1936, Hurston finished what would become her second novel. The book was published in September 1937.

DP: *And the film, what was the genesis of the film?*

VB: I interviewed Oprah Winfrey about the genesis of the film for a short piece I wrote for *Essence* magazine. I asked her to recall her first encounter with *Their Eyes Were Watching God.* She said, "I first read *Their Eyes* while on the set shooting *The Color Purple.* Alice Walker was constantly singing the praises of Zora Neale Hurston. Danny Glover said he'd read the book 23 times. I felt left out of the conversation. A story so compelling that anyone can read 23 times is a must read for me. So I got the book and remember reading it straight through and was bawlin' like a baby when Tea Cake was telling Janie she was like the roses. It's my favorite love story of all time. Because ultimately it's about learning to love what's real about yourself, so that you're free to love as you choose."

When I asked Oprah how the movie came about and how she chose Halle Berry to play the long-coveted role of Janie Crawford, she said it all seemed sort of predestined to her: "Halle seemed a natural for Janie. For years I've wanted to do this story and always saw her in the role," Oprah said. "I gave her the book to read almost a decade ago when she first appeared on my show. This was before I even had the rights to the book, but I knew if there were rights to be had, I would go to battle for them, and I did. As it turns out, I was in a bidding war—the price kept going up and up, because somebody else wanted it as badly as I did. Turns out that somebody was Quincy Jones. Alice Walker had bent his ear about Zora too. So I called him up and said,

'Hey, quit biddin' against me. I really, really want this.' He said, 'All right baby, let's split it.' And we did."

DP: *Novels and films are very different genres, of course. With novels, we certainly might want to have an appreciation of authorial intent. As the definitive biographer of Zora Neale Hurston to date, what do you see as Hurston's intent in the novel?*

VB: *Their Eyes Were Watching God* is, as you know, the story of Janie Crawford, a deep-thinking, deep-feeling black woman who embarks on a journey to know her own self—and, I believe, to know her own Highest Self. I think Hurston's intent was multifaceted. This novel is so multilayered and richly nuanced that it's difficult to deconstruct Hurston's intent, but here are just a few of the things that always strike me when I reread it. I think Hurston wanted to follow this ordinary, self-educated black woman on this inner journey of discovery. I think she wanted to give voice to this rural black female character, someone who was neither Mammy nor Jezebel, but who had an active, healthy sexuality—but who, up to this point, was completely invisible in American literature. I think she also wanted to privilege black vernacular speech and present it as the poetry that it is. I think she's also writing about the joys and limits of community. And, of course, she's also exploring the many facets of love in the novel—love of others, love of community and, especially, love of self.

DP: *And the movie, what do you perceive to be the intention of the producer?*

VB: Here's how producer Oprah Winfrey addressed that question in my interview with her. She said, "When I first read *Their Eyes*, it jumped off the page and came alive in a way I believed could translate beautifully to film. Since then, it's been a long-time dream of mine to share the story with as many people as possible, and television provides the opportunity to reach millions with the book's powerful message of strength, determination and survival."

DP: *As succinctly as you can, would you compare and contrast the general popular and critical reception of the novel and the film for us?*

VB: To put it succinctly, I think both the novel and the film received somewhat mixed receptions. When the novel was first published in 1937, it earned rave reviews; Hurston was featured in several newspaper profiles; and Pulitzer Prize-winning poet Edna St. Vincent Millay sent Hurston a telegram congratulating her on the book's success.

But then some black male critics were really harsh in their responses to the novel—at least partly, I think, because Hurston used the novel to convey her view that women were the equals of men in every way—and that their inner lives were infinitely rich and worthy of exploration. Given these proto-feminist themes, it's no surprise that Richard Wright, soon to become the best-selling author of *Native Son*, categorically dismissed Hurston's book: "The sensory sweep of her novel carries no theme, no message, no thought," he wrote. But we should remember, of course, that Wright was not exactly known for his progressive views toward women. And how dare Hurston write a novel with a self-aware, sexually desirable, financially secure, well-spoken, thoughtful black woman at the center of it?

Over the years, most critics have emphatically disagreed with Wright's dim assessment of Hurston's novel, which is now required reading in high schools and colleges throughout the country. "There is no book more important to me than this one," Alice Walker has said. And Oprah Winfrey has called *Their Eyes Were Watching God* her "favorite love story of all time."

Winfrey's admiration for the novel is what inspired her to produce the television adaptation of it, which aired for the first time on March 6, 2005. And the film, like the novel, received mixed reviews. One critic called it "a mostly successful mix of suds and substance," and I think that's probably a pretty fair assessment.

Of course, some die-hard fans of the novel didn't like the choice of Halle Berry as Janie. Personally, I felt that she didn't really transcend being Halle Berry to actually *become* Janie, but was always Halle *playing* Janie. I also might have cast a more voluptuous, more womanly actress in the role, and someone whose face was less well known to viewers—maybe an Audra McDonald. Yet at the same time, I have to say that the girlishness that Halle Berry brought to the role was delightful, and the chemistry between her and Michael Ealy, who played Tea Cake, was remarkable. So, while it's not the adaptation that I would have made, as Hurston's biographer, there is still a lot to enjoy and admire in the film. And I think it's important to note that Halle Berry was nominated for an NAACP Image Award, a Golden Globe Award, and an Emmy Award for her performance.

DP: *For you, what are the greatest points of comparison between the novel and the film, in terms of content, character, plot, etc.?*

VB: I think the film is best enjoyed when taken on its own terms, as a work of art in its own right, engaged in a kind of cinematic dialogue with the novel. When I saw the film the first time, I was very critical of it because I disagreed with the way it portrayed certain scenes from the novel. But I had to let that go. No film is a literal translation of any book. It has to be taken on its own terms.

I also realized—from interviewing Halle Berry and Oprah Winfrey—that they didn't set out to make a jacked-up movie. They love *Their*

Eyes as much as you and I do, and they were trying to do their best to bring the novel to life on the screen. Of course, they made different choices than we might make, but they were still thoughtful choices, lovingly made. So once I embraced that reality, I was able to enjoy the film and appreciate what it offers.

And here's the thing: The TV movie was watched—on that one night in March 2005—by an estimated 24.6 million viewers, which further entrenched the novel in the public consciousness and in the American literary canon. The movie also sent readers back to the novel. The TV buzz propelled the novel onto the *New York Times* Bestseller List for three weeks. This was in 2005—68 years after the novel was first published. So, in that sense, I think the film certainly served a great purpose.

DP: *Among contemporary artists, who, for you, is the most exciting writer (of any genre and more than one, if that is appropriate), and the most exciting filmmaker?*

VB: Wow, that's a tough question: THE most exciting? I haven't seen or read everything, obviously, so it's hard to answer that question with any kind of authority. I can say, though, that I like the work of filmmaker Kasi Lemmons very much. I like what she did with *Eve's Bayou* as well as *Talk to Me*. I would love to see her consider directing *Wrapped in Rainbows*, if it's ever made into a film. She has a young daughter named Zora, so I know she's a fan.

As for most exciting writers: There are many, many contemporary writers doing amazing, inspiring work. There are a couple of celebrated, Pulitzer Prize-winning writers of my generation whose work I admire very much: people like Edward P. Jones and Jhumpa Lahiri. But there are also some exciting contemporary writers of color whose work hasn't received as much acclaim, though I think it's equally compelling. I'm thinking particularly of Tayari Jones (*Leaving Atlanta*); Dana Johnson (*Break Any Woman Down*); Shay Youngblood (*Soul Kiss*); Nina Revoyr (*The Age of Dreaming*); and Phyllis Alesia Perry (*Stigmata*), all fiction writers who do beautiful work. Among nonfiction writers, I really enjoy the work of biographer Wil Haygood, who's written a powerful American trilogy of three black men: Adam Clayton Powell Jr., Sammy Davis Jr., and Sugar Ray Robinson. I also recently read a book about New Orleans by a white writer, Dan Baum, that I found really compelling. It's called *Nine Lives: Death and Life in New Orleans*. All of these books—along with classics from writers like Zora Neale Hurston, Jean Toomer, James Baldwin, Toni Morrison, Alice Walker, and others—really inspire me to do my own best work.

De-Lionizing Zora Neale Hurston?

Linda Tavernier-Almada

"It used to be a dirt road for a very long time," said my informant, a gentle-looking, 90-year-old woman. I thought about the road that she was referring to, Kennedy Boulevard, originally known as Old Apopka Road and later as Eatonville Road. It is the main thoroughfare, and really the only route, that one needs to get to anywhere in the little town of Eatonville. I had taken it to get to my informant's house today, and by now I knew every façade. Indeed, I knew Kennedy Boulevard from beginning to end, and I also knew many of the people who lived on or behind it. This was not a great achievement, as one can actually walk the whole length of Kennedy in 20 minutes.

Knowledge of Eatonville, Florida, came to me as all good things come to those of us who teach—from reading a student's paper. Her essay was actually about symbolism in one of Zora Neale Hurston's novels. However, in one line in her essay, my student mentioned that the town where the author was born was less than three miles from the school where I was then teaching. I was unfamiliar with the area, because I had only recently moved from California. Hence, I was floored when I realized my proximity to the dreamy little town so often referred to in Hurston's writings.

Salivating at the prospect of doing my own fieldwork investigation of the town that had so inspired the famous author, I was also curious about the fact that this was a town with an all-black population. At the time, I was at the peak of my anthropological plateau of excitement as I imagined the warm, loving stories the townspeople would tell me about their home girl and the impact she and her fame had had on their little community. After all, had not my colleagues and I always been fascinated by this author and her work? Her books had often resulted in interesting discussions in my classes, both at the small local school where I now taught and at UC Berkeley, where the students had no historical connection to the town or its author. To my surprise, however, things were not so clear-cut with the Eatonville citizens.

Like many before me, I attempted to celebrate the author by researching her fellow townspeople. However, it slowly dawned on me that, without exception, works done on Hurston have not properly addressed the historical reality and relevance of the legendary author's impact on the town itself or its citizenry. Yet, the complex history of this town, where the author lived all of her youth and set most of her writings, and where her legacy is archived and commemorated, is an important part of locating contemporary sociocultural questions about Hurston's narrative.

A review of the writings on the author during the past 30 years, mostly from academics, shows a clear imbalance in how Hurston's ideological remake was articulated. Only praise for her work found its way into any publication or public forum. This was a result of the pushback against the negative attacks the author had suffered during the later part of her life, when critics found her last three books wanting. After her revival, those critical of her work refrained from making public statements, for fear of appearing to be in poor taste, or concerned about being shunned or demonized by those of the intellectual community. This silencing of Hurston's critics also occurred in her hometown. Her lionizers there also only extolled her virtues, and the average citizens of Eatonville, who did not agree with the modern rhetoric being espoused by those in charge of her legacy, often felt that they would be marginalized if they spoke up. In fact, they often were.

As my fieldwork in Eatonville progressed, I became aware that there was a huge difference between those few citizens who were part of the group fighting to preserve the Hurston legacy and the average townsfolk, and that the desires and wants of those two groups were often at odds. As an anthropological folklorist, I was naturally drawn to the latter group, because they constituted the town's working-class and underclass communities and were the largest constituency in Eatonville. Their reticence to talk to outsiders, as has been repeatedly noted, was not, as presumed by previous writers, because they are a taciturn people, but rather because this was their subversive way of contesting the legacy's displacement of their lived realities. As an adherent to Antonio Gramsci's organic approach to fieldwork, I was inevitably drawn to learn more about the average citizens of Eatonville. In the process, I had no idea that, eventually for me, their story would gain precedence over that of the author's legacy.

After my first year of doing fieldwork in the town, I understood that I should not mention Hurston's name when I was interviewing the townspeople, if I did not want to gather long passive silences all day. So long as I kept the subject of Hurston out of my interviews, I generated warm and even lengthy feedbacks from the average Eatonviller. Most of the 58 of my students whom I had taken into Eatonville also noticed that it was not productive to discuss Hurston with older Eatonvillers. One student noted in her final research paper that it was not until she told her 89-year-old informant that the interview was not about Hurston that she was asked to sit down. It became clear to me that the much-written-about myth of how guarded Eatonvillers are is directly connected to their strong antipathy toward either the author or the guardians of her legacy, including the continuous flow of writers who have come through the town. When the subject of conversation is not set on extolling the author or her legacy, most Eatonvillers are generally friendly and talkative folks, who seem always ready with a story about their town and its historical attributes. However, for many of them, that approachable demeanor changes drastically at the mere mention of Hurston. A palpable exasperation was most obvious in women over the age of 60 and under the age of 25 whenever a conversation was linked to anything Hurstonian. At the protothought level, there was a fundamental difference between average Eatonvillers, members of the "Hurston crowd," and the slew of probing visitors, whose sole purpose seemed to be to own their piece of Hurston through writings or some other form of commemorative work.

As my research continued, I noted that many of the Hurstonites did not actually live in Eatonville. Still more interesting was my discovery that, even among the Hurstonites themselves, there was deep resentment toward the impact her legacy was having on the small town. Those of them who did live in Eatonville were more likely to criticize the author and the impact of her legacy on the town, if they were assured that they would not be directly quoted. It is at this point that I began to understand why so many people who had gone into Eatonville to write about the author so often came away feeling that the townsfolk are "reserved" and "guarded." After making this unexpected discovery in various interviews, I was compelled to learn more about the town itself and to give the people space to express their honest feelings.

THE HURSTON FAMILY IN EATONVILLE

My essay-writing student had not gotten the information quite right. Eatonville was not actually Hurston's birthplace, but rather the town to which her parents had moved when their daughter was a mere three years old. It was the place where the author spent most of her childhood until the death of her mother, Lucy Hurston, in 1904, when Zora was 13. Eatonville was also the place where the author's father, John Hurston, was the minister of the Macedonia Baptist Church from 1902 to 1917, and the town's third mayor, from 1912 to 1916. He helped to establish some of the town's key municipal laws, and ordered the building of the town's first jail. John Hurston clearly had a strong impact on the town's educational and religious orientation. Eatonville is approximately five miles north of Orlando. Although several all-black towns came into existence in the United States after the Civil War, and although a dozen or so still claim to be all-black, only Eatonville is truly so. For the most part, the others are either too small to be considered towns, or they have had a sprinkling of whites among them. This last point is important to the concept of what it means to be an all-black town, particularly what it meant during the years following slavery and right up to the 1960s. Throughout that century, an all-black town with all-black government officials was fundamentally more vulnerable to all sorts of predators than a town with whites—regardless of how small their numbers. During the post-Civil War era, the years of Jim Crow, and at least until the *Brown v. Board of Education* decision in 1954, a town that had some whites was somewhat insulated from the wrath of the Ku Klux Klan and other racist hate groups and individuals. In the South alone, between 1882 and 1936, it is estimated that 3,383 blacks were lynched, mostly for petty crimes or trumped-up charges.[1] Eatonville, being a true all-black town, had no internal protection against such predators. And yet, as one of my informants, a 75-year-old woman, gleefully told me, referring to the KKK, "They never came in this town!" As she said this, she seemed to grow just a little bit taller. During several of my interviews with the town's senior citizens, I found that they took great pride in the fact that, several times, groups they thought were perhaps with the KKK had come to the edge of their town, sometimes creating "all sorts of ruckus out there," but never coming into the town itself.

Comparatively, for a town to truly be considered all-black, it should have been founded and continuously governed and inhabited only by black people for most of its early existence. Eatonville meets all of these criteria, although today it has a minuscule white population, constituting less than half of 1% of the citizenry. In fact, Eatonville is the only town left in the United States that fits the all-black profile I have described here.

The town was founded in 1867 by newly freed slaves, who had been allowed to live on some unused property near a white-owned area now called Maitland, Florida.[2] The white people of Maitland had allowed this small black population to live on that land because it was

convenient for them to have manual laborers living nearby. These former slaves worked for the whites in their fields, shops, and homes.
Two black men, Joseph E. Clark and Allen Rickett, decided to purchase
part of the land in order to start a town. These were the first twelve
acres of what later became Eatonville's original 112 acres. Another ten
of those 112 were donated by the St. Lawrence African Methodist Epis-
copal Church, which still stands in Eatonville today, with a large,
mostly black, congregation that comes from all the surrounding cities
and towns. Eatonville was officially incorporated by 27 black men on
August 15, 1887, giving it the legitimate claim of "first incorporated
all-black town in the United States."[3]

As of July 2007, Eatonville had a total population of 2,379, nearly
90% of whom are black. The town's median household income for that
year was $36,438, which is considerably lower than Florida's mean
income of $47,804. Between 1994 and 2006 various improvements
were made to the town's infrastructure, including a $3 million sewer
upgrade; an upgrade of the town's police facilities; and the purchase of
21 new police cars. Before this, the town had rented police cars from
car rental companies. The town also got a new library, a new town
hall, and a complete renovation of the main thoroughfare, Kennedy
Boulevard. Also in 2006, the town's property tax base increased from
$43 million to $195 million.[4]

These days, Kennedy Boulevard looks much better than the dirt road
described by my informant. It runs through the center of town, with
two lanes paved with beautiful rich red brick, and is anchored by an
island with small palm trees and cleanly cut edges. Overall, it is pretty,
quaint, and inviting, lined with many small buildings that are painted
with vibrant colors, giving the town a toylike semblance. As one drives
along Kennedy, there is a little building that says Zora Neale Hurston
Museum. Not far from that, also at the town center, there is a new
Zora Neale Hurston Library. On Sundays, all of the town's churches
are crammed with black parishioners, who come from all over the east
central Florida region to worship in Eatonville. The little town's
churches never seem to have enough room for everyone, which may be
why the town has a church every half-mile.

Hurston's family moved to Eatonville only three years after the town
was founded, and several years before it was incorporated, so the
Hurstons were among the town's earliest residents. Current residents
who are old enough to remember the Hurston family have colorful and
endearing stories to tell about their life in the town, particularly about
the author's father. Thus, it was not the whole Hurston family that
prompted ill will among the citizens. Yet, the average Eatonviller's
reluctance to talk about Zora, outside of her family life when she was a
child, is undeniable. As a matter of fact, it sometimes seems difficult

for many of the female senior citizens to even mention the museum dedicated to her or the annual festival that celebrates her and brings tons of visitors and money to the town. As for Zora's books, the most one gets out of the townspeople is a brief, "Yes, I read them." So, why were the majority of Eatonvillers I interviewed so reluctant to talk about Zora? I was all the more puzzled that the mere mention of the author's name should bring on a curious heaviness, particularly among those over the age of 65.

ZORA AND EATONVILLE

The tense relationship between Hurston and the town started before her death. It is a well-established fact that the townspeople resented her portrayal of their community. However, it is really after Zora's death that we see an interesting correlation between the town's decline, the production of the Hurston legend, and the defensive discourse now prevalent among Eatonvillers. The birth of the legend was launched in 1975 by African American novelist Alice Walker. Hurston's resurrection from dead history was one of many that happened in the late 20th century. During the 1970s and 1980s, there was a sudden interest in resurrecting black female writers who had been archived on forgotten library shelves. Such authors as Harriet Jacobs (1813–1897); Pauline E. Hopkins (1859–1930); N.F. Mossell (1855–1948); Lucy C. Parsons (1853?–1942); and Frances Harper (1825–1911) were all given life again during that period. This movement, in fact, was a projection of the frustration felt by modern black female authors, and served as a conduit for their own unrecognized and uncelebrated voices. This literary revival period provoked much discourse about the state of black female writers, resulting in many positive changes in their position in the literary circuit. Many of the authors rescued from library death would now be sought after and read, mostly by faculty members and their students. However, unlike the others named above, Hurston's literary reincarnation came from an author whose own magnificent writings catapulted to the top of the literary world during those revival years and after, and in doing so took Hurston along with them. Hurston's name, now attached to Walker's impressive accomplishments, became an extremely desired commodity, and everyone wanted a part of it.

However, I doubt that Walker herself could ever have imagined that Hurston, whose work is worthy of praise, would one day become such an African American literary icon that she would be placed alongside, and often above, such greats as Langston Hughes, Richard Wright, Ralph Ellison, Gwendolyn Brooks, Lorraine Hansberry, Toni Morrison, and Alex Haley. In fact, Hurston's legend is now often prioritized over the tangible and substantial body of work done by Alice Walker herself.

As the Hurston legend grew with a festival dedicated to her in Eatonville in 1987, her narrative was further intertwined with the lived reality of the citizens of the town. One might think that that would have been good for Eatonville, but in fact the rise of the Hurston legend proved to coincide with the rapid decline in the quality of life for the townspeople. Before the late 1980s, there had been a steady migration into Eatonville by black people, who were seeking a safer, more wholesome life for their children. Frank Otey, the only historian of Eatonville, notes that from the 1960s to the 1980s, a "booming economy meant jobs for virtually everyone who wanted them and increased wages for those who worked. . . . People could afford a higher standard of living. They built new homes, or they painted, repaired, and modernized their old ones."[5] From the late 1980s on, however, the incoming migration stopped and the exodus of people, particularly young working-class people and their dollars, began.

As the author's narrative achieved national importance, at the local level it began to completely dominate the lives of the townspeople. Initially, the citizens of Eatonville tolerated this ubiquitous incursion, perhaps thinking that Hurston's fame would eventually benefit them. Given different circumstances, that might have happened. But the people soon began to feel that the Hurston advocates did not necessarily represent them.

THE ZORA IMPACT ON EATONVILLE

To an outsider, the charming look of Kennedy Boulevard is heartwarming, and Hurston's admirers take great pride in the fact that they defeated a plan to widen the boulevard and open a freeway access to it. One writer, who quotes her source as the executive director of the Hurston legacy in Eatonville, claims that when the road change was cancelled, "Hurston's old neighbors saw [Zora] as a savior."[6]

Many articles favoring this same conclusion were written when the road-widening project was dropped. Outsiders who do not understand the dichotomy between the town's needs and the need of Hurston's admirers to preserve her legacy often use the most affluent members of the town as their informants. They therefore congratulated the town for its success in defeating the project. What they did not understand is that the average Eatonviller had hoped that the expansion of the town's main road would help the town itself to expand economically.

What most of those who wrote about the defeat failed to understand is that the townspeople felt that the reason the Hurston lionizers fought the road project was that they were intent on keeping the town as it is described in Hurston's novels. To do this, they must keep Eatonville stuck in time. Unlike the outsiders, average Eatonvillers feel that they were deprived of a project that would bring development possibilities and jobs to the town, but were powerless to do anything about it, because the Hurston forces dominate the community.

Hence, ordinary Eatonvillers remain silent for fear of being ostracized. Because of this social subtext, however, they become more resentful of the author and everything she stands for in their town. All the while, the intellectuals remain completely out of touch with the organic reality that surrounds them, continually enabling the sociocultural continuum that marginalizes average Eatonvillers for the benefit of the long-departed author.

Once one turns off Kennedy Boulevard to visit the little streets behind it, it becomes clear how the work of the Hurston advocates has subverted the well-being of the majority of the people in this small town. Beyond Kennedy, the rest of the town's homes, with a few exceptions, seem somewhat battle-weary, as if everything needs a fresh coat of paint. I am not implying that the town looks shabby, but it certainly does not look prosperously antique. Fences need mending, and shingles need repair. The town is certainly not ugly, nor is it unpleasant. In a way, it is quietly inviting. And although behind Kennedy Boulevard things look a little sad, those less visible areas are kept as clean and neat as the town center.

For the most part, everyone's lawns are primly cut, even when they are obviously in need of fertilizer. Clean, faded, curtains frame most of the windows, even in many of the more affluent homes. Many houses have little flower and plant arrangements in front—nothing remotely elaborate, but enough to give color. The town gives the impression of a favorite old pair of shoes that one cannot bear to leave behind or throw out. Most of my informants live in these faded little houses behind Kennedy Boulevard.

The town officials once raised enough funds to have some of the sadder-looking houses painted, and many students from the local college volunteered their efforts toward this project. However, even this small effort to take the town out of the temporal image set by Hurston displeased those in charge of her legacy. It seems that anything that takes the town beyond the image painted of it in Hurston's novels is displeasing to these Hurstonites, regardless of how it may benefit the town. Yet, the fresh coat of paint on some of the houses improved the town's overall appearance without changing its sleepy dollhouse image.

As the self-appointed protectors of the Hurston legacy continuously failed to differentiate between the town's well-being and the promotion of the Hurston legend, life became more difficult for the average citizens.

Anything that did not clearly advance the legendary figure's narrative was deemed irrelevant, regardless of how important it was to the town's average citizens. Thus, since the 1980s, many of the town's old homes, some dating back to the 1800s, have been destroyed. Because they were not directly connected to the author's stories, no serious effort was made to save them. Yet, Eatonville's historical heritage as the first all-black town in the United States is just as significant to black history as the life and legacy of a single author, if not more so.

In 2005, the town officials attempted to raise awareness of the cultural importance of Eatonville in American history by building a town museum dedicated to African American culture. The museum, which would have been surrounded by new shops and a new walkway, would have merged Hurston's legacy with the works of various African American artists in the context of displaying the town's history. However, this project received no support from the Hurston lionizers, who instead threatened (idly, as it turned out) to move the Zora Neale Hurston Festival out of Eatonville into a neighboring town.

Perhaps the most striking example of the town's needs being ignored by the Hurstonites is what has happened to Eatonville's two schools, the first one of which was founded in 1889 on land donated as a trust for the special purpose of creating a "school for negroes."[7] The school was the first and only one in the area for black children. In 1951, a court decree ordered the transfer of all of the school's property (except for its chapel) to the Orange County School Board (OCSB). Instead of—as promised—using the land to benefit the community and to help the school and the black children of Eatonville, the school board sold much of the land to big corporations.[8] Recently, the OCSB voted to close down the high school in order to save the county money. In this battle for educational survival, the little town would have stood a chance if the educational system had been intertwined with the Hurston historical legacy. Instead, the school stood alone, because its demise would not noticeably affect that legacy.

During much of the 1980s and 1990s, the continuous proliferation of Hurston's narrative over that of the town left average Eatonvillers precariously vulnerable—much more vulnerable, in fact, than they had been during any time in their past. Clearly, in Eatonville, Hurston's history truncates and dislocates all non-Hurston references.

ACADEMIC RESPONSIBILITY

I believe that, for the past 30 years, we in academia have also served as funnels for the reconstruction of a legendary discourse about Hurston without seriously questioning the validity of that production. Furthermore, we have imposed this legendary narrative on our students, almost to the detriment of truly amazing writings from other African American authors. As with its dominant position in the Eatonville historical landscape, we have allowed Hurston's narrative to occupy an extraordinary space in black female literature that could well be occupied by other, more outstanding black female authors.

The power of academics to launch, remake, or undo a literary figure is enormous, and must be used with great responsibility, because our decisions reverberate throughout the lives of our students and the general public. However, I am in no way trying to take from Hurston what was originally given to her by Alice Walker and others. I am simply proposing that we consider whether or not there are other literary figures who are as deserving as Hurston is of the legendary status we have bestowed on her. I am also saying that the true Hurston narrative has been supplanted by an aggrandized version that perhaps exceeds the author's real life and work. Consider, for example, the way we in academia introduce Hurston to our students. Most of us introduce her with great fanfare, prefacing her books with all of her life history and suffering, and anything else that we feel the students will need to understand why we are asking them to favor her work. I question our motive for doing that. Is it possible that, although Hurston's writings are pleasant and interesting, they are not breathtaking or heartwrenching, like those of some of our other black female authors? Is it possible that Hurston's books cannot stand alone? Let us, for instance, consider providing our students with either *Tell My Horse* or *Their Eyes Were Watching God*, and waiting for them to come into our offices elated, astonished, or reverent. Do they come with tears, anger, or deep depression, as they do after reading *The Invisible Man*, *Native Son*, *Beloved*, or *The Color Purple*? Have intellectuals been complicit in creating a legend that everyone else has bought into?

Perhaps anxiety about being undesired or unwelcomed by the literary community means that we in academia have allowed Hurston's narrative to become too big. The average citizens of Eatonville dare not speak up, lest they be ostracized by the Hurston canonists, and we in academia appear to suffer from the same impotence.

NOTES

1. Mary Frances Berry and John W. Blasangame, *Long Memory: The Black Experience in America* (New York: Oxford University Press, 1982), 123.

2. Frank M. Otey, *Eatonville, Florida: A Brief History* (Winter Park, FL: Four-G Publishers, 1989), 1.

3. Otey, *Eatonville, Florida: A Brief History*, 1–3.

4. Anthony Grant, "To: The Association to Preserve the Eatonville Community" (Letter presented to the association, February 15, 2005).

5. Otey, *Eatonville, Florida: A Brief History*, 44.

6. Tradition of Excellence. (2008). *Honoring History and Contemporary Black Americans: Zora Neale Hurston's Eatonville Still a Florida Anomaly*. Retrieved June 18, 2009, from http://traditionofexcellence.wordpress.com/2008/10/01/zora-neale-hurstons-eatonville-still-a-florida-anomaly/.

7. Town of Eatonville Educational Advisory Committee: Recommendation on the Robert Hungerford Preparatory High School and the Robert Hungerford Elementary School, 2007.

8. Town of Eatonville Educational Advisory Committee, 2007.

"A Child Cannot Be Taught by Anyone Who Despises Him": Hurston versus Court-Ordered School Integration

Lynn Moylan

A child cannot be taught by anyone who despises him.

—James Baldwin

To say that Zora Neale Hurston's social and political views were controversial would be a classic understatement. In fact, many of her views are as contentious today as they were in her lifetime. She was, without a doubt, a highly complex individual who lived most of her life swimming upstream. Perhaps one of her most controversial stands, taken during the last decade of her life, was her opposition to the U.S. Supreme Court's 1954 *Brown v. Board of Education* decision. The pivotal ruling, which declared segregation in public schools unconstitutional, is considered the spark that launched the civil rights movement, which ultimately led to the end of American apartheid.

Hurston's position, which has been characterized as naive, short-sighted, and reactionary, earned her the reputation in some circles as a segregationist and a traitor to her race. Her critics, then as well as now, accused her of turning a blind eye to the stark realities of the black experience in America—a reality that she admittedly "had met in the flesh."

Her reputation also suffered from her friendships with conservative Southern politicians Spencer Holland and George Smathers who, along with 100 other members of Congress, signed the now infamous "Southern Manifesto," a protest document arguing that the federal government had no power to force states to integrate schools.

Considering the monumental positive outcomes of the civil rights movement, it is easy to identify with Hurston's critics. However, as we mark the 55th anniversary of the *Brown* decision in 2009, modern scholarship, which carefully examines the deleterious effects of school desegregation on the black population, has provided new insights into Hurston's misgivings and reaffirmed her social and political acumen.

Biographer Robert Hemenway contends that in her final years Hurston had become politically isolated and that her social and political philosophies had become too inflexible to accommodate changing situations or "demonstrate a future vision."[1] However, when viewing her opposition to the *Brown* decision through the retrospective lens of the 21st century, it is clear that her remonstration against the ruling was valid, insightful, and prescient.

Hurston's evolving political views were individualistic and at times eccentric, but she was neither a segregationist nor a traitor. "As a Negro, you know that I cannot be in favor of segregation, but I do deplore the way they go about ending it," she explained.[2] To her mind, the *Brown* decision was an insult to her race and its institutions as well as a dangerous exercise of judicial power. She was categorically opposed to a judicial decree that ordered culturally distinct races that had been segregated for over a century to suddenly mix—and to do so at a time of deep racial discord.

As a cultural anthropologist, folklorist, and writer, Hurston devoted the first two decades of her career trying to demonstrate the ideological, esthetic, and social significance of black culture. She held that the survival of African American culture and its traditions was central to the struggle against white dominance and racism.[3] To force black students to attend white educational institutions that excluded and devalued black culture robbed black children of those traditions that contribute to their individual and cultural identities and self-esteem.

She was appalled by the Court's insinuation that African American educational institutions were inferior and that "there is no greater delight to Negroes than physical association with whites," a misconception that, she complained, was exploited by the Communist Party to enlist black members. In a provocative letter to the *Orlando Sentinel* titled "Court Order Can't Make Races Mix," Hurston wrote: "The whole matter revolves around the self-respect of my people. How much satisfaction can I get from a court order for somebody to associate with me who does not wish me near them?" Convinced, along with many other Southerners, that the Supreme Court was usurping states' rights, Hurston warned her readers that the *Brown* decision could be a harbinger of more "ominous" things to come. In a statement consistent with the national preoccupation with the evils of Communism, she admonished: "What if it is contemplated to do away with the two-party system and arrive at government by decree? . . . Govt by fiat can replace the Constitution."[4] Taking aim at what she perceived as the hypocrisy of the NAACP in regard to the Court's implication that African American educational institutions were not adequately educating their youth, she argued:

. . . If there are not adequate Negro schools in Florida, and there is some residual, some inherent and unchangeable quality in white schools, impossible to duplicate anywhere else, then I am the first to insist that Negro children of Florida be allowed to share this boon. But if there are adequate Negro schools and prepared instructors and instructions, then there is nothing different except the presence of white people.

For this reason, I regard the ruling of the U.S. Supreme Court as insulting rather than honoring my race.

It is a contradiction in terms to scream race pride and equality while at the same time spurning Negro teachers and race association.[5]

Interestingly, W.E.B. Du Bois, a founding member of the NAACP and a staunch desegregationist, expressed similar confidence in black institutions. Writing in an editorial in the *Crisis* in April 1934, Du Bois argued that "thinking colored people of the U.S. must stop being stampeded by the word segregation . . . It is the race-conscious black man cooperating together with his own institutions and movements who will eventually emancipate the colored race."[6]

Hurston's letter to the *Sentinel* sparked a thunderous public response. Those who opposed *Brown* commended Hurston for supporting their positions, while *Brown* proponents condemned her for, among other things, her refusal to acknowledge the manifest inequalities that existed between Southern black and white schools. Instead, she argued that "Negro schools in the state are in very good shape and on the improve."[7]

Black public schools in the South, including Florida, had suffered from chronic neglect since 1885 when the Supreme Court's infamous "separate but equal" doctrine, which in reality meant "a little dab'll do ya," rendered the practice of discrimination legal and convenient. Black schools were often housed in inferior and sometimes dilapidated buildings without libraries or laboratories, and while transportation was provided for white students, black children had none.[8]

There were also significant disparities between black and white schools in the allocation of funds as well as inequalities in principal and teacher salaries. In 1940, white teachers' salaries were double the salaries of black teachers', and white principals received far greater stipends than those allotted to their black counterparts.[9]

In Hurston's defense, her claim that Florida was making progress toward improving black education was essentially true. In the early 1940s lawsuits initiated in Florida and filed by the NAACP had resulted in more equitable salaries for black and white teachers.[10] During that same period, the Florida legislature made a significant stride toward the improvement of black schools, due primarily to the efforts of Dr. D.E. Williams of the state Department of Education. Under his leadership, the state approved the Minimum Foundation Public School Program with the intention of ending the practice of allowing communities to allocate minimal funding to black and to poor white schools. Under this provision, ideally, all children in the state of Florida were assured a minimum standard of quality in the education financed by the state. But the results of the program were varied.

By 1952, according to the state Department of Education, Florida had closed the gap in capital outlays to black schools; however, the inequality in expenditures per pupil went unaddressed. During the same year, white schools received $195.01 per pupil, while black schools received $153.24.[11]

Although the rate of progress varied from state to state and from county to county, over the previous twelve years (1940–1952) the South overall had made significant gains toward raising the standards of public education to the national level. A report compiled by the U.S. Office of Education reported that the average per pupil spending, including both black and white schools, in thirteen Southern states increased more than threefold, from $46.98 in 1940 to $163.00 in 1952.[12]

While these increases were evidence of an upward trend, there still remained a substantial gap in per pupil expenditures between black and white rural school districts. Even after the passage of the Minimum Foundation Public School Program, in 1952 Florida's white rural school districts received $189.51 per pupil while their black counterparts received $119.22.[13]

But what Hurston certainly knew, and what *Brown* proponents failed to consider, was that despite these educational inequalities, most African American schools had "made a way out of no way," developing nurturing, effective, and successful educational and socialization systems that reflected their culture and values.[14]

Based on case studies of segregated schools before *Brown*, researchers have discovered that vital to the success of its students, African American schools across the South had established caring environments where every student was valued and encouraged to excel despite the oppression of a racist society.[15] Additionally, as an integral part of the community, many African American schools were the epicenters of social, recreational, and cultural life at a time when scarce resources were allocated for black communities.[16]

Hurston's concern for the loss of this vital cultural cohesion, and her confidence in African American educational institutions, was shared by many African Americans including the Reverend Dr. Martin Luther King, Jr. In 1959, in a candid conversation with two former black educators who had taught in Montgomery, Alabama's all-black Carver High School, King expressed his own concerns over the desegregation of public schools:

I favor integration on buses and in all areas of public accommodation and travel. I am for equality. However, I think integration in our public schools is different. In that setting, you are dealing with one of the most important assets of an individual—the mind. White people view black people as inferior. A large percentage of them have a very low opinion of our race. People with such a low view of the black race cannot be given free rein and put in charge of the intellectual care and development of our boys and girls.[17]

Based on historical accounts and academic studies of the desegregation era, these same concerns were echoed by African American educators and parents throughout the South. In the spring of 1954, when NAACP Legal Defense Fund representative Constance Baker Motley visited south Florida, she noted that some of the black teachers and administrators she met rejected integration in favor of equalization of facilities and resources, taking a "spend rather than blend" approach.[18]

Research conducted by Hamilton (2000) and reported in his classic article "Race and Education: A Search for Legitimacy" clearly demonstrates that before the *Brown* ruling, African Americans had every confidence in their capacity to educate their children. What they wanted was a fair share of the educational resources.[19] What they got instead were unfulfilled promises, white resistance, hostility and violence, poor educational opportunities, the loss of thousands of black teachers, hundreds of black principals, and the eradication of their institutions and traditions.

When the *Brown* decision was announced, the South's initial reaction was disbelief and indifference. But in 1955, when the Court's implementation decree (Brown II) ordered schools to desegregate with an oxymoron "with all deliberate speed," the response quickly turned from calm indifference to angry resistance. Individual communities formed citizens' councils, refuges of the Ku Klux Klan, to oppose any efforts toward desegregation, and Southern governors appointed expert commissions to study legal grounds to challenge it. Georgia and South Carolina forced the closing of desegregated schools by cutting off their funding. Alabama instituted a three-tier school system: one for blacks, one for whites, and one for those who chose to mix. Six other Southern states enacted pupil assignment laws, empowering school boards to assign white and black students to separate schools.[20] All of these tactics, meant to derail desegregation, were upheld by district courts.

In fact, from 1955 to 1957, no fewer than 120 laws were enacted in the South to oppose desegregation.[21] In strong protest in 1956, nearly every congressman in the Deep South signed the "Southern Manifesto." While state legislatures fought the legal battles and citizens' councils staged school boycotts and established private whites-only schools, violence erupted across the South as angry mobs blocked black children who tried to enter white public schools. In Kentucky, the National Guard was sent to restore law and order.[22]

These events, which Hurston described as "sickening," only served to cement her position on the folly of trying to legislate revolutionary social change. Having been welcomed as the first black student at Barnard College, she was utterly dumbstruck as to why Autherine Lucy, a black student who was denied entrance into the all-white University of Alabama in 1952, would subject herself to public humiliation and threats of violence in order to fight it through the courts, particularly when she had the option of attending quality African American colleges such as Tuskegee or Howard. "My nature would not permit me to go through what Authorine [sic] Lucy undertook. I could not bear to be so rejected. I am a sensitive soul and would rather go on to some school where I would be welcome."[23]

Given the hostility faced by black students who were forced to attend white schools, many of them might have shared Hurston's view. In their study on the effects of desegregation in Tuscumbia County in Alabama, Morris and Morris (2002) reported that black students who were forced to attend white schools were exposed to hostility not only from the students, but from the teachers and administrators as well.[24] In addition to the damaging emotional impact, black students suffered academic losses when many white schools implemented a system known as "tracking." In this system, white students were placed in accelerated or gifted classes and programs, while blacks were relegated to lower-level classes and programs.[25]

The Morris study findings, which reflect the conclusions of similar studies conducted throughout the South, illuminate the fact that despite the lofty promises of *Brown*, in addition to the low expectations placed on black students by white educators, the cultural connection and the vital sense of belonging and "ethic of caring" characteristic of their former all-black schools were in effect destroyed by the court system.[26]

Ten years after the *Brown* decision, hundreds of black school principals had lost their jobs; thousands of qualified, talented black teachers were fired; and hundreds of black schools were closed. And although the court had permanently altered the spirit of race relations, little had actually changed. By the 1963–1964 school year, a mere 1.19% of black students in the eleven core southern states were attending school with whites.[27]

Federal district judges continued to give school districts unlimited time to comply with the court's decree until 1971, when the Supreme Court ruled that lower courts had the authority to order busing of students from surrounding communities to achieve racial balance.

As a result of this ruling, white families who lived in urban school districts with court-ordered busing fled to the suburbs to avoid its reach. This exodus, which led to segregated housing patterns within cities, unfairly burdened black students who were shuffled in and out of white schools to take the places of those white students who had fled, only to be met with hostility and a curriculum that essentially ignored their needs.[28]

When the *Brown* decision was announced, former NAACP Legal Fund attorney Derrick Bell believed with near-religious fervor that it was destined to be the "Holy Grail of racial justice." But over the decades, *Brown*'s failures, losses, and broken promises to African Americans, long burdened by Jim Crow oppression, led to a broader and more sober perspective. In his book *Silent Covenant, Brown v. Board of Education and the Unfulfilled Hopes for Racial Reform*, Bell, who risked his life in support of *Brown*, contends that if he knew then what he knows now, he would have supported a different approach. He now holds that if the court had enforced "separate but equal" funding and resources for black schools, it might have been less contentious, less disruptive, and more effective: "In short, while the rhetoric of integration promised much, court orders to ensure that black youngsters actually received the education they needed to progress would have achieved more."[29]

By the time court-ordered desegregation ended in the 1990s, African Americans in the South had suffered devastating social, economic, academic, and cultural injustice. And in spite of it all, Orfield and Lee (2004) reported that K–12 schooling in the United States has experienced a "substantial slippage toward segregation in most states that were highly desegregated in 1991."[30]

African American literary critic Darwin Turner once quipped, "Miss Hurston did not always ignore the serious aspects of Afro-Americans; inexplicably, she denounced some of their efforts to secure equal opportunities in America."[31] Later, when the consequences of *Brown* were more apparent, he perceived her actions in a different light: "Perhaps history will prove Zora Neale Hurston wiser than she once seemed to Afro-Americans who optimistically looked only at the advantages of integration."[32]

Looking back at the effects of the *Brown* decision, and the high price paid by African Americans to implement it, it seems his prediction has come to pass.

NOTES

1. Robert Hemenway, *Zora Neal Hurston: A Literary Biography* (1977; repr., Urbana: University of Illinois Press, 1980), 336.

2. Zora Neale Hurston, *Zora Neale Hurston: A Life in Letters*, ed. Carla Kaplan (New York: Doubleday, 2002), 747.

3. Hemenway, *Zora Neale Hurston*, 332.

4. Zora Neale Hurston, "Court Order Can't Make Races Mix," *Orlando Sentinel*, August 11, 1955, in *Zora Neale Hurston: A Life in Letters*, 738–740.

5. Ibid., 738–740.

6. Quoted in Samuel G. Freedman, "Still Separate, Still Unequal," in the *New York Times*, May 16, 2004.

7. Hurston, *Zora Neale Hurston: A Life in Letters*, 740.

8. Edward D. Davis, *A Half Century of Struggle for Freedom in Florida* (Orlando: Drake's Publishing, 1981), 131.

9. Ben Green, *Before His Time: The Untold Story of Harry Moore, America's First Civil Rights Martyr* (New York: The Free Press, 1999), 36.

10. Ibid.

11. Harry S. Ashmore, *The Negro and the Schools* (Chapel Hill: University of North Carolina Press, 1954), 153.

12. Ibid., 152.

13. Ibid., 155.

14. Asa G. Hilliard, III, foreword to *The Price They Paid: Desegregation in an African American Community*, by Vivian Gunn Morris and Curtis L. Morris (New York: Teachers College Press, 2002), x.

15. Ibid., ix.

16. Morris and Morris, *The Price They Paid*, 3.

17. Quoted in Freedman, "Still Separate, Still Unequal," 33.

18. Brian J. Daugherity and Charles C. Bolton, eds., *With All Deliberate Speed: Implementing Brown v. Board of Education* (Fayetteville: University of Arkansas Press, 2008), 142.

19. C. Hamilton, "Race and Education: A Search for Legitimacy," *Harvard Educational Review* 38 (2000): 669–684.

20. John Bartlow Martin, *The Deep South Says Never* (New York: Ballantine Books, 1957), 11.

21. Ibid., 11.

22. Ibid., 6.

23. Hurston, *Zora Neale Hurston: A Life in Letters*, 747.

24. Morris and Morris, *The Price They Paid*, 78.

25. Derrick Bell, *Silent Covenants: Brown v. Board of Education and the Unfulfilled Hopes for Racial Reform* (New York: Oxford University Press, 2004), 112.

26. Morris and Morris, *The Price They Paid*, 79.

27. Bell, *Silent Covenants*, 96–97.

28. Ibid., 112.

29. Ibid., 4.

30. G. Orfield and C. Lee, "Brown at 50: King's Dream or Plessy's Nightmare?" *The Civil Rights Project*, Harvard University, 2004.

31. Quoted in Deborah G. Plant, *Every Tub Must Sit on Its Own Bottom: The Philosophy and Politics of Zora Neale Hurston* (Champaign: University of Illinois Press, 1995), 117.

32. Ibid., 118.

The Color Line and the Hem Line: Problem or Promise of a Post-Racial, Post-Gendered America

A. Giselle Jones-Jones

> I have asked many well-educated people of both races to tell me what this Race Problem is. They look startled at first. Then I can see them scratching around inside themselves and hunting for the meaning of the words which they have used with so much glibness and unction. I have never had an answer that was an answer, so I have had to make up my own. Since there is no fundamental conflict, since there is no solid reason why the blacks and the whites cannot live in one nation in perfect harmony, the only thing in the way of it is Race Pride and Race Consciousness on both sides.[1]

Admittedly out of step with her contemporaries of the early to mid-20th century, Zora Neale Hurston attempted to identify the loopholes or the gaps of sound reasoning concerning phrases like the "Race Problem," "Race Pride," "Race Man or Woman," "Race Solidarity," "Race Consciousness," and "Race Leader."[2] In her estimation, blacks were no better or worse than any other race. "Race pride," to her, "[was] a luxury [she could not] afford."[3] Roger Clegg, author of "Wrapped in Zora: A Rainbow without the Coalition" and contributing editor for the National Review Online (NRO), contends:

> Hurston had the right attitude, and even if one thinks it was not the right attitude then, it is most definitely the right attitude now. She was not afraid to denounce white prejudice, did so in no uncertain terms, and demanded to know why, if whites were superior, they were afraid to compete with blacks. "She would not allow white oppression to define or distort her life," however, and she "resolved to stay the course and focus on the positive, as was her way." Now more than ever, while it is fine to look at the injustices of the past, one

should not . . . stare. If Hurston, who lived in the Jim Crow South, concluded that one should not let bigotry define one's existence, how much truer is that now?[4]

Twenty-first-century Millennials, who comprise more than 80 million people born after 1981 and make up more than 41% of today's population,[5] would wholeheartedly agree with Hurston's repudiation of any color line, gender line, or any other social ill that may cause disharmony in our society. Recently tagged "New Progressives," Millennials are the most racially and ethnically diverse generation in United States history[6] who unequivocally "support gay marriages, take race and gender equality as givens, are tolerant of religious and family diversity, have an open and positive attitude toward immigration, and generally display little interest in fighting over the divisive social issues of the past."[7]

I believe Hurston would find promise in the Millennials' attempt toward humanization and social responsibility. "The fate of each and every group," Hurston proposes, "is bound up with the others. Individual ability in any group must function for all the rest. . . . There is no escape in grouping. And in practice, there can be no sharp lines drawn, because the interest of every individual in any racial group is not identical with the others. Section, locality, self-interest, special fitness, and the like set one group of Anglo-Saxons, Jews, and Negroes against another set of Anglo-Saxons, Jews, and Negroes. We are influenced by a pain in the pocket just like everybody else."[8] Zora Neale Hurston explains in no uncertain terms that people, not races, commit heinous acts oftentimes at the expense of others because of their necessity or love of money. Race becomes the culprit for greed.

The problem that Hurston might see with this burgeoning cohort, however, is its overwhelming sense of *conformity*.[9] Hurston's life repelled any station in life that resembled conventionality. "I am so put together," she exalts, "that I do not have much of a herd instinct. Or if I must be connected with the flock, let *me* be the shepherd my ownself. That is just the way I am made."[10] Further she states, "The solace of easy generalization was taken from me, but I received the richer gift of individualism. When I have been made to suffer or when I have been made happy by others, I have known that individuals were responsible for that, and not races. All clumps of people turn out to be individuals on close inspection."[11] So, while Millennials are reportedly high achieving, intelligent, and optimistic as a group, as Millennial researcher Edward Spencer postulates, they are "often under prepared for the challenges of an independent lifestyle."[12]

It is therefore at this junction that I interject the purpose for this essay: I contend that because she was a complex woman with many faces or sides or personalities, Zora Neale Hurston makes an interesting study most significantly for her instinctual proclivity for self-actualization. Throughout the course of her life, her thoughts and attitude were against the grain and unpopular at a very contentious time in our not-so-distant past; for that reason, the providence of her life and works *as a black woman* positions her for a more localized role in modeling libratory practices toward self-actualization and self-empowerment for young black women.

Why narrow the focus to only *black* women? My intention here is not to exclude anyone, for the principles asserted in the ensuing pages as *strategies* may be instructive, containing pedagogical practices proving beneficial for multiple audiences and for various and competing purposes. In that regard, the narrowing is didactic and universally purposeful.

The broader goal of this essay is to centralize Hurston's wisdom, experiences, and stories in such a way that Millennial black women may organize their thoughts and govern their attitudes and behaviors around deep-abounding concepts, such as *self-actualization* and *self-empowerment.* Most importantly, it is my hope that these young women will embrace this line of discourse as a "process" or journey *toward* becoming self-actualized and self-empowered. There are no quick fixes or easy answers. Moving *toward* something signifies a metaphysical position of "becoming."[13] In "becoming," "the basic doctrine is that the universe is essentially a creative advance and that everything in the universe is in the process of moving toward self-realization and fulfillment. . . . Process is marked by creativity; things [that] are constantly trying to create new experiences for themselves."[14] Thus, this essay is about the black woman's (and ultimately about myself as researcher) ability to negotiate space for creating and analyzing "new experiences" for ourselves and about our ongoing or continual journey toward "fulfillment" that moves us past our pain and suffering to a place of hope, potential, critical self-examination and reflection, and forgiveness.

THE SEARCH FOR *PURPOSE* IN THE TRENCHES

Perhaps it is because of my positionality at the present time that I am extremely concerned about the role my students will play in the future. I am an assistant professor of English at Bennett College for Women in Greensboro, North Carolina, and my task is not only to provide instruction in the processes and functions of human communications, but also to advance the mission of the college. Dr. Julianne Malveaux, 15th President of Bennett College for Women, quite appropriately prefaces many of her addresses to the college community with the following charge that keeps me ever mindful of my multi-layered task:

David Dallas Jones, the ninth President of Bennett College for Women was known for walking up to young women on campus and asking them, "Young lady, *what is your purpose?*" [Emphasis added.] It is our intention to help young women discover their purpose, embrace their dreams and possibilities, and move forward, with distinction, into our ever-changing world. And it is our intention to create a space that is safe, wholesome, supportive and sisterly, an oasis in our rapidly changing society. For many, it is truly an emotional anchor, an oasis.[15]

Embedded in this message is the notion of *intention*. Our intention as educators on this particular campus, which is one of two historically black colleges for women in the United States, is to take young women from where they are—regardless of their academic, social, economic, or spiritual condition as they enter Bennett's austere, yet prestigious gates—to another/higher level, a better place. Intention implies little more than what we as an institution *desire* to do or bring about; the success of our intentions has a great deal to do with what happens on a one-on-one level with our students. Though queried some 50 years ago, Dr. Jones's intuitive question resonates even more profoundly today and for good reason.

A peripheral look around the campus on any given day, one may see the appearance of an oasis. However, in the trenches, where educators are, in the classrooms or in our offices, we look squarely into the eyes of many of our students, yet we do not see purpose. Instead we see *frustration* and *wandering*. They are longing, and those of us educators who care meet them where they are and do our best to guide them. This ethical characteristic is one, in my full estimation, that separates those who are "called" to teach from those who are not. What we must do for today's Millennial students requires much more time, effort, and energy than a mere three hours in a classroom per week begets.

Particularly, many of my students just *happen to* stop by my office, at any given time (regardless of my "actual" posted office hours) desiring a moment of my time to "run something by me," which ends up being an hour-long moment. Still others linger after class offering to accompany me back to my office for the same purpose. Approximately 80% of my designated office hours are spent diagnosing problems and discussing viable solutions. The remaining percentage is split between completing administrative assignments and maybe assisting students with issues related to course content and assignments. The majority of these Millennial women are on a continual search for answers to questions they do not know quite how to ask, or they are looking for ways to deal with problems that come up—sometimes over and over again. One of my favorite students who recently graduated asked me one day, "How do you do it? How do you manage a career, a husband, three kids, us [meaning ALL the students I've claimed as 'my kids' as well], and still look good, and smile, and stay positive?" My answer to her was that I do not always get *it* right, that I cry often, that I too wander and wallow in my own self-pity at times; but at the end of the day, I know that I'm not alone. I know that there are examples of women around me, both literary and actual, who have suffered and survived in much the same way that I have, and that there is something to be gained from the conversations, prayers, and lessons learned from those who exist and persist in community.

And such is the case for the modern-day black woman. She has to understand that battles or struggles are imminent. The best line of defense, as Zora Neale Hurston's life can attest, is to keep moving. From my vantage point, I consider engagement with literature as an authoritative means to figure out life or at least to make sense of it. There is power that fuels critical and feminist/womanist theories, epistemologies, and even imaginative literature coined by black women about our experiences. These venues open lines of inquiry that reflect *connectedness* through hard-lived theories, philosophies, and characterizations of the lives of actual or fictional women, whose "stories"—again, either real or imagined—have the power to mobilize and liberate toward self-actualization,[16] as well as offer varied strategies for intervention in those venues where black women across the generations collide or converge in the classroom, in the home, or in the church, on "back porches,"[17] toward *praxis*.

The "stories" manifest themselves in a voice and subjectivity that Mary Field Belenky et al., authors of *Women's Ways of Knowing: The Development of Self, Voice, and Mind*, might define as authoritative treatises of expression/negotiation through which redefinition can take place within and around contexts of oppressive forces that have historically or culturally silenced them. Further Belenky et al. offer, "This interior voice [or "inner urges"[18]] has become, for us, the hallmark of women's emergent sense of self and sense of agency and control."[19] This state of subjectivism, then, is a critical stage in the development of actualizing black women to understand that power/strength and identity comes through *their* stories, the language of *their* experiences, and the maxims or fundamental principles of *their* philosophies about their personal life journeys and choices made along the way. Maxine Greene might further label this part of the actualizing process as "'conscientization [which] makes possible, a deepening of the attitude of awareness.' It is important to see," she asserts, "that such awareness is only available to those capable of reflecting on their own situationality, their own historical existence in a problematic world."[20]

A very relevant and salient argument arises then in the context of subjectivism and suffering, and in validating "stories" as a mechanism for releasing power for the black woman. I offer that the use of *imaginative literature* coupled with an intensive study of the *narrative lives of the creator/author* may offer an alternative angle to perhaps ferret out the sundry issues that perplex the black woman and her connectedness to society. Imaginative literature allows its readers to explore familiar and unfamiliar notions, to examine the complexities, nuances, and idiosyncrasies of "all-too-familiar" behavior of its characters, and to move to a reasonable or ironic, even surprising end, which would be that there *is* no ending—only another beginning. In the words of the popular, contemporary fiction writer Terry McMillan:

Without a doubt, writing fiction requires passion and compassion. A sense of urgency. Excitement. Intensity. Stillness. For many of us, writing is our reaction to injustices, absurdities, beauty. It's our way of registering our complaints or affirmations. The best are not didactic. They do not scream out "message," nor are they abstractions. Our stories are our personal response. What we want to specify. What we see. What we feel. Our wide-angle lens—our close-up look, and even if the story doesn't quite pinpoint the solution or the answer, it is the exploration itself that is often worth the trip.[21]

The point here is that there is some type of deliberation, some degree of critical analysis concerning an issue or issues that the author wishes to examine thoroughly. Through the authors' lens the readers are coerced or compelled to look at the events or actions of the text in a way that may illumine them by intuitive insight or wisdom. Imaginative literature allows for the greatest latitude of possibilities and space for play, a space for trying out solutions to the central problems that most often reflect real-life situations, or a space for play that "amounts to finding and creating oneself and bring[ing] alive the symbols that picture both a reality beyond the self and our experiences of uniting with it."[22]

"I HAVE A TESTIMONY": MY STORY OF "BECOMING" AS A WITNESS TO THE POWER OF LITERATURE[23]

Concerning my own subjectivity and the nature of this study, I have wrestled with the ethics, spirituality, politics, and philosophy of Zora Hurston, whose public and private lives have become intriguingly divergent and contradictory to me. My own cultural framework is strongly tied to both a religious/Christian background as well as an African American literary tradition that, on critical introspection and reflection, has informed my responsiveness or (more telling) my unresponsiveness to issues of race, class, gender, ethics, morality, religion, politics, education, scholarship, and philosophy for the majority of my life. Thus the way that I have addressed and subsequently interacted with these critical and often complex and perplexing issues as a Generation X black woman in the ever-evolving 21st century, can be conspicuously traced back to my grounding or framework of meaning.

I first became acquainted with Zora Neale Hurston in an Afro-American literature course offered at Spelman College back in the fall of 1987 when I was a sophomore student. I had just read *Their Eyes Were Watching God* and was taken. I had not quite experienced an epiphany at that particular point in my life, yet I was awakened. At that time, I was still very unsure of myself—what I wanted to do with my life. I didn't know if I was supposed to have a "voice" or not—probably wouldn't have recognized it either. What I did know was that I was in the tradition of my mother—attending an all-women's historically black college in the South and that this would be the venue (as I was told) in which I would be groomed and gain some idea of my role as a black woman. I was a "rising star," as my mother put it, continuing the journey of a second-generation educated black woman in our family. My maternal grandmother had prepared the foundation with a 6th grade education and lots of *hope*; my mother, as the eldest of six offspring, fostered that hope by paving the way as a first-generation Madison not only to graduate from high school but also to venture beyond that to attain her college, master, and doctoral degrees with an outstanding career in Education to boot; I was to continue in that tradition of hope, perseverance, and purpose. For many years, however, I didn't understand the honor bestowed on me. But then I met Janie.

The providential importance and beauty of my impending relationship with Janie Crawford is in the realm of "knowing." In my state of "unknowing," I was able to vicariously *play out* the scenarios and experiences presented in the text and to gain insight into my own queries as a non-present participant. In many ways Janie's story was my story. The cosmic power her author/creator possessed to *know* me—my sundry complexities and young soul's stirrings, as well as unbeknownst to me until our first class discussion, the stirrings of my yearning classmates—captivated me and launched an epistemic questing of my own to *know* myself better.

For me, *Their Eyes Were Watching God* served as that one poignant catalyst that would ignite an internal sense of urgency as a reader, as a student, and most importantly, as a black woman at a time when my soul was searching for sanctuary, yet release—for a concerned listener, yet an arsenal of alternatives. I had questions like Janie, and like her, I did not desire convenient responses to pacify me. The same is true even today as young black women have similar questions and concerns about life and living. In my daily conversations, the following queries have been made: "Why are we so poor at developing meaningful relationships with men?" "Why are men less attracted to women who are well spoken, well educated, and able to take care of themselves financially?" "Why is there such a communication gap between us and our men?" "Why is it that black *accomplished* women have a much more difficult time embarking on *stable* relationships with black men?" "Why is it that we as black women are still under the delusion that we have to conform to someone else's standard of beauty and success?" "How will we ever effectively transition ourselves into confident women of strength who are proud of our natural strength, character, and physical beauty?" "Why has the media made women in general as the ones who are to pursue the man and the relationship?" "What happened to a man pursuing a woman and her standing her ground and not lowering her standards to be accepted by him?" "Why do our mothers feel that their way of worshipping God is better than how we women of today express our love?" "Why must some women in this day and age, either black or any other race, still appear to be less than her man in order for their relationship to work?" "Why in such a so-called progressive society are we still playing catch-up to the rest of the population?"

Pondering these questions, I surmise that the pulse of black women's progressive thoughts is similar, despite time, age, and circumstances. There exist powerful strongholds in our society that seek to disempower black women despite certain advances and progresses they have made in the media, corporate, and entertainment industries. From my perception, it also appears that the social constructs informing black women's reaction to issues of relationships, gender roles in society, beauty, and so on, have persisted through history and remain as shackles on their feet. Therefore forging conversations between the generations of women to centralize their "stories" is paramount. Each woman reaches a point along her journey when she *needs* other women for support, mentorship, and the like, as a matter of preservation and survival. I felt a kindred connection to Janie Crawford, the heroine of *Their Eyes Were Watching God*. Janie, as she tells her story, is a young woman whose desire was to follow the guidance of her grandmother, the woman who raised her and instilled conservative and traditional values of what a black woman's role was to be. How she was to act, how she was to strive to serve or accommodate men to ensure a life of security and stability were all prescribed. Love was an afterthought or the icing on the cake, if one could achieve it, but the lack of discussion in that area would lead Janie on a continuous search throughout the book for it/love in her relationships in order to feel a sense of validation about her "self" as a woman and of completeness as a human being. If love were a mutual expectation in relationships, then there would be no problem with validation or self-worth of the parties involved, as it would be less of a *condition* of love leading to the subsequent or eventual inequality of power, than a *result* of love leading to a healthy balance of power.

The philosophy of Nanny, Janie's grandmother, was neither necessarily incorrect nor mal-intended; it was more an engraining of oppressive conditioning. Nanny was conditioned to train her offspring to seek after that which was denied or taken away from her and her ancestors—a sense of security at the expense or sacrifice of love and meaning, those things which ensure wholeness. That is the way most people who are oppressed instruct their young. One thing at the exclusion of the other. One cannot expect to have her cake and eat it too in Nanny's eyes. She reasoned this way:

Honey, de white man is de ruler of everything as fur as Ah been able tuh find out. Maybe it's some place way off in de ocean where de black man is in power, but we don't know nothin' but what we see. So de white man throw down de load and tell de nigger man tuh pick it up. He pick it up because he have to, but he don't tote it. He hand it to his womenfolks. De nigger woman is de mule uh de world so fur as Ah can see. Ah been prayin' fuh it tuh be different wid you. Lawd, Lawd, Lawd![24]

It would definitely take a widening of spaces in dialogue to embrace such concepts as balance and love in a society that for centuries has viewed the sexes as unequal and for those with power to manipulate and exploit the supposed "weaker" sex to attain their desires. Nanny urges further in her coaxing of Janie about the non-necessity for loving the first husband in the marriage she arranged, "'Tain't no use in cryin', Janie. Grandma done been long uh few roads herself. But folks is meant to cry 'bout somethin' or other. Better leave things de way dey is. Youse young yet. No tellin' whut mout happen befo' you die. Wait awhile, baby. Yo' mind will change."[25] Of course, Janie's mind *does not* change; not long after her grandmother dies, Janie runs off with another man to Florida—Mr. Joe Starks, who "spoke for change and chance"[26]—in search of the horizon and hope for the love she craved.

Conversations going on around me in Atlanta during my collegiate years at the time of my acquaintance with Janie, especially within the pearly, austere gates of the illustrious Spelman College, were obviously contradictory at best because of how we were all engrained (as "Spelmanites"). On the one hand, I was being told to "be myself" and to follow the stirring of my soul as far as career and relationships were concerned; yet on the other hand, I was told that my direction was predestined to be in Education and that I had to have a mate by a certain age in order to make my life complete. My rebellious nature (although I couldn't explain its roots then) mirrored Janie's in that I found myself initially majoring in degree areas other than Education—Economics first, then Music—and refusing to embrace the idea of marriage, up until age 27 when fate and purpose would converge in my life. In my mind, before that moment of truth hit me in my life, I had convinced myself that I didn't want to be tied down and that I wasn't going to be an educator either—period.

Again, Janie's approach to life and love as a black woman made sense of the contradictions in my head to a certain degree. Janie indeed was my sophomoric hero because we understood each other; we were on the same page in theory and action, in taking chances and questing to find our way, but I had not yet met the author. The brief biography I would read of Ms. Hurston's life and eventually have to report on for my Afro-American Literature course, however, puzzled me initially, but I couldn't dwell long on the causes of my puzzlement because our class moved on to another author and then another, and so on. I wouldn't have the occasion to read Hurston again until my years of study at North Carolina Agricultural and Technical State University where I pursued a master's degree in Afro-American literature. It was as if I would *need* to read her autobiography, *Dust Tracks on a Road*, at the time it was assigned because I had yet reached another juncture in my life that required intervention and insight. As a mid-20s aspiring black woman whose life was careening in the direction of the predestined life I fought furiously to oppose in both career and relationship, I endeavored to know just *whose* life I was living and if I was truly happy with the way life was turning out for me.

Accompanied with the study of Robert Hemenway's essential work entitled *Zora Neale Hurston: A Literary Biography*,[27] which confirmed the enigma of her life that I too experienced, my read of *Dust Tracks* would further confound me and turn into a type of melancholy that would haunt my dreams until now, some 17 years after my first read of Hurston. Why this woman died in obscurity when she had so passionately written and lived was entirely beyond me. More had to be to her story than met the eye.

"In Search of Zora Neale Hurston," written by Alice Walker, is a tribute to the quest of "finding" Zora.[28] Hurston's unmarked grave was found in a field full of weeds in the Garden of the Heavenly Rest in Fort Pierce, Florida, not in her hometown of Eatonville, Florida, the beloved, pastoral setting of the majority of her folklore. Why was this? The sundry questions in the back of my mind persisted: Why wasn't she buried in her hometown of Eatonville? Why hadn't her family tried to locate her body and properly handle the burial details on Hurston's behalf? Why did it take 13 years for her to be memorialized and her works to be exhumed and celebrated for *their* brilliance, *her* genius?

In another article entitled "On Refusing to Be Humbled by Second Place," Alice Walker surmises that there *is* more to her story and life than meets the eye, and for good reason. Hurston was an anomaly, a woman who resisted at a time when it was unpopular and ultimately fatal, yet she persisted because she had to. Walker intimates:

We live in a society, as blacks, women, and artists, whose contests we do not design and with whose insistence on ranking us we are permanently at war. To know that second place, in such a society, has often required more work and innate genius than first, a longer, grimmer struggle over greater odds than first—and to be able to fling your scarf about dramatically while you demonstrate that you know—is to trust your own self-evaluation in the face of the Great White Western Commercial of white and male supremacy, which is virtually everything we see, outside and often inside our own homes. That Hurston held her own, literally, against the flood of whiteness and maleness that diluted so much other black art of the period in which she worked is a testimony to her genius and her faith.[29]

Further research and history reveal that during the height of her career, Hurston was a noted and well-read author, especially during the 1920s through the 1950s in which she was heralded as "the daughter or heir of the Harlem Renaissance."[30] To me, there is evidence of pioneerism, i.e., accomplishments and sacrifices being made. So, in light of these things, were Hurston's contemporaries not the slightest bit curious about her disappearance from the literary scene? What had she done to create the disconnect? Had she been ousted by the literary and black communities? Indeed her literary career had made an unfortunate radical, yet pejorative change after World War II as she became a political writer. What kind of revolution had she started that made her so uncomfortable to discuss among her contemporaries or to study as a writer? Why did it seem as if my literary grandmother, so to speak, fell off the face of the earth?

The need to *find* Zora on my own behalf as well as Alice's and countless other women stems from a yearning to not only understand the enigma surrounding the rise and fall of such a worthy heroine, but also to find answers for our own "selves." Walker writes further,

We do not love her for her lack of modesty (that tends to amuse us: an assertive black person during Hurston's time was considered an anomaly); we do not love her for her unpredictable and occasionally weird politics (they tend to confuse us); we do not, certainly, applaud many of the *mad* things she is alleged to have said and sometimes actually did say; we do not even claim never to dislike her. In reading through the thirty-odd-year span of her writing, most of us, I imagine, find her alternately winning and appalling, but rarely dull, which is worth a lot. We love Zora Neale Hurston for her work, first, and then again (as she and all Eatonville would say), we love her for herself. For the humor and courage with which she encountered a life she infrequently designed, for her absolute uninterest in becoming either white or bourgeois, and for her *devoted* appreciation of her own culture, which is an inspiration to us all.[31]

The compelling nature of my desire to *know* this complex, determined, and self-assured woman is that against all odds, she never ceased in trying to "make it" in a career nor in expressing "the folk" and herself. Walker adds, "Someone who knew her has said: 'Zora would have been Zora even if she'd been an Eskimo.' That is what it means to be yourself. . . ."[32] Hence Zora offers black women a way to know ourselves however complex, perplexing, frustrating, or contradictory we may be.

THE BENEFITS OF PEDAGOGICAL STUDY TOWARD SELF-ACTUALIZATION

It is not difficult to fathom why this woman, her life, and literature would serve as a precursor to the epistemological development of women in contemporary society. She always knew that she lived before her time—yet she had to live *then* in order to be of aid in the development toward self-actualization for the black woman *now*.

The benefit of this pedagogical study for self-actualization as examined through the eyes of Zora Neale Hurston is that we as black women and readers alike can analyze our own "searches for meaning." Our real-life experiences often reveal (if we would openly admit this) an ongoing, unceasing quest to find ourselves. I contend that the pattern of Hurston's works and travels is epitomized by the themes in her own personal life, which more often than not translated into an African American community ethic of collective or communal mutability and survival as opposed to just her individual struggles and transcendence. I am also compelled by Hurston's evolution of "becoming" and the way in which she used her literature, notably *Their Eyes Were Watching God*, to explore intense characters (much like ourselves), to break through "masks of suffering" toward the direction of *becoming*, of finding peace and validation of self. Hurston wrote with a sense of passion and urgency. Her pen, in whatever medium she found most expedient, was used to bridge the gap or to potentially open critical spaces for dialogue between social constructs and personal awareness. In my estimation, Hurston's writings and *life* were a precursor to postmodernism as they were derived within her own horizon and out of her own experiences as a woman.

CONCLUSION

It is just as important to know where we've been as to understand where we are in the present. This state of mind is an affirmation of truth—a historical reality. Self-actualization is a stimulus to move beyond the uncertainties or doubts arising out of unfulfilled desires and goals, as well as frustration and wandering. Zora Neale Hurston provides an ideal example in such transitions of life. This is my mantra and keeps me on task.

NOTES

1. Zora Neale Hurston, *Dust Tracks on a Road: An Autobiography*, 2nd ed. (1942; repr., Urbana: University of Illinois Press, 1984), 326.

2. Hurston, *Dust Tracks*, 324.

3. Hurston, *Dust Tracks*, 324.

4. Roger Clegg, "Wrapped in Zora: A Rainbow without the Coalition," in *National Review Online*, April 2004, <http://www.nationalreview.com/script/printpage.p?ref=/clegg/clegg200404130910.asp> (24 May 2009).

5. Paula Gleason, "Meeting the Needs of Millennial Students," *InTouch Newsletter* 16, no. 1 (2007), <http://www.csulb.edu/divisions/students2/intouch/archives/2007–08/vol16_no1/01.htm> (7 May 2009).

6. Gleason, "Meeting the Needs."

7. Center for American Progress, "New Progressive America: The Millennial Generation" by David Madland and Ruy Teixeira (May 2009), 5.

8. Hurston, *Dust Tracks*, 327–328.

9. Gleason, "Meeting the Needs."

10. Hurston, *Dust Tracks*, 344–345.

11. Hurston, *Dust Tracks*, 323.

12. "Student Affairs Administrator Shares Research on Millennial Generation," Division of Student Affairs, Virginia Tech (12 January 2006), <http://www.studentprograms.vt.edu/publications/millennials.php> (7 May 2009).

13. H.H. Titus, M.S. Smith, and R.T. Nolan, *Living Issues in Philosophy*, 8th ed. (Belmont: Wadsworth Publishing, Inc., 1986), 408.

14. Titus, Smith, and Nolan, *Living Issues*, 408.

15. "Mission Statement," Bennett College for Women official website, <http://www.bennett.edu>.

16. bell hooks, *Teaching to Trangress: Education as the Practice of Freedom* (New York: Routledge, 1994).

17. In *Their Eyes Were Watching God*, the protagonist Janie Crawford shares her story with friend Phoeby Watson on Janie's porch. Zora Neale Hurston, *Their Eyes Were Watching God* (1937; repr., New York: Negro Universities Press, 1969).

18. Zora Neale Hurston, "How It Feels to Be Colored Me" from *The World Tomorrow* (1928), <http://people.whitman.edu/~hashimiy/zora.htm> (24 May 2009).

19. Mary Field Belenky, Blythe McVicker Clinchy, Nancy Rule Goldberger, Jill Mattuck Tarule, *Women's Ways of Knowing: The Development of Self, Voice, and Mind* (New York: Basic Books, 1986), 68.

20. Maxine Greene, *Landscapes of Learning* (New York: Teachers College Press, 1978), 102.

21. Terry McMillan, ed., *Breaking Ice: An Anthology of Contemporary African American Fiction* (New York: Penguin Group, 1990), xxiii.

22. Ann Belford Ulanov, *Finding Space: Winnicott, God, and Psychic Reality* (Louisville: Westminster John Knox Press, 2001), 13.

23. This section of the paper emanates from Chapter 1 of the author's dissertation research entitled "More Than a State of Being. The Process of Actualizing 'Self' in the Midst of Limitations and Contradictions: Establishing Pedagogy of Self-Actualization and Survival through Zora's Eyes" (May 2005).

24. Hurston, *Their Eyes*, 29.

25. Hurston, *Their Eyes*, 43.

26. Hurston, *Their Eyes*, 50.

27. Robert Hemenway, *Zora Neale Hurston: A Literary Biography* (1977; repr., Urbana: University of Illinois Press, 1980).

28. Alice Walker, "In Search of Zora Neale Hurston," *MS Magazine* (March 1975): 74–79, 85–89.

29. Alice Walker, "On Refusing to Be Humbled by Second Place in a Contest You Did Not Design: A Tradition by Now," in *I Love Myself When I Am Laughing and Then Again When I Am Looking Mean and Impressive*, ed. Alice Walker (New York: The Feminist Press, 1979), 4.

30. Michael Cooke, *Afro-American Literature in the Twentieth Century: The Achievements of Intimacy* (New Haven, CT: Yale University, 1984), 139.

31. Alice Walker, "On Refusing," 1–2.

32. Alice Walker, "On Refusing," 105.

Organic Universalism in Zora Neale Hurston's *Their Eyes Were Watching God*[*]

Joanne M. Braxton

Ah wanted to preach a great sermon about colored people sittin' on high, but there wasn't no pulpit for me . . . nothin' Ah been through ain't too much if you just take a stand on high ground lak Ah dreamed.
                              —Zora Neale Hurston, *Their Eyes Were Watching God*

The age of prophetic living must not stay imprisoned in the past; it must be revived in every generation as our own.
                              —John A. Buehrens, foreword to
                              Richard L. Gilbert's *The Prophetic Imperative*

Books, not which afford us a cowering enjoyment, but in which each thought is of unusual daring; such as an idle man cannot read, and a timid one would not be entertained by, which make us dangerous to existing institutions,—such I call good books.
                              —Henry David Thoreau, *A Week*
                              on the Concord and Merrimac

Sometimes, when I look at the life and work of Zora Neale Hurston (1891–1960), I feel as if I were looking at Moses' burning bush. We read and we read, but the work is not consumed; each new reading reveals infinite variety and newness of meaning as if one were looking at a miracle hidden in plain sight. Revelation is not sealed.

Theologian and ethicist Sharon Welch sees Afra-American[1] writers as "Bearers of Dangerous Memory,"[2] and I agree. According to many sources, the values of the pre-integration black community put the community first, sometimes suppressing individualism and originality. When I was growing up in the 1950s as part of a segregated and oppressed community in Prince Georges' County, Maryland, that community expressed and acted on values of wholeness and shared identity, so that when I entered the "white" world, I had to *learn* how to "get ahead." Even today, I see the elders of my community of origin—people in their 80s and 90s—sacrificing personal comfort for the well-being of others who will inherit a future they will not see. Though these acts may be secular in nature, they are closely related to the spiritual tradition of "bearing witness," and they exemplify James Luther Adams' definition of religious faith, "giving oneself in the wholeness of his being, so far as he is able"[3] to Love and the greater good. There is indeed transformative power in such acts, both for the individual and the community. This power resides in part in the collective consciousness and the "dangerous memory" of Afra-American writers like Zora Neale Hurston and her linguistic and spiritual progeny, empowering our work with prophetic imperative, a power "not of our own making."[4]

This prophetic tradition of bearing witness derives from an unspoken covenant with those who have gone before us in struggle, and, to borrow a theological concept from Rebecca Ann Parker, stands as an invisible marker of our "membership in a community of resistance to oppression."[5] Sharon Welch's distillation of what Katie G. Cannon calls "womanist ethics"[6] and her read of the literary works of Afra-Americans as "a fundamental challenge to the presuppositions of Western moral theories" holds up; she may see Afra-American writers as "Bearers of Dangerous Memory,"[7] but the bearing of witness and memory has in fact been a life-sustaining activity for both the bearers and the communities they represent.

In my monograph, *Black Women Writing Autobiography*, I argue that:

Black women autobiographers are grounded in a chosen kinship with their literary antecedents from blueswomen and evangelists to the works of the founding fathers, black and white. Like the blues, most autobiographies by black Americans, male and female, tend to have a dominant internal strategy of action rather than contemplation. And, like the blues singer, the autobiographer incorporates communal values into the autobiographical act, sometimes rising to function as the "point of consciousness" of her people. Thus, black women writers are joined together by forces tangible and real, no more mystical than Du Bois' veiled seventh son of the seventh son, and insist on their own terms. For while "mysticism" cannot define a tradition, there *are* unwritten texts and contexts that black women bring to the reading or creation of written literature. [T]he text is accessible to whoever would first establish the proper cultural context, thus gaining access to a sphere of privileged (and valuable) knowledge—which was often what Toni Morrison called "discredited knowledge."[8]

Zora Neale Hurston, autobiographer, biographer, novelist, and ethnographer *extraordinaire* working at the intersection of literature and the oral tradition, was the possessor of such discredited visionary knowledge. Her work bears prophetic witness, chastising and warning, while at the same time showing possibilities for harmony, humanity, and wholeness. Like 19th-century black Shaker eldress Rebecca Cox Jackson (d. 1871) who wrote, "I had started to go to the promised land, and I wanted husband, brother, and all the world to go with me, but my mind was made up to stop for none. I had no friends at home or abroad,"[9] Hurston would always be something of an outsider. In many ways, including her solitary travels throughout the American South, Hurston resembled Jackson, who often preached on her own authority and experienced dreams and visions.[10]

As revealed most literally in her autobiography, *Dust Tracks on a Road*, Hurston may not have been a mystic, but she was a visionary. In the chapter "The Inside Search," Hurston writes of experiencing a series of visions when she was about seven years old:

I do not know when the visions began. Certainly I was not more than seven years old, but I remember the first coming very distinctly . . . I saw a big raisin lying on the porch and stopped to eat it, and soon I was asleep in a strange way. Like clear cut stereopticon slides, I saw twelve scenes flash before me, each one held until I had seen it well in every detail, and then replaced by another. There was no continuity as in the average dream. . . . I knew they were all true, a preview of things to come and my soul writhed in agony and shrunk away. But I knew there was no shrinking. These things had to be. . . . I had a feeling of difference from my fellow men and I did not want it to be found out. Oh, how I longed to be just as everybody else! But the voice said No. I must go where I was sent. The weight of this commandment laid heavy and made me moody at times. . . . It gave me a terrible feeling of aloneness.[11]

Hurston spent much of the rest of her life reflecting on what she had experienced; her revelations marked her as being different; they also marked a tear or disruption in her psychic landscape and her theological inheritance. Like 19th-century Universalist[12] minister and theologian Hosea Ballou (1771–1852), Hurston was the child of a Baptist minister. However, whereas Ballou was ordained and radical (radical because he advocated universal salvation, rejecting the belief that God would divide humanity into the saved and the damned), Hurston, black and female, did not have the option of following in her father's footsteps.[13] Even today, ordination for a woman is controversial in most Baptist denominations; that path was closed to her. She did not choose the path of being a missionary or a licensed preacher, as some black women had and she eschewed formal religious expression in her adult life. When she did refer to her own religious beliefs, she described herself as an agnostic. Yet it seems strange that an agnostic would produce works with titles like *Their Eyes Were Watching God* (1937), *Moses, Man of the Mountain* (1939), and *Herod the Great* (n.d.). For these and other reasons (some of which I will illustrate), I like to think of Zora Neale Hurston and Hosea Ballou as *organic universalists*.

In coining this term, *organic universalist*, I refer to the work of Antonio Gramsci (1891–1937), the Italian Marxist who influenced Frantz Fanon, Michel Foucault, Paulo Freire, Noam Chomsky, Homi Baba, Cornel West, and others. Gramsci thought of every human being as a creature of reason and intellect, but distinguished between the *traditional intellectuals* who isolated themselves from the masses and served the prevailing ideology of the culture, and those *organic intellectuals* who articulated the thoughts and feelings of the multitudes and thereby advanced their agency as transformers of society. I also refer to a theological tradition that resists the division of humanity into the saved and the damned and is concerned with the salvation of all souls/all beings—a theological tradition that dissents from religion that functions oppressively. *Organic universalism*, as I define it, is not a religion, but rather a philosophical approach that is inclusive of theological understandings; it includes rather than excludes all manner of diversity, with respect for nature, people, living things, and interdependent relationships.

Organic universalism bridges the scholarly and the scientific as well as the artistic and aesthetic, the secular and the sacred; living under prophetic imperative as an organic universalist means living as if the dream of humanity and wholeness is the truth. Organic universalism holds tragedy and heartbreak, yet it is nurtured by beauty. It requires the poet-prophet to bear witness continually with or without hope of reward. Writing is grounded speech/action; the artist bears witness in her creative work both because she does not want to be lost in a society that is profit-driven rather than prophet-driven and also as an affirmation of faith because she knows that the dream is the truth. The organic universalist, like the organic intellectual, articulates the knowledge and experience (or life-wisdom) of what Freire calls the "submerged" masses who participate in a dominant/dominating culture with a dissident spirit that often remains unvoiced.[14] Going beyond the dualism of the organic intellectual's Marxist framework, the organic universalist embraces wholeness, even with its contradictions. In testifying, singing, writing, or preaching, the organic universalist raises the voice of the oppressed, resists subjugation, and advances an inclusiveness that counters the fragmentation and exclusion typical of oppressive social systems.

Hurston, a political conservative, might not have liked being classified by this hybrid terminology with leftist connotations;[15] however, she fits this model of organic and spiritual faithfulness to her roots among ordinary black folk. In the beginning, Hurston, a professional anthropologist trained by noted scholar Franz Boas (1858–1942) at

Barnard, would go out to collect folklore in her perfect "Barnardese," asking people if they knew any Negro folktales, the epitome of the detached scientific observer. Later, after some discomfort, she would become fully immersed in black folk culture, blurring the rigid boundaries that had kept her apart; she even participates in rituals of hoodoo and conjure, as recorded in *Tell My Horse* (1935). In communion with those she has joined, she moves from being a passive recipient of dominant culture, as represented by her formal social science education and its requisite distancing, to becoming an active agent of cultural transformation and resistance.

I consider Ballou an *organic universalist* because his Universalism resisted a dominating religious culture that divided humanity into the elect and the damned, an orthodoxy that, in Ballou's folk wisdom provided religious justification for cruelty and oppression. Ballou did not subscribe to Jonathan Edwards's fear-provoking notion of "an angry God" or the Puritan idea of "election." He considered Christ "a man, but with a divine mission . . . to demonstrate God's all-consuming love for humanity,"[16] a humanity that is saved not by the atoning death of Christ on the cross, but by the beauty of God manifest in Christ's character and the natural beauties of the earth.[17] Both Hurston and Ballou came from poor to modest backgrounds. Each grew up with a strong foundation in Bible study and practical Homiletics, hearing their Baptist fathers preach. Both spoke to and for the common folk and articulated the thoughts and feelings of ordinary people in a way that addressed the social location and spiritual condition of the working underclass. Though Hurston lived long after Ballou and was better educated than he, both writers love story-making and produced works infused with orality, which is the quality of speaking, and specifically the spoken quality of the language of common people. This orality and love of story is evident in Ballou's speeches and writings; he also loved argument as a rhetorical form suited to reaching and teaching his audience. Here is a well-known illustration from one of his talks:

Your child has fallen into the mire, and its body and garments are defiled. You cleanse it and array it in clean robes. The query is, Do you love your child because you have washed it? Or Did you wash it because you loved it?[18]

On the subject of universal salvation, Ballou argued, "God saves men to purify them; that's what salvation is designed for. God does not require men to be pure in order that he might save them."[19]

Hurston embraces the concept of universal salvation as a participant-observer in her secular anthropological scholarship; to this day, however, the theological implications of Hurston's intellectual labor, both literary and scientific, have been largely overlooked. "Mother

Catherine" is a religious figure who appears for the first time in a vignette of the same name in *The Sanctified Church* (1981), a posthumous volume including some pieces, like "Mother Catherine," from Hurston's previously unpublished work. The cover artwork from a photograph of Mother Catherine's tomb in New Orleans features a sculpture of Mother Catherine with her arms lifted in prayer in the classic posture of the *orante*. This posture is described in the early third century by Clement of Alexandria (c. 150–215):

For this reason also we raise the head and lift the hands in the closing outbursts of prayer, following the eager flight of the spirit into the spiritual world. And while we thus endeavor to detach the body from the earth by lifting it upwards along with spoken words, we spurn the fetters of the flesh and constrain the soul, winged with the desire of better things, to ascend into the holy place.[20]

Given that Origen (c. 185–c. 254), Clement's student who succeeded Clement as head of the catechetical school in Alexandria, Egypt, when Clement died in 215, is thought of by many as the father of universalist Christianity, this may well be the very posture in which the first universalists prayed. She stands there, captured in a life-sized stone image atop her tomb in flowing biblical dress, much like that which Hurston describes her as wearing in life. Hurston stayed with Mother Catherine in her "Manger" two weeks; she tells us that no money was ever solicited there. The "Manger" was topped by a Greek or Byzantine cross.[21] Hurston wrote that Mother Catherine's religion was matriarchal. Her compound was "called the Manger, and is dedicated to the birth of children in and out of wedlock."[22] Describing the "Manger," Hurston wrote about Mother Catherine's belief system as being catholic or universal: "There was a catholic flavor about the place, but it is certainly not catholic [sic]. She has taken from all the religions she knows anything about any feature that pleases her."[23]

Mother Catherine preached that everything born was sacred; the Manger included "four mongrel dogs," three canaries "singing and chirping happily all through the service," a donkey, "a mother goat with her kid, numbers of hens, a sheep—all wandering in and out of the service without seeming out of place." "A Methodist or Baptist church—or one of any denomination whatever—would have been demoralized by any of these animals."[24] Here is Mother Catherine, whose universalism goes beyond our wildest dreams—recorded once in this life only by Zora Neale Hurston in her role as trained anthropologist:

God tells me to tell you (invariable opening) that He hold the world in the middle of His hand. "There is no hell beneath this earth. God wouldn't build a hell to burn His breath.

"There is no heaven beyond dat blue globe. There is a between world between this brown earth and the blue above. So says the beautiful spirit.

"When we die, where does the breath go? Into trees and grass and animals. Your flesh goes back to mortal earth to fertilize it. So says the beautiful spirit.

"Our brains is trying to make something out of us. Everybody can be something good.

"It is right that a woman should lead. A womb was what God made in the beginning, and out of that womb was born Time, and all that fills up space. So says the beautiful spirit . . . "Don't teach what the apostles and prophets say. Go to the tree and get the pure sap and find out whether they were right."[25]

This is not some "respectable" version of African American religious experience sanitized to make it palatable as a tool of racial uplift. Mother Catherine saw herself as "an equal of Christ." Her radical "concept of the divinity of Christ is that Joseph was his foster father as all men are foster fathers, in that all children are of God and all fathers are merely the means." She healed through "the laying on of hands, by suggestion and copious doses of castor oil and Epsom salts." According to Hurston, Mother Catherine was also a practitioner of distance healing. "Mother Catherine was not converted by anyone," she writes. "Like Christ, Mohammed, Buddha, the call just came. No one stands between her and God."[26]

In some ways, Mother Catherine's universalist ideas as recorded by Hurston bear at least a semblance to Ballou's universalist belief that all are "chosen people" destined for happiness and holiness, and his assertion that "a false education has riveted the error in the minds of thousands that God's law required endless misery to be inflicted on the sinner."[27] That "God wouldn't build a hell to burn His breath" is not a new idea, but for many it is still heretical. Mother Catherine's religion resembles what today might be called "the gospel of inclusion," as advanced by Carlton Pearson an African American Pentecostal religious leader and formerly a leading disciple of Oral Roberts, who argues, "We do not need to be saved from God; we need to be saved from religion . . . We need to stop worrying about other people's lifestyle and start building our 'love style.'"[28] Mother Catherine was already building her "love style" down in the Manger, as Hurston recorded it sometime in the 1920s or 1930s. This is the love that we need right now.

We also need new and more theoretically inclusive ways of reading. In her study *Spiritual Interrogations: Culture, Gender and Community in Early African American Women's Writing*, Katherine Clay Bassard has identified "three primary metanarratives of African American intertextuality/intersubjectivity" related to women's literary traditions: 1) the *tropological/vernacular*, which seeks "an 'indigenous' vernacular trope or controlling metaphor as a descriptor," 2) the *familial*, which "constructs a literary historical lineage for black women writers" using tropes of "sisterhood" or "matriliny," and 3) the *social/ideological*, which "understands relationships between African American women's texts as a function of the writers' responses to prevailing discourses and ideologies of 'blackness' and/or 'womanhood.'"[29] I am not in agreement with all of Bassard's categories and find some of her definitions to be over-simplified misreadings (perhaps an inevitable consequence when gathering such a cloud of scholars as Henry Louis Gates, Jr., Hortense Spillers, Houston Baker, Harold Bloom, Alice Walker, Hazel Carby, May Henderson, and Michael Awkward). While these concepts are useful starting points for literary conversation, the typological approach may need to be de-constructed as just another form of rhetoric, a form often found in the literature reviews of books that emerge from former doctoral dissertations that seek to "defeat and displace" their intellectual progenitors.[30] For now, I will offer what could be viewed, at the very least, as another category of metadiscourse contributing to the formulation of African American literary theory: *the ethical and/or theological*. And why not? After all, the line between the sacred and the secular is often slim, especially in the African American community. It has long been a practice in the academic world to separate this aspect of our literary discourse into a different sphere of study, but it belongs in both literary and theological conversations and without this both/and consideration our theorizing and contextualization is incomplete.

Some writers, like Zora Neale Hurston, write as if they believe in *prophetic imperative* and they have received "the legacy of Nommo—the empowering engendered word" described so well by Fahamisha Patricia Brown. Brown suggests that the black poet "achieves a kind of written orality. Writing in the presence of an implicit community/ congregation, the poet responds to both oral and written cultural calls,"[31] invoking the power of words to change things and the necessity of making change. The implicit community/congregation, I would argue, includes both writers and readers, blues singers and preachers, the living and the dead, a multigenerational "community of saints" in covenantal relation for struggle against oppression.

In addition to the legacy of Nommo, there is another tradition, a tradition equally ancient, equally powerful and at least as influential as the tradition of *Nommo* operating in Hurston's literary consciousness; this is the Old Testament tradition of prophetic testimony, the tradition of Miriam, Isaiah, Amos, and Jeremiah, some of the earliest recorded literature. Speaking of Thoreau's prophetic testimony in *Walden* and several other works, Paul Lauter observed that: "Active and literary testimonies are often interdependent, so that the word can refer to a distinctive expression in public action *and* literary affirmations of one's faith. . . . [L]iterary 'testimonies' of the prophetic sort gain their power . . . precisely by the virtue of this double referent." The prophet also regards her-/himself as "the *Nabi* or 'mouthpiece' of a God predominantly manifest through his *Ruach*, his breath, literally, or 'spirit.'" This is not altogether unlike the concept of Nommo, which means, literally, breath.[32] Because Nommo is present in all waters, seas, storms, torrents and coasts, it also implies a relationship with nature.[33] What if "God is still speaking?"

Multiple referents, both secular and sacred, converge in *Their Eyes Were Watching God* (1937). Prophetic imperative grounded in ancestral covenant is foundational to *Their Eyes*, a work marked by Hurston's transcendent vision of humanity and wholeness; this dream, which implies respect for nature, people, living things, and their dynamic and interdependent relationships is her truth. "Ole Massa is doin' His work now," says her first-person narrator, Janie Starks, when the storm begins down on the 'glades, "Us oughta keep quiet."[34] Hurston shows the communality of hope and death and grief before God:

They huddled closer and stared at the door. They just didn't use another part of their bodies, and they didn't look at anything but the door. The time was past for asking the white folks what to look for through that door. Six eyes were questioning *God*.

As soon as Tea Cake went out pushing wind in front of him, he saw that the wind and water had given life to lots of things that folks think of as dead and given death to so much that had been living things. . . .

They passed a dead man in a sitting position on a hammock, entirely surrounded by wild animals and snakes. Common danger made common friends. Nothing sought a conquest over the other.[35]

Bearing prophetic witness, Janie tells the stories of poor folk who waited too long to leave and could not find a ride out, gives us the sights and sounds of levees breaking. Everything is equal in this vision. Men, women, blacks, whites, rattlesnakes too scared to coil and bite.

Racism presents a disruption to this relation of organic wholeness; Janie depicts racist whites holding the high ground and forcing blacks away:

Everybody was walking the fill. Hurrying, dragging, falling, crying, calling out names hopefully and hopelessly. Wind and rain beating on old folks and beating on babies. Tea Cake stumbled once or twice in his weariness and Janie held him up. So they reached the bridge at Six Mile Bend and thought to rest.

But it was crowded. White people had preempted that point of elevation and there was no more room. They could climb up one of its high sides and down the other, but that was all. Miles further on, still no rest.[36]

So what does this have to do with us? My contention is that the pro-phetic imperative[37] is often present in literary works by black women writers that are not specifically theological and that we overlook this prophecy because we are not prepared to receive it. Because we are not prepared to receive it, we do not allow ourselves to see it. What if we had read *Their Eyes Were Watching God* as prophecy as well as fic-tion? How many lives could have been saved on the Gulf Coast in Hurricanes Katrina and Rita if we had listened to Hurston's prophetic witness? Could Hurston's vision have helped forestall the incredible, unnecessary, and tragic loss?

What if we re-envision Zora Neale Hurston as prophet as well as poet? Can we envision a world where trees and dogs and snakes and children born in or out of wedlock are holy, holy, holy? How would we begin? Let us go back to Hosea Ballou's question: "Do you love your child because you have washed it? Or Did you wash it because you loved it?"[38] Remember the appellation of the "nigger woman" as "de mule uh de world" as rendered by Nanny in chapter two of *Their Eyes*? Later Jody buys Janie Matt Bonner's yellow mule and when the mule dies, Jody stands on the belly of the mule giving a "sermon," mocking "everything human in death . . . the sisters got mock happy and had to be held up by the menfolks." Finally the buzzards descended on the mule and the buzzard parson gave his sermon in a parody of human call and response, then "he picked out the eyes in a ceremonial way, and the feast went on." And the questions are these: Do we praise Hurston because we love her or do we love her because we praise her? Are we keeping faith with Zora Neale Hur-ston and her prophetic imperative, or are we picking her bones like so many buzzards? Are we making "faithful choices"?[39] How could we begin?

We could begin to hold each other accountable for the ways in which we read our poet/prophets and what we do with their words and visions. We might also begin by eschewing either/or thinking and embracing the multiple contexts and referents that frame some of our most important texts. Reading across the boundaries of literary criti-cism, religious studies, and theological studies activates the prophetic imperative in Zora Neale Hurston's work. This practice in turn engen-ders a responsibility to read and theorize holistically, without frag-menting or reducing the text into "literature" or "the moral of the story." We might include in our interpretive communities those ethi-cists and theologians who are not only reading black women writers, but raising questions about the ways in which we order our presump-tive notions of the ways conflict is structured. Some of what we have inherited theologically may represent oppressive religion that is not in our own best service or that of our communities; it goes against the deeper ancestral covenant, harking back to the master's imperial narrative where religion becomes a means of social control.

We could begin by acknowledging that religion has most often been the tool of empire and that revelation is not sealed. Dissident religious perspectives, resistant to the unholy alliance of religion, violence, and subjugation, have been present when and wherever religion has functioned to sanction injustice; new scholarship in religious and theological studies—especially that written by women of color—unveils these resistant strains. Perhaps we would learn that much of institutionalized Christianity, as constructed as a series of conflicts based on guilt, exclusion, and fear, is incompatible with the teachings of the early church as well as our deeper humanistic goals. Inviting progressive theologians and ethicists like Katie G. Cannon, Emilie Townes, Karen Baker-Fletcher, M. Shawn Copeland, Sharon Welch, Rebecca Ann Parker, Rita Nakashima Brock, James Cone, and their students into our literary conversations will challenge and enrich our traditional theoretical approaches to literature and culture. This inclusion will open new communities of discourse, produce new ways of reading and theorizing by postcolonial activist readers, and create new communities of resistance across traditional academic boundaries.

Their Eyes Were Watching God embodies Hurston's values of humanity and wholeness and her best attempt to move others toward their new testimonies of these values. Hurston therefore becomes not only a literary and aesthetic model but also a model for just how an artist might go out into the wilderness and live. In the end, she didn't require much: a bed, a small burner for cooking her simple meals, a bean bag chair, a typewriter, a crate to hold it up, some paper, her garden, and her dog. Like Rebecca Cox Jackson, she testifies that the prophet often works alone, but her work is not about going it alone. As Freire notes, "the pursuit of full humanity . . . cannot be carried out in isolation or individualism, but only in fellowship and solidarity."[40] Even as the solitary narrator, Hurston wraps the voices of a beloved community around her as she tells their tales.

When we are open to continuing revelation and female prophethood, we can read the work of Zora Neale Hurston, Toni Morrison, and Maya Angelou respecting that the prophetic imperatives they pronounce are real. We can stop shunning (the way the porch sitters do in the early pages of *Their Eyes*) and start building our "love style" to include those we have excluded in often hypocritical practices of religious or academic bigotry—especially against people who believe differently from what we believe or engage in personal choices that are different from ours. Sometimes we shun to avoid being shunned ourselves. *We know all the reasons.* Janie Starks was shunned because she married a younger man who was considered to be beneath her social station. Hurston herself did not escape this personal affliction; when she was falsely accused of a terrible crime, some were happy to see an independent woman brought down; they viewed Hurston's originality of expression as a threat and made her a social outcast. Though she is celebrated today, she died in poverty. If we love Hurston, we must embrace what June Jordan called, "the responsibility that love implies," and make the recognition of prophetic imperative and the sheltering of prophets a priority. We have only to open our eyes, remember the words of Mother Catherine, and speak that we might speak again. In this way, we advance the quest for humanity and wholeness and the legacy of Zora Neale Hurston, keeping alive her "dangerous memory" and her organic universalism.

NOTES

1. Beginning with the publication of *Black Women Writing Autobiography: A Tradition within a Tradition* (Philadelphia: Temple University Press, 1989) and *Wild Women in the Whirlwind: Afra-American Culture and the Contemporary Literary Renaissance* (New Brunswick: Rutgers University Press, 1989) , I have used *Afra-American* to designate that which is distinctive about the literature and culture of African diaspora women. Use of the term *Afra-American* as a political choice and an affirmation of wholeness requires no modifiers.

2. Sharon Welch, "A Theology of Resistance and Hope," in *A Feminist Ethic of Risk* (Minneapolis: Fortress Press, 1990), 153–199. Welch writes that "Dangerous memories fund a community's sense of dignity; they inspire and empower those who challenge oppression. Dangerous memories are a people's history of resistance and struggle, of dignity and transcendence in the face of oppression." Welch takes the term *dangerous memory* from Johannes Metz who "identifies the power of dangerous memories in resisting communities." She explains that her "use of the term is derived from his exploration of the task of Christian theology, which he defines as 'speaking about God by making the connection between the Christian message and the modern world and expressing the Christian tradition in this world as a dangerous memory.' This memory," she writes, "leads Christianity to a critique of what is commonly accepted as plausible: dangerous memory leads to political action." See also, Johannes Baptist Metz, *Faith in History and Society: Toward a Practical Fundamental Society* (New York: Seabury Press, 1980), 77, 89–90, 236.

3. James Luther Adams, *The Prophethood of All Believers*, edited with an introduction by George K. Beach (Boston: Beacon Press, 1989), 252.

4. James Luther Adams, *The Prophethood*, 252.

5. Rebecca Ann Parker, "What They Dreamed Be Ours to Do: Lessons from the History of Covenant," in *Redeeming Time: Endowing Your Church with the Power of Covenant*, ed. Walter P. Herz (Boston: Skinner House, 1999), 83–97.

6. Katie G. Cannon was one of one of the first to explore "The Black Woman's Literary Tradition as a Source for Ethics," in *Black Womanist Ethics* (Atlanta:

Scholar's Press, 1988). *Womanist ethics* is a widely used term derived from the title of Katie G. Cannon's pioneering book.

7. Sharon Welch, "A Theology of Resistance," 153–199.

8. Joanne M. Braxton, *Black Women Writing Autobiography: A Tradition Within a Tradition* (Philadelphia: Temple University Press, 1989), 5–6. The same transcendent impulses found in the blues are found equally in the spirituals; blues songs and spirituals are often sung by the same people and they can be virtually indistinguishable.

9. Rebecca Cox Jackson, *Gifts of Power: The Writings of Rebecca Cox Jackson, Black Visionary, Shaker Eldress* (Amherst: University of Massachusetts Press, 1971), 87.

10. Joanne M. Braxton, *Black Women Writing Autobiography*, 59–72, 146–158.

11. Zora Neale Hurston, *Dust Tracks on a Road* (1942; repr., Urbana: University of Illinois, 1984), 58–59.

12. In this essay, Universalist (capitalized) refers to a theological perspective held by a denominational body, specifically the Universalist Church of America and/or the views of a religious leader regarded as a forebear of this denomination. Universalist (lowercase) refers to a philosophical or theological view or approach as defined in the body of the essay.

13. According to biographer Deborah G. Plant, "Hurston's relationship with her father was of an oedipal nature. Though rebuffed, she longed for her father's affection. . . . Hurston could not win her father's love, so she resignedly contented herself with being like him." Plant argues that "John Hurston's rejection of his daughter is as much a determining factor in her self-image and self-concept as her mother's love." See Deborah G. Plant, *Every Tub Must Sit on Its Own Bottom: The Philosophy and Politics of Zora Neale Hurston* (Urbana: University of Illinois Press, 1995), 160–161. See also, *Zora Neale Hurston: A Biography of the Spirit* (Westport: Praeger, 2007).

14. See Paulo Freire, *Pedagogy of the Oppressed* (New York: Herder and Herder, 1990), 60–68. Freire advocates "the emergence of consciousness and critical intervention in reality" (68).

15. See Zora Neale Hurston, "Why the Negro Won't Buy Communism," *American Legion Magazine* 50 (June 1951), 13–55, 55–60.

16. Hosea Ballou, quoted by Ernest Cassara, in Hosea Ballou, *A Treatise on Atonement*, Edited and Introduced by Ernest Cassara (1804; repr., Boston: Skinner House Books, 1986), xix.

17. Hosea Ballou, *A Treatise on Atonement* (1804), objects to religion that instills fear; characterizing such religion is an insult to God and a danger for human society. Those who profess to believe in a God who is satisfied by the miserable humiliation and crucifixion of his only son, have "done more injury to the Christian religion than the writings of all its opposers . . . all those principles which are to be dreaded by men, have been believed to exist in God; and professors have been moulded into the image of their Deity, and become more cruel. . . ." (104–105). Instead, Ballou argues that the purpose of religion is to happify humanity. Jesus saves, not by dying, but by inspiring love: "While our minds are darkened by the veil on the heart . . . the beauties of the ministration of life are hidden from our eyes, and its excellent glories are out of our sight."

But Jesus has the power to "cause us to love holiness . . . to reveal the divine beauties . . . to take the veil from the heart . . . and to cause us to see himself altogether lovely." Salvation is akin to earth's springtime, "when the increasing majesty of the sunbeams gently removes the chains of frost, and warm zephyrs are breathed on the surrounding snow, removing it from the land; the embryo blossom . . . swells with genial heat; and the leaf, so nicely folded in winter's chest, now displays its matchless green, and the whole forest rejoices in expanded delights" (133). Ballou contends: "It is impossible for anyone to be willing to be endlessly miserable. Happiness always was, and always will be, the grand object of all rational beings" (130).

18. Ballou, *A Treatise on Atonement*, xix.

19. Ibid., xviii.

20. Clement, Stromateis, quoted in Margaret R. Miles, *The Word Made Flesh: A History of Christian Thought* (Malden, MA: Blackwell, 2005), 59−60.

21. Zora Neale Hurston, *Sanctified Church* (Berkeley, CA: Turtle Island, 1981), 23.

22. Ibid., 28.

23. Ibid., 26.

24. Ibid., 25.

25. Ibid., 26.

26. Ibid., 27−28.

27. Ballou, *Treatise on Atonement*, 128.

28. Bishop Carlton Pearson, *The Gospel of Inclusion: Reaching Beyond Religious Fundamentalism to the True Love of God* (New York: Azusa Press International, 2006), 5. ". . . [A]s I grew older and got more involved in the broader religious world, I discovered that the seductive vices of religious prejudice far outstripped those of race hatred. Religious prejudice stands in the way of truth. It arrogantly presupposes that there is nothing more one can learn about God, the Bible or faith" (58).

29. Katherine Clay Bassard, *Spiritual Interrogations: Culture, Gender and Community in Early African American Women's Writing* (Princeton: Princeton University Press, 1999).

30. In "A People Blinded from Birth: American History According to Sacvan Bercovitch," David Harlan argues that "Typology is a particular form of rhetoric" that helps to "constitute the basic arrangement of, and directs the basic operation of the myth-making mind." He suggests that Bercovitch's *The American Jeremiad*, was part of a struggle to replace his "intellectual progenitor," Perry Miller: "In fact, Bercovitch has come not to honor Miller but to bury him; Bercovitch's interpretation of American Puritanism is not an extension and completion of Miller's work, but its denial and negation." It could be argued that Bassard's typology stands in a somewhat similar relation to those progenitors who have helped define Afra-American literary tradition. See David Harlan, "A People Blinded from Birth: American History According to Sacvan Bercovitch," *The Journal of American History* (December 1991), 941−952.

31. Fahamisha Patricia Brown, *Performing the Word: African American Poetry as Vernacular Culture* (New Brunswick: Rutgers University Press, 1999), 25.

32. Paul Lauter, "Thoreau's Prophetic Prophecy," *The Massachusetts Review,* Vol. 4, No. 113. Lauter observed, "The 'testimony' which is a prophetic book not only embodies the prophet's testimony of action and that which informs it, but it also attempts, by its 'testimony' to get its readers to accept its truths, to live by them."

33. See D.A. Masolo, *African Philosophy in Search of Identity* (Bloomington: Indiana University Press, 1994), 71; "These spirits, called Nommo, were two homogeneous products of God, of Divine essence like himself, conceived without outward incidents and developed normally within the womb of the earth. Their nature is identical with Word, just like vapor is identical with breath."

34. Zora Neale Hurston, *Their Eyes Were Watching God* (1937; repr., New York: Harper, 2006), 159.

35. Ibid., 159–164.

36. Ibid., 164.

37. See Richard L. Gilbert, *The Prophetic Imperative: Social Gospel in Theory and Practice* (Boston: Skinner House, 2008), 4; "Here at the cusp of the millennium, it is time once more to take our spiritual and moral bearings," writes Gilbert. "The militantly conservative nineties have been too much for us, and more than ever we need to assert our justice-making capacity before we are swept away."

38. Ballou, *A Treatise on Atonement*, xix.

39. John A. Buehrens, "Foreword," in Richard L. Gilbert, *The Prophetic Imperative,* ix.

40. Paulo Freire, *Pedagogy of the Oppressed*, 73–74.

Conclusion

Deborah G. Plant

There is only one consciousness. Individualized consciousnesses are permutations of the one consciousness. Though perceived as individuated and distinct, individualized consciousness is never separate from the whole.[1] Yet, in *The Souls of Black Folk*, W.E.B. Du Bois would write that "the American Negro" was compelled to negotiate an imposed double consciousness which undermined a true sense of self in the Negro, as it also enervated creative action:

After the Egyptian and Indian, the Greek and Roman, the Teuton and Mongolian, the Negro is a sort of seventh son, born with a veil, and gifted with second-sight in this American world,—a world which yields him no true self-consciousness, but only lets him see himself through the revelation of the other world. It is a peculiar sensation, this double-consciousness, this sense of always looking at one's self through the eyes of others, of measuring one's soul by the tape of a world that looks on in amused contempt and pity. One ever feels his twoness,—an American, a Negro; two souls, two thoughts, two unreconciled strivings; two warring ideals in one dark body, whose dogged strength alone keeps it from being torn asunder.[2]

Du Bois characterizes the history of the Negro in America as "the history of this strife": the desire "to be a co-worker in the kingdom of culture" while also resisting being perceived as a problem. In the presence of white Americans, Du Bois sensed the ever-present tacit question: "How does it feel to be a problem?"[3] The perception of "the Negro" as the cause of America's problems is interwoven into

American political and legal history and into the fabric of American popular culture. *Birth of a Nation*, for instance, is a landmark film in U.S. history. Produced in 1915, it was proclaimed 15 years later as "having stood the test of time and still considered the best picture ever made."[4] In the opening scenes of *Birth of a Nation*, the eighth caption reads: "the bringing of the African to America planted the first seed of disunion." This sentiment became part of the social discourse and permeated every sphere of American life, not only continuing the legacy of a house divided, but also continuing the conviction that black people were innately inferior—intellectually, physically, socially, and morally. This film stereotyped African Americans as crazed, traitorous, abusive, lascivious, violent, and—a problem. Books like *The Bell Curve* and documentaries like "Bowling for Columbine" inform us that these sentiments are still deeply embedded in the minds and hearts of many Americans.[5]

As a cultural anthropologist of the Boasian school of cultural relativity, Zora Neale Hurston worked to dispel the myth of race and its attendant pseudo-scientific theory—biological determinism. She found the idea of racial and cultural superiority or inferiority to be fallacious. Race Pride and Race Consciousness, she determined, were illogical and abhorrent—among blacks as well as whites—and rather poor nourishment for the soul.[6] Although African Americans, collectively, had made remarkable progress since Emancipation, Hurston did not attribute those accomplishments to race. Race, like class, was a social construction that had no value in and of itself. Hurston described both as "scourges of humanity":[7]

Why should I be proud to be a Negro? Why should anyone be proud to be white? Or yellow? Or red? After all the word "race" is a loose classification of physical characteristics. It tells nothing about the insides of people. Pointing at achievements tells nothing either. Races have never done anything. What seems race achievement is the work of individuals.

Instead of Race Pride being a virtue, it is a sapping vice. It has caused more suffering in the world than religious opinion, and that is saying a lot.[8]

"Race Consciousness" was only nuanced in its difference from "Race Pride." One was saying, "Be continually conscious of what race you belong to so you can be proud." But what use was that, she asked:

I don't care which race you belong to, if you are only one quarter honest in your judgment, you can seldom be proud. Why waste time keeping conscious of your physical aspects? What the world is crying and dying for is less race consciousness. The human race would blot itself out entirely if it had any more.[9]

Unfortunately, racial dogma, racial stereotyping, and racist practice prevailed, keeping social groups separate from and fearful of one another. For many African Americans, racial pride was the response to racial denigration. A motivating desire of the Harlem Renaissance movement was to acquaint white America with black genius. This, for Harlem Renaissance pundits like W.E.B. Du Bois, was tantamount to acquainting whites with the humanity of black people. Surely, then, they would recognize that African Americans were intelligent, culturally rich, patriotic, and thus, worthy of full citizenship. However, this was not the case. The pain and anger over the "carnival of blood and passion" that flowed during the Civil War rested squarely on the shoulders of black people. Who could hear the longing of once-chattel blacks when whites were yet in anguish over their loss. So whatever the accomplishments and efforts of African Americans, they would not be invited to step into the heartbeat of America.

Away back in the days of bondage they thought to see in one divine event the end of all doubt and disappointment; few men ever worshipped Freedom with half such unquestioning faith as did the American Negro for two centuries. To him, so far as he thought and dreamed, slavery was indeed the sum of all villainies, the cause of all sorrow, the root of all prejudices; Emancipation was the key to a promised land of sweeter beauty than ever stretched before the eyes of wearied Israelites. In song and exhortation swelled one refrain—Liberty; in his tears and cures the God he implored had Freedom in his right hand. At last it came,—suddenly, fearfully like a dream. With one wild carnival of blood and passion came the message in his own plaintive cadences:
  "Shout, O children!
  Shout, you're free!
  For God has bought your liberty!"
Years have passed away since then,—ten, twenty, forty; forty years of national life, forty years of renewal and development, and yet the swarthy spectre sits in its accustomed seat at the nation's feast. In vain do we cry to this our vastest social problem:—
  "Take any shape but that, and my firm nerves
  Shall never tremble!"
The nation has not yet found peace from its sins; the freedman has not yet found in freedom his promised land. Whatever of good may have come in these years of change, the shadow of a deep disappointment rests upon the Negro people,—a disappointment all the more bitter because the unattained ideal was unbounded save by the simple ignorance of a lowly people.[10]

This disappointment is expressed in W.E.B. Du Bois' iconic statement that "the problem of the twentieth century is the problem of the color-line." He expounded further that the problem of the color line entailed "the relation of the darker to the lighter races of men in Asia and Africa, in America and the islands of the sea." And he concludes matter-of-factly:

It was a phase of this problem that caused the Civil War; and however much they who marched South and North in 1861 may have fixed on the technical points of union and local autonomy as a shibboleth, all nevertheless knew, as we know, that the question of Negro slavery was the real cause of the conflict.[11]

Du Bois made his prediction at the beginning of the 20th century, in 1903. He was prescient. Griffith's 1915 film was also prescient, as it was indicative of the ensuing civil wars the nation would face. During the last decade of the 20th century, in light of the growing disparities between blacks and whites, John Hope Franklin also felt compelled to say "categorically that the problem of the twenty-first century will be the problem of the color line":

This conclusion arises from the fact that by any standard of measurement or evaluation the problem has not been solved in the twentieth-century, and this becomes a part of the legacy and burden of the next century. Consequently, it follows the pattern that the nineteenth century bequeathed to the twentieth-century and that the eighteenth century handed to its successor.[12]

Rather than prophecy, however, Franklin's statement might be interpreted as a caveat. Later in his discourse, he states,

To find the way out of this morass, these dilemmas, is the great challenge of this decade. It is also our final opportunity to prevent the color line from being a most important legacy for the twenty-first century.[13]

Therefore, this legacy is not inevitable. We have the ability and the creative energy to change things. A decade into the 21st century, we have been reminded of the "audacity of hope." Though we have not yet created a post-racial society—racial disparities in education, housing, employment, health, and security being what they are—and the problem of the color line is far from being a memory of the past, it is not necessary that we carry racial and color prejudice into our future. As the presidency of Barack Obama has clearly demonstrated, the future is what we make it. Though he was an "unlikely" candidate and an "unlikely" choice, 66 million voters of all ethnic, economic, social, and cultural backgrounds elected him to lead the nation. They responded to one of the most profound aspects of Obama's campaign: his appreciation for the American desire for wholeness, for oneness—*e pluribus unum*. The perception that Griffith's *Birth of a Nation* clearly portrays is that white Americans of the South and the North were brothers (and sisters)—until the advent of the Civil War. The attitudes and events that led to the war are not typically examined in relation to the resulting hostilities between "the North and the South." Rather, the attitudes, particularly those infused with racialized notions, have remained in the unconscious memory and hostilities have morphed over time into hostilities between Republicans and Democrats, between conservatives (neo-cons) and liberals (progressives), and between the right and the left.

"When I meet people for the first time," writes Obama, "they sometimes quote back to me a line in my speech at the 2004 Democratic National Convention":

There is not a black America and white America and Latino America and Asian America—there's the United States of America.[14]

Their focus on this idea of a unified America reflected their audacity of hope, which Obama saw as "the best of the American spirit":

having the audacity to believe despite all the evidence to the contrary that we could restore a sense of community to a nation torn by conflict; the gall to believe that despite personal set backs, the loss of a job or an illness in the family or a childhood mired in poverty, we had some control—and therefore responsibility—over our own fate.[15]

In recognizing common values and common dreams, Obama sounded a common chord that recalled the nation's motto. He reminded us that we can create the nation we want. In order for the nation to succeed, its ideals must be grounded in our common humanity. The idea that "one isn't confined in one's dreams" is central to understanding the American character, says Obama. And more and more, this is the characterizing attitude of many of the new generation of African Americans who reject any limits to their possibilities. He states further that this idea "represents a radical break from the past, a severing of the psychological shackles of slavery and Jim Crow."[16]

As we peer into the past, we see that no one was more radical about breaking from the psychological shackles of oppression than Zora Neale Hurston:

I see nothing but futility in looking back over my shoulder in rebuke at the grave of some white man who has been dead too long to talk about. That is just what I would be doing in trying to fix the blame for the dark days of and the Reconstruction. . . . I have no intention of wasting my time beating on old graves with a club. I know that I cannot pry loose the clutching hand of Time, so I will turn all my thoughts and energies on the present. I will settle for from now on.[17]

Zora Neale Hurston, like the protagonists in her short stories and novels—John Redding, Hi John, Janie Woods, Moses, Arvay and Jim

Merserve, among others—defied imposed and perceived limitations and spoke of far horizons. They knew the dream to be the truth, because, as Obama wrote, there are no limitations in dreams. In dreams everything is possible. *This* is the human condition: possibility. Hurston's work as a cultural anthropologist contributes to the appreciation of our common humanity. She looked ahead to a day when humankind would know its creative potentiality and realize its higher Self:

Consider that with tolerance and patience, we godly demons may breed a noble world in a few hundred generations or so.[18]

The presidential campaigns of Hillary Clinton and Barack Obama encourage our movement into a noble millennium. The election of Barack Obama to the presidency of the United States encourages and inspires the possibility of a nation in living out the full meaning of its creed, that all people are created free and equal and endowed with unalienable human rights. It was altogether fitting and proper that the Reverend Joseph Lowery, Jr., opened the closing Inaugural prayer with verses from the Negro national anthem, "Lift Every Voice and Sing":

God of our weary years, God of our silent tears
Thou who has brought us thus far along the way,
Thou who has by thy might, led us into the light,
Keep us forever in the path we pray
Lest our feet stray from the places our God where we met thee,
Lest our hearts drunk with the wine of the world we forget thee,
Shadowed beneath thy hand, may we forever stand,
True to thee o God, and true to our native land.

The lyrics, originally a poem, were penned in 1900 by James Weldon Johnson. His brother, J. Rosamond Johnson, wrote the score. The words were written to introduce speaker Booker T. Washington and were sung on the occasion of the birthday celebration of Abraham Lincoln, the president who sought to prevent secession and fragmentation, and thereby, establish a more perfect union. Lincoln, the 16th president from whom Barack Obama, the 44th president, drew so much of his inspiration. Even as the lyrics of "Lift Every Voice" pledged dedication "to our native land," Barack Obama, right hand on Lincoln's Bible, pledged to protect and uphold the Constitution of the United States.

Standing on the steps of the Capitol, a building erected with the labor of enslaved Africans, Barack Obama reminded the nation of America's promise. He reminded the nation that each has his and her part to play in the realization of freedom, liberty, and democracy. Just as he and others vowed to uphold their responsibilities as public servants, he impressed on each citizen the need to acknowledge and accept individual responsibility for her and his own destiny, or, as Zora Neale Hurston would put it, "Every tub must sit on its own bottom, regardless."[19]

A woman who lived through the weary years of Jim Crow and who stood in sorrow's kitchen crying silent tears, looked within to her own light and tapped into her own creative energy to walk a pathless path as a cultural anthropologist, folklorist, novelist, journalist, playwright, and musical producer. As one who stood on the peaky mountaintop, wrapped in rainbows, with a harp in one hand and a sword in the other, Hurston inspires us to create a new, inclusive, and life-affirming legacy in the 21st century.[20] The voices of the scholars in this collection bring new perspectives, new angles of vision, to the works of Zora Neale Hurston, as they also introduce Hurston to new generations of readers in a new millennium. Their interpretations and analysis give us an appreciation of Hurston in the 21st century, and they help to raise our consciousness, as Americans, as world citizens, as enlightened beings knowledgeable of our creative energy and ability to create a society that reflects the best of the American Spirit.

NOTES

1. Paramahansa Yogananda, *God Talks with Arjuna, The Bhagavad Gita: Royal Science of God-Realization, The Immortal Dialogue Between Soul and Spirit* (Los Angeles: Self-Realization Fellowship, 1995), 131–132, 859–879.

2. W.E.B. Du Bois, *The Souls of Black Folk* (1903; repr., New York: Signet, 1969), 45.

3. Ibid., 45.

4. D.W. Griffith, *Birth of a Nation* (Reel Enterprises), 2006.

5. Richard Herrnstein and Charles Murray, *The Bell Curve: Intelligence and Class Structure in American Life* (New York: Free Press, 1994); Michael Moore, *Bowling for Columbine* (Iconolatry Productions, 2002).

6. Zora Neale Hurston, *Dust Tracks on a Road* (Urbana: University of Illinois Press, 1942), 326–327.

7. Hurston, *Dust Tracks*, 323.

8. Ibid., 325.

9. Ibid., 326.

10. Du Bois, *The Souls of Black Folk*, 47–48.

11. Ibid., 54–55.

12. John Hope Franklin, *The Color Line: Legacy for the Twenty-First Century* (Columbia: University of Missouri, 1993), 5.

13. Ibid., 50.

14. Barack Obama, Democratic Convention Speech, 2004, 231.

15. Barack Obama, *The Audacity of Hope: Thoughts on Reclaiming the American Dream* (New York: Crown, 2006), 356.

16. Obama, *The Audacity of Hope*, 241.

17. Hurston, *Dust Tracks*, 282–284.

18. Ibid., 286.

19. Ibid., 325.

20. Hurston, *Dust Tracks*, 280.

We Be Theorizin

Kendra Nicole Bryant

They thought we was over here
shuckin and jivin
when all the while we been theorizin
how else you think black folks survivin
they try to keep us down
but we keeps on thrivin
Can't no oppression keep us from strivin
they try to break our souls
but we keeps on smilin
and through grins and lies
we master guisin
gotta be a trickster for humanizin
but we'll wear the mask
cause we be theorizin

So right on Zora Neale
Write on
Right on W. Du Bois
Write on
Right on Booker T.
Write on
cause we been watchin God
while they been in the dark
the souls of black folks
produce the purest heart
and our plantin seeds
is just a start
see we sowin wisdom
with literary arts

and through performances
that's how we impart
the theory they claim, rename, and bogart
so Right on Langston Hughes
Write on
Right on Richard Wright
Write on
Right on James Baldwin
Write on
cause the negro speaks of rivers
and the weary blues
he's the native son
the outsider
if she choose
and if beale street could talk
it would share some news
cause we've gone a piece of the way
in our travelin shoes
and though our cuttin the rug/might seem our muse
we be theorizin and maskin the clues
so Right on Nella Larsen
Write on
Right on Countee Cullen
Write on
Right on Claude McKay
Write on
cause just as quick as sand
we can change our tune
we speak in vernaculars
they call us a coon
but once they're outta our way
and have left the room
out comes Harlem wine
and intellectuals bloom
and when the Harlem dancer/makes her body croon
that's our theory that esoterically looms
so talk that talk money
and walk that walk
black feeling and judgment/compels them to gawk
it's our colorful brilliance
that makes them balk/at the notion that we be a theory

cause we be theorizin
in our baptizin
in churches and clubs
we signifyin
gospel jazz/blues got us cryin
oral traditions keep us from dyin
we flyin on tryin
we hypnotizin

and dance floors are our silver linin's
creatin the arts keep us glidin
so we paintin faith and buildin horiz'ns
keepin hope alive and eyes on prizes
and writin poetry makes us the wisest
we are the ones that we've been waitin for

we soar . . .
like . . . birds . . . in . . . the sky . . .

so high five
Gwendolyn Brooks and James Weldon Johnson
Nina Simone and Alice Walker
Give me some skin
Malcolm X and Leopold Senghor
Toni Morrison and Martin Luther King
Tell me something good
Audre Lorde and Jamaica Kincaid
Houston Baker and Frantz Fanon
Throw me a shimmy
bell hooks and Lauryn Hill
Angela Davis and Assata Shakur
Pass me the mic
Marcus Garvey and Henry Louis Gates
Aime Cesaire and Cornel West
Bet that up
Mos Def and Wole Soyinka
Huey Newton and Amiri Baraka
All givin life to Barack Obama!

See our theorizin
Be our salvation
through the Middle Passage and their plantations
through Jim Crow laws and humiliation
COINTELPRO and subjugation
Our theorizin so bright it's blazin
We are the light that gives them life
blacker than the blackest night
we're the blues on the left tryin to be the funk on the right
magical and dynOmite—
we are the world's good time. . . .

Cause we be theorizin
Which is our uprisin
No reparations/but we're enterprisin
Creatin life to keep us from dyin
singin, dancin, paintin, and writin
we are the Titans
and our hue gives the world humanity.

Index

About the Editor
and Contributors

DEBORAH G. PLANT is Associate Professor and Chair of the Department of Africana Studies at the University of South Florida in Tampa, Florida. She is author of *Every Tub Must Sit on Its Own Bottom: The Philosophy and Politics of Zora Neale Hurston* and *Zora Neale Hurston: A Spiritual Biography*.

ELIZABETH BINGGELI is a Post-doctoral Instructor in the Departments of Cinema and Media Studies and English at the University of Chicago. Her research focuses on American modernist literature and cinema. She is currently completing the book manuscript "Hollywood Dark Matter: Race and the American Novel in Studio Narrative Culture."

VALERIE BOYD is author of *Wrapped in Rainbows: The Life of Zora Neale Hurston* and the forthcoming *Spirits in the Dark: The Untold Story of Black Women in Hollywood*. She is Associate Professor and Charlayne Hunter-Gault Distinguished Writer-in-Residence at the Grady College of Journalism at the University of Georgia.

JOANNE M. BRAXTON is Frances and Edwin L. Cummings Professor of the Humanities and Director of Africana House at the College of William and Mary. Her works include *Sometimes I Think of Maryland* (1977), *Black Women Writing Autobiography* (1989), and her edited volume, *Collected Poetry of Paul Laurence Dunbar* (1993).

KENDRA NICOLE BRYANT is Poet, Instructor, and Ph.D. student of English at the University of South Florida. Her interests include Contemplative Pedagogy, Hip Hop Music, and African-American Literature. She is author of *AS I ROC the MIC* and editor of *Power to the Pen: Finding Agency through Argument*.

GURLEEN GREWAL, PH.D., Associate Professor of English, and Director of the Center for India Studies, teaches at the University of South Florida, Tampa. She is author of *Circles of Sorrow, Lines of Struggle: The Novels of Toni Morrison*, and several articles on postcolonial writers.

SCOTT HICKS is an Assistant Professor of English at the University of North Carolina, Pembroke. He teaches and studies African American and environmental literature, and his essays appear in *Callaloo* and *Interdisciplinary Studies in Literature and Environment*. His current research explores globalization, agriculture, and environmental consciousness in 20th-century American literature.

DR. EMILY M. HINNOV is Assistant Professor of English at Bowling Green State University, Firelands College. She teaches British literature, transnational literary modernism, gender studies, and women's literature. She is author of *Encountering Choran Community: Literary Modernism, Visual Culture and Political Aesthetics in the Interwar Years* (Susquehanna U P, 2009).

PIPER G. HUGULEY-RIGGINS is a Temporary Assistant Professor at Spelman College. She received her Ph.D. in Twentieth Century American Literature from Georgia State University. She has taught at Georgia State University, Georgia Institute of Technology, Spelman College and Berry College. Her research interests are Autobiography, Women Writers and Multi-Ethnic Literature.

LUCY ANNE HURSTON is Associate Professor of Sociology at Manchester Community College in Manchester, CT. She earned her MA degree from the Ohio State University. Author of *Speak So You Can Speak Again: The Life of Zora Neale Hurston*, her research focuses on women-centered issues of inequality in the Caribbean.

MICHELLE JARMAN is Assistant Professor of Disability Studies at the University of Wyoming. Her research interests include U.S. literature, women's studies, and cultural representations of disability. Her current project traces eugenic discourse in the United States through key modernist texts to frame an intersectional analysis of race, gender, and disability.

CATHERINE A. JOHN is an Associate Professor of English at the University of Oklahoma. She published *Clear Word and Third Sight: Folk Groundings and Diasporic Consciousness in African Caribbean Writing* (Duke U P, 2003). Author of several articles, she is currently writing *The Just Society and the Diasporic Imagination*.

DR. A. GISELLE JONES-JONES is Assistant Professor and Chair of the Department of English and Foreign Language at Bennett College. Her areas of teaching and research include African American Literature, Educational Leadership, and Cultural Foundations.

ANTHEA KRAUT is Associate Professor in the Department of Dance at the University of California, Riverside, where she teaches courses in critical dance studies. Her book *Choreographing the Folk: The Dance Stagings of Zora Neale Hurston* was published by the University of Minnesota Press (2008).

JOHN LOWE, Professor of English and Director of the Program in Louisiana and Caribbean Studies at Louisiana State University, is author or editor of seven books, including *Jump at the Sun: Zora Neale Hurston's Cosmic Comedy* and *Approaches to Teaching Hurston's Their Eyes Were Watching God and Other Works*.

PHYLLIS MCEWEN is a Poet, Librarian, and Performance/Visual Artist. She has been portraying Dr. Hurston in a Chautauqua-style one-woman show since 1991. Phyllis is a member of Cave Canem Poetry Collective and BRAVA, a Florida-based women's visual arts cadre.

E. ETHELBERT MILLER is a Literary Activist. He is board chair of the Institute for Policy Studies. The author of several collections of poems, his latest book is *The 5th Inning*, a second memoir, published by Busboys and Poets/PM Press. Mr. Miller is often heard on National Public Radio.

LYNN MOYLAN is an Independent Scholar, veteran Educator, and author of the forthcoming biography *Zora Neale Hurston: The Finale Decade 1950–1960*.

KERSUZE SIMEON-JONES is Assistant Professor of Francophone Literature and Africana Studies at the University of South Florida. Her teaching and research interests include Diasporan Women's History; Comparative Africana Literature; and Black Internationalism. She is author of the forthcoming *Literary and Socio-Political Writings of the Black Diaspora: 19th and 20th Centuries*.

DR. DAWOOD H. SULTAN is an Assistant Professor of Health Policy and Management at the University of South Florida. His research focuses on health outcomes and healthcare in the United States and health outcomes in East Africa. He also studies the political economy and structural vulnerability of African American communities.

DR. LINDA TAVERNIER-ALMADA is Assistant Professor of Anthropology and African American Studies at Rollins College. Utilizing an ethnohistorical approach, she investigates the unique values and the diversity of African Diaspora communities.

DR. SHIRLEY TOLAND-DIX, Assistant Professor of English at the University of South Florida, teaches and engages in research on Africana Women Writers and the Black Atlantic. Author of several articles, she is completing the book manuscript "'Half the Story Has Never Been Told': Black Women Novelists, History and Imagined Community."

DEANNA J. WATHINGTON, MD, MPH, FAAFP, is Interim Associate Dean for Academic and Student Affairs and Director of the Public Health Practice program at University of South Florida's College of Public Health. Research focus includes health disparities, family violence and diversity in health professions. Publications address maternal health and infant mortality.